A Critical Introduction to Phonetics

Continuum Critical Introductions to Linguistics

A Critical Introduction to Phonology
Daniel Silverman

A Critical Introduction to Phonetics

Ken Lodge

continuum

Continuum International Publishing Group
The Tower Building   80 Maiden Lane, Suite 704
11 York Road   New York
London SE1 7NX   NY 10038

© Ken Lodge 2009

Ken Lodge has asserted his right under the Copyright, Designs and Patents Act, 1988, to be identified as Author of this work.

All rights reserved. No part of this publication may be reproduced or transmitted in any form or by any means, electronic or mechanical, including photocopying, recording, or any information storage or retrieval system, without prior permission in writing from the publishers.

British Library Cataloguing-in-Publication Data
A catalogue record for this book is available from the British Library.

ISBN: 978-0-8264-8873-2 (hardback)
       978-0-8264-8874-9 (paperback)

Library of Congress Cataloging-in-Publication Data
The Publisher has applied for the CIP data.

Typeset by Newgen Imaging Systems Pvt Ltd, Chennai, India
Printed and bound in Great Britain by The MPG Books Group

Contents

	Preface	vii
1	Why Phonetics?	1
2	Articulation	13
3	The Articulators in Combination	51
4	Transcription	67
5	Segmentation	96
6	Prosodic Features	110
7	Continuous Speech	135
8	Varieties of English	161
9	Acoustic Phonetics	183
	Glossary of Phonetic Terms	225
	References	235
	Index	239

Preface

This book is the outcome of some thirty years teaching phonetics, mainly articulatory phonetics to undergraduate and postgraduate students with a variety of interests, though their core has always been students on a linguistics programme. As an introduction to phonetics, it will take a somewhat different stance from a traditional approach on the presentation of basic phonetic skills for students of linguistics and others (e.g., speech and language therapists). It assumes that

(i) natural, everyday speech is the true reflection of the linguistic system (the phonology in particular);
(ii) speech is not a concatenation of discrete segments (whatever sort of phonology we may wish to establish);
(iii) universal characteristics of phonetic realization of the linguistic system are at best poorly understood; and
(iv) ear-training, production and acoustic analysis should be taught in equal measure, since all three should be used hand-in-hand, as they are complementary rather than superior to one another.

In this book, however, my main focus is on articulation and ear-training with a final chapter on how spectrograms can help us interpret what is going on in speech and sharpen our observations of it.

Assumption (i) means that linguists should always consider connected speech as well as or even in preference to the phonetic characteristics of individual words, in particular their citation forms, that is the sound of the word spoken in isolation. After all, in most circumstances we do not communicate with one another in single-word utterances, and even if we do, we do not necessarily pronounce the words we use as though we were reading them out of a dictionary. Assumption (ii) means that, whereas as an introductory platform to phonetics the description and transcription of individual sounds may make sense, this alone cannot achieve a full appreciation of the nature of continuous speech, which requires a non-segmental approach to the contributory rôles of the various parameters of articulation, that is, vocal cord activity, manner of constriction, nasality, and so on.

Assumption (iii) relates to a large extent to the assumptions made by phonologists about the most appropriate way of representing a native speaker's knowledge of phonological structure. Of course, phonologists are often phoneticians, too, and they wear different hats on different occasions. So, it is not impossible for one and the same researcher to stress the continuous nature of the articulation and the acoustics of speech from a phonetic point of view, and then to opt for a purely segmental kind of phonological analysis. The problem is that all too often there is no discussion of how the two different kinds of interpretation are connected. My contention is that, if we are to understand the nature of the relationship between the two, phonetic detail and phonological structure, then we need as much information as possible about the nature of spoken language from a physical point of view, as well as the continuing investigations into the psycholinguistic aspects of phonological knowledge. This book is an introduction to the complexity of the physical characteristics of speech. In this task it tries to avoid presenting the phonetics in such a way as to make mainstream phonological theory seem obvious; for instance, it rejects the notion that if phonological structure is based on strings of segments, then let's present phonetics in the same way.

Assumption (iv) reflects my belief that a good ear is as important as a good eye and good analytical and observational skills. Ear-training and an ability to transcribe as accurately as possible what is heard (impressionistic transcription) is the starting point for a phonetician, despite the many excellent advances in instrumental support for the observation of speech that have occurred since the Second World War. And if the phonetician is also a phonologist, no amount of equipment and software will give her/him answers of an analytical nature. What it will do, of course, is provide even more detail for consideration.

During the very long gestation period of this book I have been grateful to have had the opportunity to try out my approach in teaching phonetics to several cohorts of students, without whom none of this would have been necessary. I am also grateful to the many colleagues over the years with whom I have discussed the issues laid out above. I have appreciated the opportunity to argue my case over the years, even if sometimes I have failed to convince and at other times I have been preaching to the converted. There are too many to mention or even remember, but I would particularly like to acknowledge my indebtness to the following friends and colleagues. They are in no particular order, and have contributed a variety of input from information about languages of which I am not a speaker to offering technical facilities for the preparation of the material that supports the text of the book. So, thanks to: Dan Silverman, whose sister book to this on phonology convinced me I should finally put pen to paper (and fingers to keyboard!), Zoe Butterfint, Lela Banakas, John Local (one of the converted), Richard Ogden (another of them), Peter Trudgill, John Gray; Francis Nolan and Geoff Potter, who kindly offered their laboratory facilities at Cambridge; and Janette Taylor for her illustrations of the human speech organs. As regards getting all this into print, I have to acknowledge the help, encouragement and, in particular, patience from Jenny Lovel, who initiated the project, Gurdeep Mattu, who took over halfway through, and Colleen Coalter, all of Continuum Books.

I hope that in the end at least some people feel that it has been worth all the effort.

Ken Lodge
Norwich
March, 2008

THE INTERNATIONAL PHONETIC ALPHABET (revised to 2005)

© 2005 IPA

CONSONANTS (PULMONIC)

	Bilabial	Labiodental	Dental	Alveolar	Postalveolar	Retroflex	Palatal	Velar	Uvular	Pharyngeal	Glottal
Plosive	p b			t d		ʈ ɖ	c ɟ	k ɡ	q ɢ		ʔ
Nasal	m	ɱ		n		ɳ	ɲ	ŋ	ɴ		
Trill	ʙ			r					ʀ		
Tap or Flap		ⱱ		ɾ		ɽ					
Fricative	ɸ β	f v	θ ð	s z	ʃ ʒ	ʂ ʐ	ç ʝ	x ɣ	χ ʁ	ħ ʕ	h ɦ
Lateral fricative				ɬ ɮ							
Approximant		ʋ		ɹ		ɻ	j	ɰ			
Lateral approximant				l		ɭ	ʎ	ʟ			

Where symbols appear in pairs, the one to the right represents a voiced consonant. Shaded areas denote articulations judged impossible.

CONSONANTS (NON-PULMONIC)

Clicks		Voiced implosives		Ejectives	
ʘ	Bilabial	ɓ	Bilabial	ʼ	Examples:
ǀ	Dental	ɗ	Dental/alveolar	pʼ	Bilabial
ǃ	(Post)alveolar	ʄ	Palatal	tʼ	Dental/alveolar
ǂ	Palatoalveolar	ɠ	Velar	kʼ	Velar
ǁ	Alveolar lateral	ʛ	Uvular	sʼ	Alveolar fricative

OTHER SYMBOLS

ʍ Voiceless labial-velar fricative
w Voiced labial-velar approximant
ɥ Voiced labial-palatal approximant
ʜ Voiceless epiglottal fricative
ʢ Voiced epiglottal fricative
ʡ Epiglottal plosive

ɕ ʑ Alveolo-palatal fricatives
ɺ Voiced alveolar lateral flap
ɧ Simultaneous ʃ and x

Affricates and double articulations can be represented by two symbols joined by a tie bar if necessary. k͡p t͡s

VOWELS

Front — Central — Back

Close: i•y — ɨ•ʉ — ɯ•u
         ɪ ʏ   ʊ
Close-mid: e•ø — ɘ•ɵ — ɤ•o
                   ə
Open-mid: ɛ•œ — ɜ•ɞ — ʌ•ɔ
        æ   ɐ
Open: a•ɶ — — ɑ•ɒ

Where symbols appear in pairs, the one to the right represents a rounded vowel.

SUPRASEGMENTALS

ˈ Primary stress
ˌ Secondary stress   ˌfoʊnəˈtɪʃən
ː Long   eː
ˑ Half-long   eˑ
˘ Extra-short   ĕ
| Minor (foot) group
‖ Major (intonation) group
. Syllable break   ɹi.ækt
‿ Linking (absence of a break)

DIACRITICS

Diacritics may be placed above a symbol with a descender, e.g. ŋ̊

̥	Voiceless	n̥ d̥	̈	Breathy voiced	b̤ a̤	̪	Dental	t̪ d̪
̬	Voiced	s̬ t̬	̰	Creaky voiced	b̰ a̰	̺	Apical	t̺ d̺
ʰ	Aspirated	tʰ dʰ	̼	Linguolabial	t̼ d̼	̻	Laminal	t̻ d̻
̹	More rounded	ɔ̹	ʷ	Labialized	tʷ dʷ	̃	Nasalized	ẽ
̜	Less rounded	ɔ̜	ʲ	Palatalized	tʲ dʲ	ⁿ	Nasal release	dⁿ
̟	Advanced	u̟	ˠ	Velarized	tˠ dˠ	ˡ	Lateral release	dˡ
̠	Retracted	e̠	ˤ	Pharyngealized	tˤ dˤ	̚	No audible release	d̚
̈	Centralized	ë	̴	Velarized or pharyngealized	ɫ			
̽	Mid-centralized	ẽ	̝	Raised	e̝ (ɹ̝ = voiced alveolar fricative)			
̩	Syllabic	n̩	̞	Lowered	e̞ (β̞ = voiced bilabial approximant)			
̯	Non-syllabic	e̯	̘	Advanced Tongue Root	e̘			
˞	Rhoticity	ɚ ɑ˞	̙	Retracted Tongue Root	e̙			

TONES AND WORD ACCENTS

LEVEL			CONTOUR		
e̋ or ˥	Extra high		ě or ˧˥	Rising	
é ˦	High		ê ˥˧	Falling	
ē ˧	Mid		᷄ ˦˥	High rising	
è ˨	Low		᷅ ˨˧	Low rising	
ȅ ˩	Extra low		᷈ ˧˦˨	Rising-falling	
↓ Downstep			↗ Global rise		
↑ Upstep			↘ Global fall		

Why Phonetics?

Chapter outline

1.1 How do we describe speech?	1
1.2 Speech versus writing	2
1.3 Intonation	4
1.4 Phonology	8
1.5 Segmentation of the speech chain	11
1.6 Other applications	12
1.7 Further reading	12

The reasons for the study of phonetics should be made clear at the outset. This chapter is intended to set out the reasons why linguists (and any other people interested in spoken language of any kind) need phonetics as a tool of investigation.

1.1 How do we describe speech?

Traditional education largely ignores spoken language; even in drama and foreign language learning, little attention is paid to the details of speech in an objective way. We, therefore, need a method of describing speech in objective, verifiable terms, as opposed to the lay approaches which typically describe sounds as 'hard', 'soft', 'sharp' and so on, which can only be properly understood by the person using such descriptions. Such an approach to any subject of study is totally subjective: since only the person carrying out the descriptions can understand them, other people are expected to be 'on the same wavelength' and clever enough to follow them. So, if we are to observe and describe speech in any meaningful way, we need some kind of objectively verifiable way of doing so. In fact, there are three ways of approaching the task.

What is speech exactly? The expression 'a lot of hot air' is rather a good starting point. Speech is made by modulating air in various ways inside our bodies. The organs of speech – the lungs, throat, tongue, nose, lips and so on, which we shall discuss in detail in Chapter Two – can be moved into many different configurations to produce the different sounds we perceive when listening to spoken language. A study of the ways in which these **articulators** of speech behave is called **articulatory phonetics**. In this book the detailed investigation of articulation will take up in eight out of the nine chapters.

Basically, air is pushed out of the body and disturbs the outside air between the speaker and anyone in the vicinity who can hear him/her. These disturbances are known as **pressure fluctuations**, which in turn cause the hearer's eardrum to move. The molecules of the air move together and then apart in various ways, producing a **sound wave**. The study of the physical nature of sound waves is **acoustic phonetics**. We shall look at this aspect of speech and the relationship of articulation to acoustic effects in Chapter Nine.

The third way of considering speech, **auditory phonetics**, deals with the ways in which speech affects and is interpreted by the hearer(s). This aspect of the investigation of speech will not be considered in this book.

To simplify, the three separate but interacting aspects of speech relate to the speaker (articulation), the hearer (audition) and what happens between the speaker and the hearer (acoustics).

1.2 Speech versus writing

Another way in which untrained people describe and discuss speech is by means of seeing it as a (funny) version of writing. Of course, it is equally possible to see writing as another form of speech, but writing tends to be given central, superior status as a means of linguistic expression. In such a view, letters represent the sounds that people utter, in some unspecified way, and so spelling must be a reliable guide to pronunciation. This view of speech took hold of all forms of linguistic description in particular during the eighteenth century (for a fascinating discussion of this period in England, see Beal, 1999). Indeed for many people, written language has come to represent the 'real' language, a basis on which one is in a position to determine all other aspects of a language. As a consequence many people believe that a language can be captured and set in stone in an authoritative dictionary, for example, the Oxford English Dictionary. What belongs to English is what is in the dictionary; what is not in the dictionary is not worth bothering with in serious studies. This is an untenable position. Not only do we find considerable variation across different written languages, but even within one language we find variability in the representation of sounds in the orthographic (i.e., writing) system; consider, for example, the different sounds represented by *ch* in English, French and German, and consider the different values of the letter *c* in *receive*, *conduct*, *indict* and *cappucino*. It is also the case that in two important senses, speech is prior to writing. First, when children acquire language naturally, it is the spoken language that is acquired. Writing is artificial and has to be taught, as is noted in Table 1.1. Children will not acquire the ability to write with the Roman alphabet (or any other kind) naturally with no adult intervention in the form of teaching. Second, in the development of human beings, speech evolved and then writing was invented much later when the social need arose. So, to understand all the facets of language, we need to study both speech and writing.

The differences between speech and writing should be considered in some detail here: for example, speech is transient, while writing is permanent;

Table 1.1 Some characteristics of speech and writing

WRITTEN	SPOKEN
1. Occurs in space	1. Occurs in time
2. Permanent inscription on material	2. Evanescent occurrence in behaviour
3. Source can be absent	3. Sources of speech often conversational, face to face
4. Is transcribed by definition	4. Can be transcribed from recordings
5. Skills: writing, reading – literacy	5. Skills: speaking, listening – oracy
6. Acquired by formal education	6. Naturally acquired by about age 5
7. Must be taught	7. Not taught, appears innate
8. Must be acquired second	8. Acquired first naturally
9. Allows detailed planning	9. Spontaneous
10. Allows complex interpretative procedures, which may not relate to speaker's intentions	10. Usually comprehended in terms of speaker's communicative intentions (speaker has authority)
11. Based on sentences	11. Based on intonational groups
12. Space between words	12. Continuous stream of speech
13. Sentence construction according to conventions of writing	13. Performances include semi-sentences, repetitions, re-statements, corrections, false starts and hesitations
14. Standardized spelling	14. Accent variation
15. Enables all practices involving writing – administration, business, bureaucracy, literature, history, note-taking, letter-wrting, etc.	15. Constitutes conversational and all other spoken uses of language – telling narratives, jokes, etc
16. Segmental mode of transcription	16. Continuous articulation

speech is usually carried out face-to-face, whereas writing is designed for communication at a distance in space or time. There have also been changes to the traditional types of medium brought about by recent technology. In the first instance, both speech and writing should be considered completely separate media; one is then in a position to consider what the relationship between the two might be, a topic that will not be elaborated in this book, which focusses on the nature of speech.

As a starting point, Table 1.1 gives a simplified list of several features of speech and writing in a contrastive way.

I will take a few of these to exemplify the differences in more detail.

1.3 Intonation

Given that writing is relatively permanent (we can still read original Shakespearean manuscripts, consult the Dead Sea scrolls or ancient Egyptian inscriptions), whereas speech is transient (although we have been able to record and replay speech for a little over a century, we do not do so as a general rule), this difference has certain consequences. By its very nature, speech has to be processed virtually instantaneously by the hearer(s), so a lot of cues as to the speaker's meaning have to be reliably identified. Writing has the luxury of being able to be returned to for numerous re-readings to determine the meaning, if need be. One of the most important cues (in English, at least) in spoken language in determining interpersonal meaning is what is called **intonation**. By 'interpersonal meaning' I mean those aspects of communication that are not determined by the lexical meaning of words nor by some aspects of the syntax. Intonation patterns can convey a speaker's attitude to the content of what (s)he is saying to the hearer(s); in interaction with the order of syntactic phrases they can also indicate what the speaker believes to be new information for the hearer(s).

We shall be looking at the physical characteristics of intonation further below (see Chapters Six and Nine), but the term refers to the rise and fall of the pitch of the voice, brought about by the change in rate of vibration of the vocal cords. (Many non-specialists call this 'inflection of the voice'; this is not the usage of linguists, because the term 'inflection' is reserved for quite a different linguistic phenomenon, namely, the system of endings on words of the same grammatical category that give them different functions in a sentence, e.g., *live, live+s, liv+ing, live+d.*) For now let us take a number of examples of how intonation works in English to indicate differences of meaning. Example (1.1), in its written form, is an ambiguous sentence.

(1.1) They are sailing ships.

In fact, not only does this sentence have (at least) two different meanings, it has two different syntactic structures.

(1.2) They are NP[`sailing ships].

On the one hand, (1.2) means that *sailing ships* is a complex NP with a high falling tone starting on the syllable *sail* and continuing to fall through to the end of the utterance. This is indicated by [`] in front of the NP.

(1.3) They V[are ˌsailing] NP[`ships].

In (1.3), on the other hand, *ships* is the simple object NP of the verb *are sailing*, indicated by a low tone [ˌ] on the syllable *sail* and a high fall on *ships*.

In speech no native speaker could be confused about the meaning of either one of them. (1.4) represents yet another instance of written ambiguity versus spoken clarity.

(1.4) You might have told me.

With a high fall on *might* and a low rise on *told*, the sentence means 'It is possible that you told me'.

(1.5) You `might have ˌtold me.

With a high sliding fall over *might have* and a fall+rise [ˇ] on *told* the meaning is 'You didn't tell me', implying that you should have done, so the sentence is clearly a reproach to the hearer(s).

(1.6) You `might have ˇtold me.

In Chapter Nine, we will discuss the acoustic characteristics of intonation (and they are mentioned briefly in section 6.1), but basically it can be presented as a plot of the changes in the **fundamental frequency** of the utterance, which clearly shows the ups and downs of the speaker's intonation pattern (basically changes in the frequency of the signal caused by change of rate of vibration of the vocal cords). I give the two versions of *You might have told me* as Figure 1.1 (= (1.5)) and Figure 1.2 (= (1.6)).

6 A Critical Introduction to Phonetics

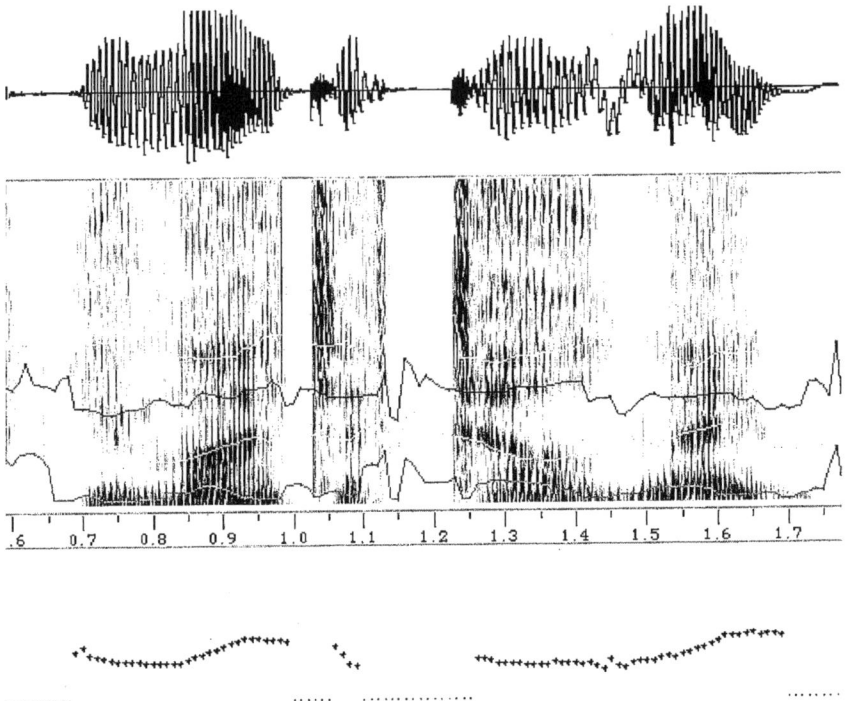

Figure 1.1 Fundamental frequency (F0) plot of example (1.5).

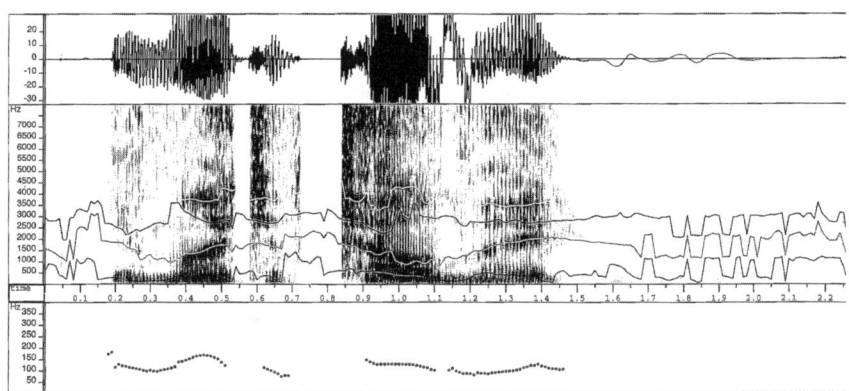

Figure 1.2 Fundamental frequency (F0) plot of example (1.6).

In the written form of a language there are usually ways of indicating a very limited number of the effects of intonation on the interpretation of an utterance, for example, !, ?, . . ., or by using lexical descriptions, for example, 'he said in a high-pitched, whining voice', but these hardly reflect the nuances that the human voice can bring to speech.

Another way in which speech is organized differently from writing relates to the fact that speech is usually carried out in a face-to-face context where the interlocutors can see one another and often share the same cultural background. Consequently, a lot of the conventions of speech are known to each interlocutor and so at least part of the meaning of utterances can be left unspoken. For example, a hearer will understand the second part of the example (1.7) as the reason for the first part, though no explicit connection has been made.

(1.7) I'm sorry I'm late. I missed the bus.

In writing it is not so easy to rely on implicit meanings in this way, as the reader may be very distant in space and time. Connections between parts of a written text tend to be more explicit than in speech, in particular by means of syntactic connectives such as pronouns or conjunctions. Here again, speech often uses intonational devices to indicate connections, and, equally importantly, points in conversational interchanges where other speakers can join in. This is a vast area for detailed investigation, and we cannot include it in this book, but it is mentioned here to give an idea of the importance of being able to study the fine detail of phonetic performance to help us to understand how language works in its many forms.

None of this is intended to argue that one of the linguistic media is superior to the other, merely that they are very different from one another. Each has its own characteristics and its own strengths. It should also be pointed out that it is not really a matter of a simple choice between speech and writing. There are instances where language is written down to be spoken out loud, for example, news bulletins, plays; or even spoken to be written down, for example, dictation, lectures. Modern technology has blurred the distinction even further and there are several mixed media varieties of language today, for example, text messaging, which incorporates aspects of speech in a written format, largely because of limitations of space and the transitory nature of such messages, or computer programs which convert, with varying degrees of success, speech into writing or writing into speech.

The point of this brief comparison of the characteristics of speech and writing is to demonstrate that since the two are so different, we need very different ways of treating them. Writing, as relatively permanent marks on a page, is already captured for us to analyze and comment on. Most educated people have had some training in looking at writing from an analytical point of view of some kind (even if it is not informed by linguistic analysis), but by its very nature, speech is not captured for us to analyse in the same way. Before we carry out any form of higher analysis, that is, phonological analysis, we have to understand its nature, and capture something that is essentially transient. This is what we need phonetics for.

1.4 Phonology

This is not a book about phonology. There is an excellent companion to this book in the same series about phonology (Silverman [2006]). However, it would be odd to say nothing about it at all and not to explain a little why it is different from phonetics, especially as most linguists would assume that the main reason for studying phonetics is to enable us to talk about the phonological systems of the world's languages. Furthermore, the relationship between the two, phonetics and phonology, is coming under ever-increasing scrutiny, and an assumption that the relationship between the two is obvious and straightforward can no longer be accepted. In very general terms, phonetics is about the physical nature of human speech sounds, irrespective of which language is being spoken, and phonology is the study of the way native speakers organize and store the knowledge of the sounds of their own language that enables them to use it appropriately on all occasions.

Phonology, then, is the study of linguistic systems, specifically the way in which sound represents differences of meaning in a language. In English, native speakers know that the words *pin* and *bin* mean something different and that the difference resides in the two different initial sounds. For the time being I am using a standard, segmental view of the situation whereby each word is made up of three segments, and *p* and *b* can be isolated from the other two. We shall discuss the phonetic details of such articulations in due course, but even without that information we can see the phonological point that is being made: these two words have meaningfully different sounds in English. We could go through the whole language in a similar vein, establishing the distinctive consonants and vowels, stating the ways in which they can be put together to form legitimate words, for example, *pin*, *bin*, *nip* and *nib* are legitimate English words, but **ipn*, **ibn*, **pni* and **nbi* are not. (The asterisk indicates an impossible form for a particular language.) This knowledge of English phonological structure has nothing to do directly with the phonetic detail of how actual words are pronounced; it has to do with more abstract organizational principles.

In most forms of phonological theory it is assumed that each language or language variety (see Chapter Eight) has a single system of contrasts which may vary slightly depending on position in the syllable, for example, the beginning (**onset**) or the end (**coda**). So each language has a system of consonants and vowels to distinguish each of its lexical items from each other. (This does not rule out **homophony**, that is two or more words sounding the same, but that issue need not concern us in this simple explanation.) So in English, for example, the words in (1.8) give the meaningfully distinct onset consonants. I have given a simple phonetic transcription in each case, especially as the orthographic form can be misleading or ambiguous. I put the IPA alphabet symbols in square brackets; consult the chart on p. x for the time being. The basic principle is that each different symbol represents a different sound with no ambiguity.

(1.8)
pin [pɪn]	fin [fɪn]	get [get]
bin [bɪn]	thin [θɪn]	let [let]
tin [tɪn]	sin [sɪn]	yet [jet]
din [dɪn]	shin [ʃɪn]	van [væn]
kin [kɪn]	Lynn [lɪn]	than [ðæn]
chin [tʃɪn]	win [wɪn]	Jeanne [ʒæn]
gin [dʒɪn]	rest [ɹest]	zest [zest]
mit [mɪt]	knit [nɪt]	hit [hɪt]

It is not possible to find words for all the onset consonants that have the same sounds in the **rhyme**, that is the vowel + its coda, for example, there is no English word *[gɪn] or *[zɪn], and some sounds are clearly less common than others in this position (e.g., [ʒæn] is a loanword from French.). But these are historical, chance implementations of the system.

Irrespective of the phonetic details of the pronunciation of these consonants it is possible to appreciate the system of contrasts and to see which the important consonants at the beginning of English words are. In most versions of phonology the distinctive phonological units are called **phonemes** (see, for example, Davenport and Hannahs [2005]). In phonemic transcriptions each phoneme is represented by a different symbol, usually one which approximates some of the phonetic detail, and is placed between slant lines, for example, /pɪn/, rather than [pɪn]. I deal with various kinds of transcription in Chapter Four.

The constraints on English phonological forms, of the kind referred to above in connection with *pin, bin, *ipn, *nbi* and so on, are not necessarily the same in all languages. In other words, the constraints are not a result of some universal phonetic inability on the part of humans to pronounce certain sequences of sounds. By way of exemplification, let us take the sounds [h] and [ŋ]; the latter is the final sound in standard English *king* and *song*. In English [h] can only occur in initial position of a stressed syllable, as in *hat, hoop, ahead, behind*; [ŋ] can only occur at the end of a syllable or followed by an unstressed syllable, as in *king, hang, singer, hanger*. So a form such as **ngah* [ŋæh] could not be a word of English. From a phonetic point of view this is not unpronounceable, and there are languages which do allow [h] and [ŋ] to occur in such syllabic positions; for example, Comaltepec Chinantec, an Otomanguean language spoken in Mexico, has words such as [loh] "cactus", [ŋi] "salt" and even [ŋɪh] "chayote" (a kind of tropical fruit). (I have ignored, and therefore not indicated, the inherent tones associated with these words; for more details of the language, see Silverman [2006: pp. 144–152].) So, it is a matter of linguistic structure, not pronounceability that determines what combinations of sounds are allowed in any particular language system. In other words, it is a matter for phonology to deal with, not phonetics. We may note here that a speaker's native knowledge of their phonology may lead them to believe that what does not occur in their language is indeed unpronounceable, and would remain so for them without special training, as in learning a foreign language.

It is at the interface between phonetics and phonology that we find traditionally assumed interconnections between the two areas, not all of which have been investigated thoroughly enough to determine their usefulness in understanding the nature of language. It is at this point where the notion of sound slips back and forth between the two areas. Speakers make sounds that are linguistic in nature, as part of their system of meaning, but, as we have just seen, there are two separate aspects to these 'sounds'. They are physical entities, which can be described in objective ways, for example, [p] in *pin* is a voiceless, oral, bilabial plosive with a delay in the onset of vocal cord vibration (voicing) in the following vowel; but they are also abstract elements in a system, which are used by native speakers to store information about how the individual words of their language behave, including how to utter them. The question that has to be asked (but which we will not attempt to answer in this book) is: is it legitimate, and, more to the point, helpful to call both these entities 'sounds'? It is also at this point where the notion of a segment in the phonology (which may or may not be legitimate) can determine our view of speech as being made up of phonetic segments (phones), because it makes life much easier if both levels, phonology and phonetics, work on roughly the same principles. This alignment of views of structure is what is referred to as isomorphism, which has become more of a dogma over the years since the Second World War, during which time great advances have been made in our understanding of acoustic phonetics, than a helpful tool to give us greater insight into the nature and functioning of language. This takes us to a fundamental question as to what a sound is. The answer is complicated and I hope by the end of the book, you will have a clearer idea of what the answer (or may be answers) might be.

Linguists are interested in generalizable features of all kinds, so a concern with universal characteristics of language, including phonological systems, is central to many people's research interests. In this research programme the relationship between phonological universals and phonetic universals is of central importance.

1.5 Segmentation of the speech chain

One very important issue involving the assumed relationship between speech and writing concerns the nature of the vehicle of writing itself. Many languages, and certainly the world-dominant European ones, use an alphabet to represent the spoken form, for example, Roman, Cyrillic, Greek, Cufic. In such alphabets it is assumed and claimed that each letter represents 'a sound'. In other words, speech is represented as a sequence of discrete segments (letters) strung together like beads on a thread, with gaps between clusters of them (words). On this model the International Phonetic Association (IPA) alphabet was established in the late 19th century and is still with us today, having undergone a number of fairly minor modifications in more recent times. Indeed, it will be used in this book, and it is important to learn how to use it to transcribe speech. However, it is one thing to have a convenient notation for indicating details of speech that are ignored by conventional orthographies, but quite another to assume that somehow speech can be segmented in the same way that writing can be. In this respect we will need to consider some of the possible answers to the question we raised at the end of the previous section: 'What is a sound?' We should note in passing that not all writing systems are alphabetic, for example, the standard Chinese writing system, and the earliest Ancient Egyptian hieroglyphs. Because this is such a central issue to the understanding of the nature of speech, I intend to devote Chapter Five to a more detailed consideration of it, after the basics of articulation have been presented. It will reappear as an issue at various points in the book, as appropriate.

1.6 Other applications

I pointed out in the previous section that most linguists consider that the main reason for studying phonetics is to enable us to understand the sound systems of the world's languages. There are, however, other reasons for the study of speech, which apply our knowledge of language to other specific areas. Language learning and teaching, speech processing (synthesis and recognition), speech therapy, forensic linguistics, drama and singing all benefit from an understanding of how speech works. One might even wish to argue that for any area of investigation relating to language, even syntactic theory, a thorough knowledge of what spoken language is like is a basic prerequisite. After all, we don't want the standard written language to masquerade as speech.

1.7 Further reading

There are a number of introductory textbooks on phonetics and phonology. Sometimes they are incorporated into the same book, sometimes not. Personally, I prefer the latter, even though it is necessary to talk about phonology in general terms in a book about phonetics, as we shall see in later chapters. Some introductions to phonology include brief introductions to phonetics, but these are intended to be résumés rather than basic training in the subject. The list of phonetics books below is not intended to be exhaustive, and it is often instructive to go back to earlier treatments of phonetics, such as Pike (1943). It is always worthwhile following up some of the references in the introductory books for more detailed treatments of particular aspects of phonetics: Ball and Rahilly (1999); Clark and Yallop (1995); Davenport and Hannahs (2005); Ladefoged (2006).

For a discussion of some fundamental issues in phonology that are often taken for granted, see Kelly and Local (1989), Docherty and Foulkes (2000), Silverman (2006). For a useful discussion of the issue of isomorphism between phonetics and phonology, see Appelbaum (1999). A useful survey of views of the interface between phonetics and phonology is provided by Scobbie (2005).

Articulation 2

Chapter outline

2.1 The lungs and airstream mechanisms	14
2.2 The vocal cords and the glottis	15
2.3 The pharynx	21
2.4 The epiglottis	22
2.5 The velum	22
2.6 The tongue	23
2.7 The lips	25
2.8 Active/passive articulators	26
2.9 Degree of occlusion	33
2.10 Non-pulmonic airstreams	46
2.11 Some pseudo-phonetic terms	48
2.12 Further reading and advice	49

I have introduced a few technical terms in the previous chapter. It is now time to present articulation and the technicalities we need to describe it in a much more organized way. I shall take each of the contributory mechanisms of speech in turn and consider what rôle each has to play. By way of organizing this survey, I shall start with general descriptions at the furthest point of the vocal apparatus, the lungs, and follow the direction of the airflow. The operation of the vocal cords and the velum are particularly important, and are discussed en route. However, in order to introduce the details of the mechanisms used in the mouth in sections 2.8 and 2.9, I shall start at the lips and go

14 A Critical Introduction to Phonetics

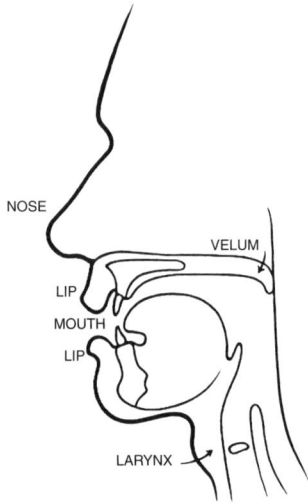

Figure 2.1 Cross-section of the vocal apparatus.

backwards into the mouth to enable you in the initial stages to appreciate the more obvious and manipulable aspects of the articulations you use.

Figure 2.1 is a cross-section of the head and neck along their median line, showing the major mechanisms that we shall deal with in turn.

The major areas of articulation are the **larynx**, **velum**, **mouth** and **lips**. We shall look at the details of each in its contribution to speech. In addition we shall consider the rôle of the lungs, the pharynx and the epiglottis, as well as the way in which air is used generally in articulation. I will put technical terms in bold on their first occurrence; they are also listed in the glossary (pp. 230–239).

In working through all the possibilities of human articulation it is important both to hear examples of them and to try to produce them yourself. This is best done with the aid of the phonetician teaching you.

2.1 The lungs and airstream mechanisms

Speech is produced by moulding and moving the articulators of all kinds around an airstream. In most cases this air comes from the lungs. During speech the volume of air in the lungs has to be greater than is used in ordinary breathing (try speaking with just normal breath and little will happen). Humans are capable of a special breathing pattern which can take in a large amount of air and release it in a controlled way over a period of time, usually more than enough time to utter a sentence or two. Such air, when it is expelled from the lungs for linguistic purposes, is called **egressive pulmonic air**. This is by far the easiest method of producing speech, especially as it can continue over quite a period, but it is not the only way in which air can be used.

There are two ways in which air can be trapped in the oral cavity:

(i) by closing the **glottis** and making some other closure in the mouth; and
(ii) by closing the **velum** and making a **velar** closure with the back of the tongue, and making some other closure in advance of this.

(i) produces a **glottalic airstream**, (ii) a **velaric airstream**. The glottalic airstream is used to produce two types of sound, **implosives** and **ejectives**; the velaric airstream is used to produce **clicks**.

I shall deal first with the egressive pulmonic airstream and the modulating mechanisms, and then consider the more restricted types of airstream at the end of the chapter.

2.2 The vocal cords and the glottis

Within the **larynx** are the **vocal cords** (also called **vocal folds**), two muscular flaps which can be moved into various positions to interfere with the airflow. The part of the windpipe that goes through the larynx is called the glottis. We need to consider the ways in which the vocal cords operate in more detail in relation to egressive pulmonic air.

The larynx is a casing made of cartilage and muscle around the windpipe (**trachea**), containing the vocal cords stretched across the glottis. At the front of the larynx the thyroid cartilage is seen from the outside of the throat as the 'Adam's apple' in men and 'Eve's wedding ring' in women; the protusion of the thyroid cartilage is usually greater in men than in women. The vocal cords can be moved into different positions by the operation of the arytnoid cartilages to which they are attached. The arytenoid cartilages are generally thicker in men than in women, and the cords themselves are generally longer in men than in women. (Note that since the vocal cords are primarily intended to stop foreign substances entering the lungs, tar from smoking cigarettes becomes lodged on them; this means that heavy smokers often develop deep voices because they cannot vibrate their cords quickly enough to produce the usual higher pitch ranges.)

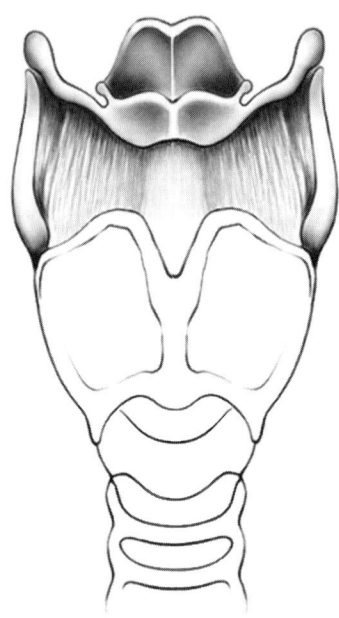

Figure 2.2 The larynx.

There are basically five different ways in which the vocal cords can be placed in relation to one another across the glottis. The resultant effects these different positions of the cords have on speech are referred to as **phonation**.

2.2.1 Closed glottis

As we saw in section 2.1, the vocal cords can be shut tight together, completely obstructing the flow of air through the glottis. This simple mechanism is known as the **glottal stop**.

The glottal stop is used in many languages and can be heard as an interruption of sound when it occurs between vowels. It is symbolized [ʔ]. Many accents of British English have it between vowels in words and phrases like [bɛʔə] *better*, [bʌʔə] *butter*, [gɒʔə] *got a*, [bɔʔə] *bought a*. (Notice that for the moment I have not separated the words in the phonetic transcription in the way we do in standard orthography.) Try saying a simple vowel interrupted by the glottal stop at regular intervals, for example, [aʔaʔaʔaʔaʔa]. (Note that an utterance of this kind is used by adults to young children as a warning.)

Although this simple glottal closure can be interpreted as a 'sound' in linguistic terms, as demonstrated for English above, it can also be used in conjunction with a **supraglottal** closure, that is, a closure above the glottis in the

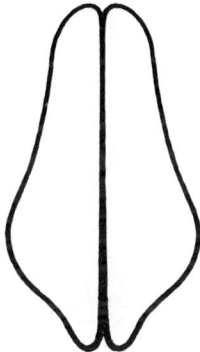

Figure 2.3 Closed glottis.

oral cavity. If the airstream is trapped and released in a particular way that we will look at later in section 2.10.2, such combined articulations result in ejectives. If the two closures are unreleased, symbolized by [˺], before another closure or the general relaxation of the articulators at the end of an utterance, we are dealing with **glottal reinforcement**, as in English [kæʔp˺] *cap*, [kæʔt˺], *cat*, [kɪʔk˺] *kick*, which have unreleased oral closures (see section 2.9.1). Glottally reinforced sounds do not have the upward movement of the larynx to compress the supralaryngeal air that we find in ejectives; glottal reinforcement is produced by stopping the egressive pulmonic air. In some accents of British English such glottal reinforcement can occur **intervocalically** (= between vowels); for instance in Norwich and Norfolk we find forms such as [æːʔpi] *happy*, [sɪʔti] *city*, [pʊuʔkə] *poker*, and in many parts of Lancashire and Yorkshire, where the definite article is pronounced [ʔ], we find glottal reinforcement in syllable-initial position, as in [ʔpʊb] *the pub*, [ʔtɹeːn] *the train*, [ʔkʊkə] *the cooker*. We even find oral stops in which the phonation changes to voicing before the stop is released, as in [ʔbʊs] *the bus*, [ʔdɹeːn] *the drain*, [ʔgeːm] *the game* (see section 8.4.2).

2.2.2 Open glottis

The opposite extreme position for the vocal cords to complete closure is to have them wide apart.

In this position the air flows freely through the glottis, giving an effect to the speech chain known as **voicelessness**. This feature is a component in some of the English stops and fricatives: [p t k tʃ f θ s ʃ], which are all labelled [voiceless]. (Note that from this chapter onwards I will put phonetic feature labels in square brackets, e.g., [voiced].)

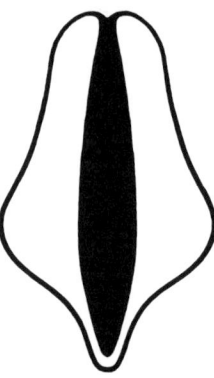

Figure 2.4 Open glottis.

We should note here some of the contradictory classifications of some sounds in the IPA chart. The glottal stop [ʔ] is placed to the left of its cell, thereby indicating that it is voiceless. But this cannot be the case; [voiceless], as we have just defined it, means 'with an open glottis', whereas the glottal stop is produced with closed vocal cords. The vocal cords cannot be both open and closed at the same time. Of course, a phonologist might argue that [voiceless] actually means 'not having any vibration of the vocal cords', which would cover the glottal stop production, but such an interpretation does not distinguish between any of the phonation types (other than [voiced]) that we are discussing, and so is not very specific from a phonetic point of view. In other words, such an interpretation would need further features to distinguish the other phonatory types.

2.2.3 Vibrating vocal cords

It is possible to hold the vocal cords loosely together so that they impede the flow of air without stopping it completely. If the cords are in this position across an egressive airflow, they produce a build-up of pressure beneath them until it becomes too great for them to hold it back. The pressure beneath the cords (**subglottal**) becomes greater than the air pressure above them (**supraglottal**) so the subglottal air pushes the cords apart and equalizes the air pressure for a fraction of a second. But with the drop in pressure and the muscular tension used to hold the vocal cords in this position, they snap back together again, and the whole process starts again. The banging together of the vocal cords in this way produces vibration, which is what produces the feature [**voiced**].

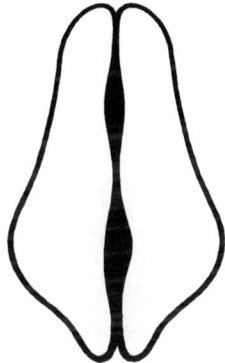

Figure 2.5 Vibrating cords.

In many languages we find that pairs of sounds are distinguished by being either voiceless or voiced; the voiceless English stops and fricatives listed above have voiced partners: [b d g dʒ v ð z ʒ]. To appreciate the difference between voicelessness and voice, try saying an alveolar fricative (because it is continuous, unlike the stops) and alternate between the voiceless one and the voiced one without interrupting the friction: [szszszszszszsz]. While doing this, place your hand on your larynx or close your ears with your fingers, and you will be able to feel the vibration as it is switched on and off.

Vibration of the vocal cords has another major function in linguistic terms: it enables the speaker to change the pitch of his/her speech by varying the rate of vibration. The quicker the rate of vibration, the higher the pitch will be. Pitch changes are a vital part of language production, both in terms of an intonation system, as we saw in English in section 1.3, and as a marker of lexical contrast in what are called tone languages (see section 6.1). Another test whereby you can appreciate voicing is to try to sing the sounds: voiced ones are singable, voiceless ones are not. This means that when we are listening to singing we 'think' the melody through the voiceless sounds; it's just as well for singers that voiced sounds outnumber voiceless ones in the world's languages.

2.2.4 Murmur

The vocal cords can be kept apart, but closer together than for voicelessness. The force of the airflow causes vibration of a different type from voicing. This phonation type is called **murmur** or **breathy voice**.

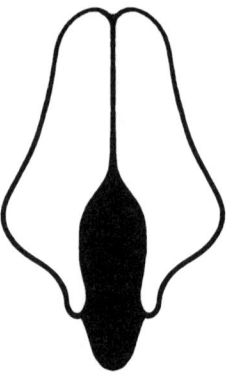

Figure 2.6 Murmur.

Some English speakers use breathy voice at the beginning of the second syllable in *ahead*, between the two vowels. Some Indian languages, such as Hindi, use it in contrast to voicelessness and voicing, giving three types of stop, voiceless, voiced and murmured.

Whereas voiceless and voiced stops and fricatives have their own distinctive symbols: [p,b t,d s,z] and so on (though this is not the case for the most part for other types of sound; see Chapter Three), murmur is represented by [..] beneath the symbol for a voiced sound: [b̤ d̤ ṳ].

2.2.5 Creak

If the vocal cords are only open at one end and are vibrated very slowly, the result is **creak** or **creaky voice**.

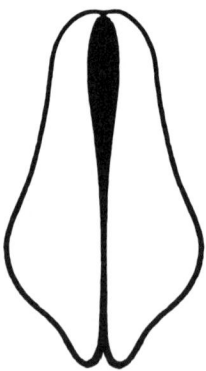

Figure 2.7 Creaky voice.

This is a feature of some speakers of English; the creak can be heard, sometimes sporadically, through the speech chain. It is also a feature of anyone who is suffering from a cold, where there is a build-up of mucous on the cords themselves, making them difficult to operate properly; the same applies to habitual smokers, who often have creaky voices as well as deep ones.

We will consider an example of creak further in our discussion of Chong in section 5.3; it is represented by [̬] under the appropriate symbol for a voiced sound: [b̬ d̬ u̬].

2.2.6 Whisper

We can whisper in one of two ways: a very quiet whisper, which is only audible in very close proximity to the speaker, and a more energetic one, that can be heard further away. In the first case the normal position for voicelessness is used; in the second the cords are shut except for a small aperture near the arytenoid cartilages at the back of the larynx, through which air can escape, but without any vibration of the vocal cords. In either case all changes in pitch available to the speaker during voicing are excluded.

2.3 The pharynx

If we move up the vocal apparatus in the direction of egressive air, immediately above the larynx is the pharynx. Part of it can be seen in a mirror looking through the opening at the back of the oral cavity (**faucal opening**) and is referred to by non-specialists as well as specialists as the throat. Typically, phoneticians do not use this more general term.

The size of the pharynx can be altered either by tightening the muscles surrounding it or by moving the tongue back into it, or both. Any such change in the size of the pharynx causes a change in the quality of the sounds being produced. The **root** (**radix**) of the tongue can be moved from its position of rest either forwards slightly or backwards slightly. The former movement will expand the size of the pharynx, the latter will reduce it. We will return to the effects of this when we consider the rôle of the tongue in section 2.6. Tightening the pharynx is often a correlate of certain vowel articulation, but it can also be a general feature of individual speakers' speech. Mimics who caricature(d) John Major, the most recent Conservative Prime Minister of Great Britain, use pharyngeal tightening in an exaggerated way to replicate his voice quality.

When we come to consider places of articulation in section 2.8, we will find that the back wall of the pharynx has a limited rôle to play as a passive articulator.

2.4 The epiglottis

The epiglottis is a small upward-pointing flap at the extreme base of the tongue (see Figure 2.9). A few languages use it as an alternative to the root of the tongue in pharyngeal articulations, and a few Caucasian languages use both articulations for phonological contrast (see Ladefoged [2006]: pp. 166–167).

2.5 The velum

We have referred to the soft palate or velum on a number of occasions so far. If you run your tongue along the roof of your mouth starting at the teeth, you will find that the hard, boney part gives way to a softer section towards the back. This is the velum. (It is customary in phonetics to use the term 'velum' for the soft palate, and 'palate' to refer to the hard palate.)

Again, we will return to the rôle of the velum as a passive articulator in section 2.8, but for the moment we need to see it as an on/off switch for channelling the airflow. At the top of the pharynx the air passages divide into two: one route goes into the mouth, the other into the nose. The velum, which hangs down during normal (non-linguistic) breathing to allow the air to escape through the nose, can be moved up against the back wall of the pharynx near to the start of the nasal cavities (**nasopharynx**). This closes off the nasal cavities and sends the egressive air into the mouth alone. When the velum is open (=is hanging down), the air flows into both the mouth and the nose. The two positions of the velum give the features [oral], when it is closed, and [nasal], when it is open. (Although there can be individuals who do not close off the nasal cavities completely and so produce 'nasal leakage' in that the air leaks into the nose to some extent, the idea of a two-way mechanism is sufficient for most purposes.)

This two-way mechanism also gives us pairs of sounds, oral versus nasal. In English we can hear the following: [b,m d,n g,ŋ]. This pairing means that the sounds are produced in the same way, except for the position of the velum. It is difficult to be aware of the movement of the velum. This is because there are fewer nerve endings in this part of the mouth in comparison with areas nearer the front, so direct awareness of feelings and movement are less obvious.

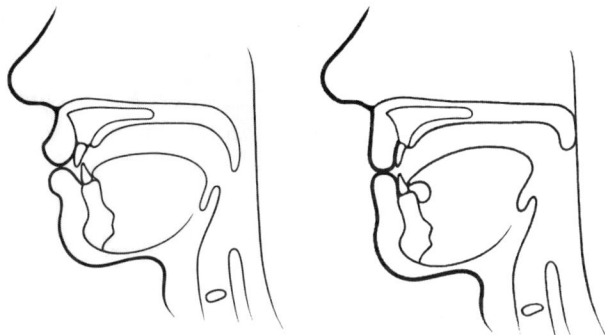

Figure 2.8 Open and closed velum.

If I tell you to touch your lips with your finger, or touch the alveolar ridge with the tip of your tongue, you can do it without difficulty and in full awareness of what you are doing. (This is referred to technically as **proprioceptive observation**, a very useful technique in learning phonetics.) On the other hand, if I tell you to move your velum, you will not know what to do (even though you now know what the velum is). If you are a native speaker of English, you can practice using words of your own language that involve just the movement of the velum one way or the other. For instance, say the word *hand*. The coda of this word has voicing and alveolar contact, [-nd]. The transition from [n] to [d] is achieved simply by closing the velum. So, say the word again and try to feel the movement of the velum from the open to the closed position. This may take several attempts before you appreciate what is happening, but it is well worth the effort to understand and feel what is going on when you speak.

Now try to perceive the movement from closed to open. This can be achieved by saying the word *hidden* with no vowel in the final syllable: [hɪdn]. (This is normal and natural to someone of my age, but may not be to younger native speakers of English.) In this case the transition from [d] to [n] is achieved solely by the change in position of the velum from closed to open.

2.6 The tongue

The tongue is a piece of flexible, non-compressible muscle, which is anchored to the floor of the mouth. Flexible means it is mobile and can change its shape, especially outside the mouth. For example, if you stick your tongue out, you can make it long and thin, roll it up at the sides or touch the end of your nose with it – in varying degrees according to the individual. Non-compressible muscle means that its volume cannot be reduced or enlarged, despite its flexibility. So any movement in one part of the tongue will be compensated for in another. If you stick your tongue out of your mouth the root of your tongue and the whole of the back portion will have to move forwards too. In most languages the tongue is not used in articulation beyond the teeth, that is, it is contained within the oral cavity. There is one language known to have a labio-lingual articulation (Pirahã, spoken in the Brazilian Amazonian jungle by a few hundred speakers, has a sound produced by the flick of the tongue tip against the top lip, in which the tongue is projected out of the mouth. Otherwise, labio-lingual articulations are restricted to abnormal speech, as in the case of some speakers with Down's syndrome.

With regard to the movements involved in normal speech, roughly speaking, a bunching of the tongue at the front of the mouth will involve an advancement of the root of the tongue; a bunching at the back of the mouth will involve a retraction of the root of the tongue. This particular phenomenon has been much discussed in phonology over recent years with arguments revolving round the features [ATR] (= advanced tongue root) and [RTR] (= retracted tongue root), but early investigations indicated that movement of the tongue

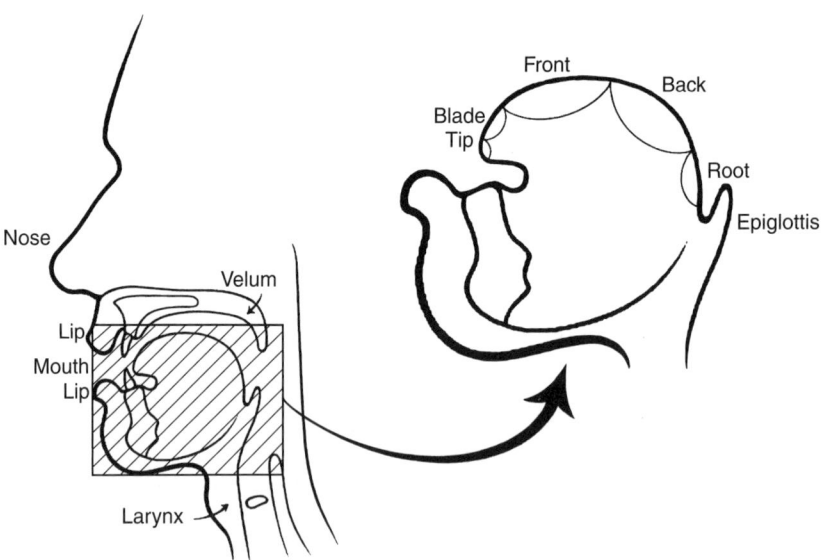

Figure 2.9 Areas of the tongue + epiglottis.

in most cases was a direct correlate of moving the bunching of the tongue on the front-back axis of the mouth (see, e.g., Lindau et al. [1973]). This is not the place to debate the pros and cons of such a feature in phonology, but a hint at the complexity of the articulations involved can be found in Local and Lodge (2004).

In physical terms the tongue is one entity, but for linguistic purposes it is divided up into particular zones that are used in articulation. Note that these zones have no physical boundaries, unlike, say, the boundary between the alveolar ridge, the palate and the velum, but are designations of specific areas that are relevant for articulation of various kinds.

The main areas of the tongue used in articulation (with their Latinate equivalent in brackets) are: **tip (apex)**, **blade (lamina)**, **front**, **back (dorsum)**, **root (radix)**. Some phoneticians distinguish three areas of the surface of the main body of the tongue: front, centre and back. Each of these areas is used in combination with an area of the oral cavity above the tongue, as we shall see in more detail in section 2.8. Whereas the tip and blade can be moved quite freely to make contact with an area from the teeth to the front of the hard palate (further back such a posture becomes uncomfortable and awkward), the front and back are only approximated in varying degrees to the part of the roof of the mouth immediately above them. It is also important to remember that the surface of the tongue is continuous, and that it will vary from speaker to speaker how much of the tip, blade or tip and blade together are used in any particular articulation. In English, for example, it makes little difference to communication whether a speaker uses the tip, the blade, or a bit of each when articulating alveolar stops and fricatives.

2.7 The lips

The lips are elastic and are operated by the musculature surrounding the mouth. From the position of rest, which we can term **neutral**, they can be spread, by pulling the sides away from one another, or they can be rounded, by pushing the sides towards one another. This gives the features [**spread**] and [**rounded**], respectively. Rounding can be achieved in either of two ways: by pursing the lips, which involves pushing them forwards at the same time as pulling the sides in, or without the pursing. Different languages use different degrees of rounding and spreading, and speakers themselves vary. French speakers have to differentiate clearly between rounded and spread vowels, as in [ly] *lu*, 'read' (past participle) versus [li] *lit*, 'bed', whereas English speakers may or may not

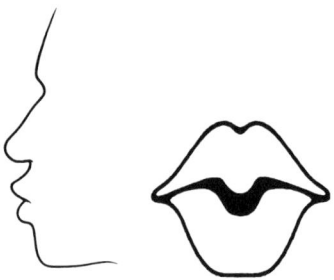

Figure 2.10 Front and side pursed lips.

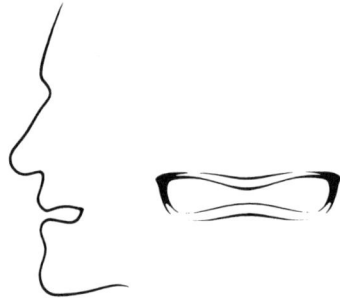

Figure 2.11 Front and side spread lips.

use rounded lips in words like *food, put, got, caught* (see Chapters Four and Eight).

2.8 Active/passive articulators

Once the egressive air is in the mouth, there are many articulators that can help to modify the airstream. Generally speaking, the oral articulators can be divided into two types: the active and the passive ones. They are listed in Table 2.1. Note that the velum belongs to both groups.

The way in which air is modulated in the mouth is by putting together an active and a passive articulator (in ways that we will discuss in more detail in section 2.9). For example, the tip of the tongue can be put against the alveolar ridge to produce sounds that we label [alveolar].

The different combinations of the oral articulators are dealt with under the general heading of **place of articulation**. There is a set of features that are used to describe which articulators are being used. I shall take each of the possibilities in turn, and symbolize a number of relevant examples of each.

Table 2.1 Active and passive articulators

Active	Passive
Lips	Teeth
Tongue	Alveolar ridge
Velum	Palate
	Velum

Further details of possible combinations of articulation are given in Chapter Three.

2.8.1 Bilabial

When both lips are used in the articulation of a sound, such a sound is labelled [**bilabial**]. [p b m] are all bilabial.

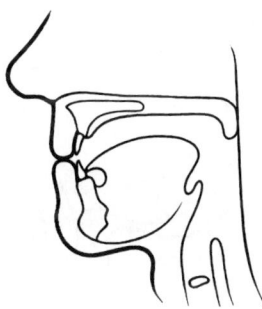

2.8.2 Labiodental

The top teeth can be placed just inside the bottom lip to produce **labiodental** sounds. [f v] are both labiodental. Note that the combination of the bottom teeth and the top lip is not a normal combination; only people with a prognathous jaw, such as many members of the royal house of Habsburg, use such articulations.

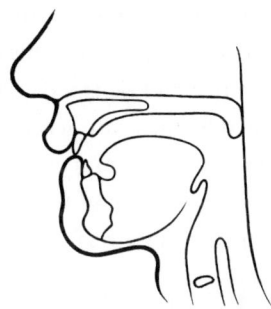

2.8.3 Dental

The tip or blade of the tongue can be placed on the back surface of the top teeth or between the teeth to produce **dental** sounds. If one wants to give even more detail that is inherent in [dental], one can specify [interdental], if the sound is produced with the tongue tip between the teeth, and specify which part of the tongue is being used to make contact, as in [apico-dental] or [lamino-dental]. Dental sounds include [θ ð], the initial sounds in English *think* and *this*, respectively. (Don't be misled by the English spelling system which represents both the voiceless and the voiced versions with the same two letters; also note that these are single, simplex sounds. Don't let the spelling lead you to think there are two sounds stuck together.) Say [θ] and [ð], and see what kind of dental contact you use.

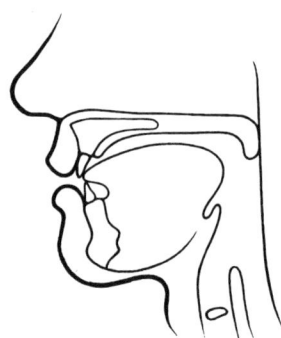

It is important to note that all obstruents involving the tongue tip, blade or front as an articulator have a concomitant side contact with the upper molars. This is to prevent air escaping round the sides of the tongue, something we will return to in section 2.9.

2.8.4 Alveolar

The **alveolar ridge** is the boney protuberance at the start of the roof of the mouth into which the teeth are set. Again, either the tip or the blade can be put into contact with it. [t d s z n] are all alveolar. (This word is pronounced in any one of three ways in standard British English, depending on which syllable is given the main stress, indicated by the acute accent on the orthographic form: [ˈælvjələ] *álveolar*, [ælˈviːələ] *alvéolar*, [ælvɪˈoʊlə] *alveólar*. Try pronouncing each of these transcriptions with the help of the IPA chart or my adaptations of it below.) Note that alveolar stops and fricatives have lateral contact with the upper molars.

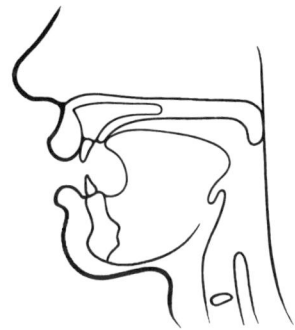

2.8.5 Retroflex

The tongue tip can be flexed backwards so that the under surface is towards the roof of the mouth. Contact is made with the area just behind the alveolar ridge or just in front of the (**hard**) **palate** to produce **retroflex** sounds. Notice that, unlike the other features described in this section, the term refers to the position of the tongue tip rather than designating the passive articulator. An alternative method of producing retroflex sounds is to pull the tip back from the alveolar ridge to make contact with the same part of the roof of the mouth, without flexing it backwards. (To describe these sounds, we could equally well refer to them as **post-alveolar** or **pre-palatal** by using the point of contact, but [retroflex] is the customary usage.) There are accents of English that use retroflex articulations, such as parts of urban Lancashire and the West Country, and many of the Indian languages have retroflex articulation, which many speakers of English from the subcontinent use in their variety of English. Retroflex sounds include [ʈ ɖ ɳ ʂ ʐ]. Notice that all the symbols have a tail curved to the right.

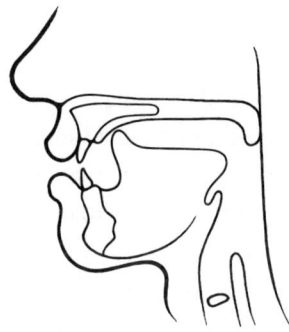

2.8.6 Palatoalveolar

Since the tongue surface and the roof of the mouth are, in fact, continuous surfaces, the amount of each that is used to make contact in articulation can vary considerably. We can put the tip of the tongue on the back of the alveolar ridge and the blade on the front of the palate and produce **palatoalveolar** sounds. (The more recent editions of the IPA chart label these sounds 'post-alveolar'. The reason for this change is unclear to me; I persist in using [palatoalveolar] along with many others, e.g., Davenport and Hannahs [2005].) We shall see in section 2.9.1 that such sounds are restricted in their manner of articulation. English has [ʃ ʒ tʃ dʒ] as in [ʃuu] *shoe*, [pleʒə] *pleasure*, [tʃɜtʃ] *church*, [dʒʌdʒ] *judge*.

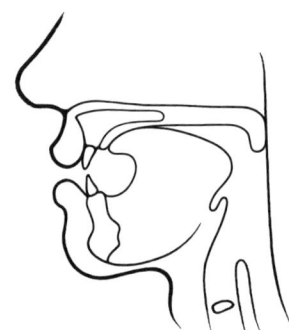

2.8.7 Alveolo-palatal

An equally restricted type of articulation involving a different relationship between tongue, alveolar ridge and palate from that used in palatoalveolar sounds is referred to as **alveolo-palatal**. More of the front of the tongue is placed against the palate in these fricatives: [ɕ ʑ]. Polish, for example, has both types of fricative: [ʃ ʒ ɕ ʑ].

2.8.8 Palatal

Instead of using the tip or blade of the tongue, the part immediately adjoining the blade, the front, can be used to articulate sounds by raising it into contact with the area of the roof of the mouth immediately above it in the rest position, the palate. The sides make contact with the upper molars, as with all the previous sounds using the tongue. Palatal sounds include [c ɟ ç ɲ]. The first two are oral stops, the third a voiceless fricative and the fourth a nasal stop. The fricative is found in German, as in [ɪç] *ich* 'I', and is used by many English speakers at the beginning of *human* or *huge*. The nasal stop is found in French, as in [mɔ̃taɲ] *montagne* 'mountain'.

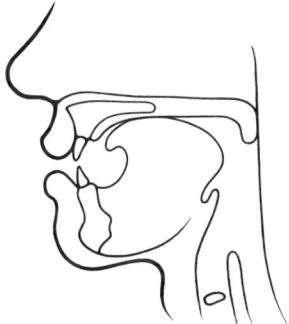

2.8.9 Velar

By raising the back of the tongue to make contact with the velum, velar sounds are produced. These include [k g x ŋ]. The third one is a voiceless fricative, which occurs in German, as in [dax] *Dach* 'roof'; the fourth one is a nasal stop, as in English [sɪŋ] *sing* and [θɪŋk] *think*. Velar articulations only involve side contact between the tongue and the upper molars in the area of the velar contact.

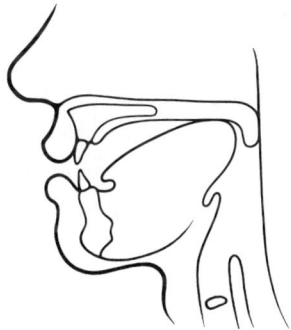

As we have emphasized already, the roof of the mouth is a continuous surface, so the exact point of contact can vary considerably for both palatal and velar sounds. In a sense the two-term system of dividing up the surface based on the edge of the bone above the hard palate is misleading. If we take English as an example, the point of contact for the stops [k g] varies slightly according to the following vowel. (We shall consider the articulation of vowels in detail in section 2.9.4.) Basically, vowels can be distinguished on a front-back dimension below the roof of the mouth: words such as *keep, king, kept* have front vowels, *come, curl* have central vowels, and *coot, could, caught, calm* have back vowels. (Note that words such as *coot, food, groom* are usually described as having a back vowel, but many young speakers, in fact, have a central or even front vowel in these words, so my description here may not equate with your own pronunciation; for various accents of English, see Chapter Eight.) Each word will have a slightly different point of contact for the initial [k]. It is possible to transcribe *king* as [cɪŋ], *keep* as [cɪip], and *curl* as [k̟ɜɫ], in an attempt to indicate these differences. (The plus sign underneath the [k] indicates that the tongue is slightly further forward than for a canonical velar [k].) However, such transcriptions for English are rare, because the focus of many transcriptions is not this kind of phonetic detail; we shall return to different types of transcription in Chapter Four.

Note that there are three adjectives derived from 'velum', each with a different meaning: **velar** refers to the use of the velum as a passive articulator against which the back of the tongue can be placed, as described in this section; **velic** refers to the closure of the nasal cavities by the raising of the velum, as described in section 2.5; **velaric** refers to the airstream mechanism described in section 2.10.3.

2.8.10 Uvular

At the back end of the roof of the mouth, as a continuation of the velum, there is a small soft part that hangs down into the faucal opening to the pharynx. This is the **uvula**. It can be brought into contact with the extreme back part of the tongue to produce uvular sounds. (Note the difference in spelling between the noun *uvula*, with no *r*, and the adjective *uvular*, with one. Both are pronounced the same in standard British English: [ˈjʊuvjələ].)

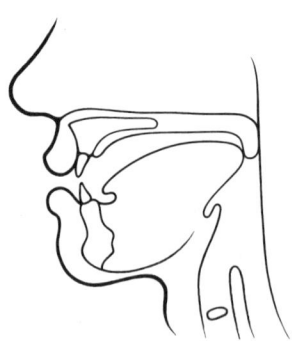

2.8.11 Pharyngeal

As mentioned above, the back wall of the pharynx can be used as a point of contact by retracting the root of the tongue to enable the extreme back of it to touch the pharynx wall. It appears that this is quite a difficult movement to carry out, as there are only a limited number of sounds produced in this way. No stop can be produced (at least not with the ease necessary for connected speech), but fricatives and **approximants** (see sections 2.9.2 and 2.9.3) can be: [ħ ʕ ʕ̞]. The first two are fricatives and the last one is an approximant. The mark beneath the symbol indicates that the articulators are approximated to one another in such a way that no local friction is produced (see section 2.9.3). (The marks situated above, below or to the side of a main symbol, e.g., [̥ ̈ ̃ ̩ ̃] are called **diacritics**.)

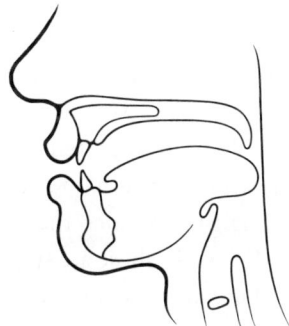

2.9 Degree of occlusion

We have now surveyed the possible points of contact that can be used in speech. What we need to consider now are the different ways in which the articulators are put together or near one another to modify the airstream. We have already referred to some of these in the course of our discussions so far: [stop], [fricative], [approximant], [lateral], but we now need to present a full picture of what is involved. We shall see in what follows that at some places of articulation the full range of modifications is possible, whereas at others only a limited number occur. This aspect of articulation is referred to as **degrees of occlusion** or **manner of articulation**.

2.9.1 Stops

The most extreme occlusion of the airstream is a complete stoppage of it. We saw this above in the case of the glottal stop, but, of course, this is made in the larynx, not in the mouth, so should be classified as a type of phonation. (Note that this is not how the IPA classifies [ʔ].) The same principle applies in the mouth, however, though in most cases the mechanism is more complicated than for the glottal stop. If the tongue tip is used as the main point of contact, the rest of the airstream has to be closed off as well, by means of contact between the sides of the tongue and the upper molars, as we noted above in section 2.8. Try saying [n] and holding it for a long time; you should be able to become aware of the side contact as well as the contact on the alveolar ridge.

The term [stop] is a general label for a number of different but similar mechanisms all of which have a complete closure of the vocal tract in the mouth. First of all let us consider the movements involved in creating a stoppage. In a sequence like [aba] the articulators are brought together, held together and then drawn apart. These three phases can be termed **closure : hold: release**. The crucial phase for any stop is the hold. With all three phases such an articulation can be called a **plosive**. Note that the IPA uses [plosive] as a generic term in the chart; this is misleading and the usage should be avoided. Use [stop] as the generic term for reasons that will be explained in what follows. The illustrations in section 2.8, except the last one, represent the hold phase of a stop.

However, provided there is a hold phase, the other phases need not occur. As we saw in section 2.2.1, English utterance-final stops are often unreleased: [kæʔp̚] *cap*, [kæʔt̚], *cat*, [kɪʔk̚] *kick*. These are stops but not plosives. We also saw in section 2.5 that the [d] in *hand* did not have a closure phase because the closure was already in place for the [n]. In the case of *hidden* with no vowel phase between the [d] and the [n], which we also discussed above, the oral stop has no release phase, since it remains in place for the [n], but the air is released through the nose. This is sometimes referred to as a **nasal release**, but note that it is the air that is released, not the oral closure. If we are to be consistent in our descriptions, then we must be very clear about the details of the mechanisms involved and our definitions of those mechanisms. Either we talk about the release of the air or we talk about the release of the stop mechanism; we should not mix up the two, which is easy to do, if we use the term 'release' for both. Is there any reason why one is better, or more general, than the other? If we return to utterance-final stops (in English, but in other languages, too), we have noted that these too can be released or unreleased. So, [kæʔp̚] or [kæʔp] *cap*, [kæb̚] or [kæb] *cab*, where the unmarked [b] represents a released plosive, are all equally possible. However, the release of such final stops is very weak and virtually no air is expelled (unlike in initial or intervocalic position), so using the term 'release' to refer to the release of the oral closure seems to be the more appropriate of the two possible usages. As regards the airstream, we can talk of the **escape** of the egressive air, which is a consequence of the release of a stop or some other mechanical intervention such as lowering the velum. For a discussion of the interplay between stop release and vocal cord activity, see sections 3.3 and 5.3.

We shall now consider other types of release. The assumption in the description of plosive release given above is that it is sudden, the articulators parting cleanly and swiftly. However, it is possible to part the articulators relatively slowly causing a short phase of local audible friction (see next section) following the release of the stop. This is usually referred to as **affrication** or **delayed release**; it is indicated in transcription by a small raised symbol for the fricative made at the same place of articulation: [p$^\phi$ t^s d^z k^x]. Such articulations are found in Liverpool accents, and [t^s] is common in many accents of British English, especially in the South East.

We noted above that palatoalveolars are restricted in their manner of articulation. Because quite a large area of the tongue is used, it is difficult to release a stop mechanism cleanly. For this reason palatoalveolars are usually fricatives or affricates, as in English [ʃ ʒ tʃ dʒ]. If a nasal stop precedes one of these sounds, it, too, will be palatoalveolar. In the conventions of the IPA there are no separate symbols or diacritic for palatoalveolar sounds except [ʃ ʒ]. If we need one in a transcription (see Chapter Seven), we can adapt an existing one.

It was emphasized above that all articulations involving the front parts of the tongue (dental to palatal) have an accompanying side contact with the upper molars to prevent air escaping along the sides of the tongue in stops and fricatives. However, it is possible to produce a stop and then release it by lowering the sides of the tongue away from the upper teeth; this is **lateral release**. We can find it in many accents of English in words like *bottle, hospital, middle, model*, when there is no vowel phase in the second, unstressed syllable: [-tɬ], [-dɬ]. For more detail of lateral articulations, see section 2.9.5.

Finally, we must note that stops can be oral or nasal. An oral stop is produced with the velum shutting off the nasal passages; a nasal stop has air going through the nose as well as into the mouth behind the stoppage. We should note that the IPA chart is misleading in this respect: it gives the impression that nasality is a manner of articulation just like stops, fricatives, and so on, as listed down the left-hand side of the chart. But in fact, as we shall discuss in more detail in the next chapter, any sound which is oral can also be nasal, except for the sounds that do not use an egressive pulmonic airstream, the implosives, ejectives and clicks. Otherwise we can produce nasal fricatives, nasal laterals, nasal vowels, and so on.

2.9.2 Fricatives

Instead of making a complete, firm contact between the articulators, we can put them almost together but leave a very small gap between them to allow the airstream to escape. When the air passes through a narrow gap, it is subject to turbulence, which produces local audible friction. This is similar to wind passing noisily through a small gap between a window and its frame. The resultant sounds are called **fricatives**. (A somewhat older term for them is **spirants**, which is used by some American and European phoneticians and phonologists.) Some of the fricatives are higher pitched than others, as we shall see in more detail when we consider their acoustic characteristics in Chapter Nine; those with the highest pitch are sometimes called **sibilants**: [s z ʃ ʒ]. Non-sibilant fricatives include: [f θ χ v ð ʁ]. Both stops and fricatives can be classed together as **obstruents**, that is, they are produced with a major obstruction in the mouth.

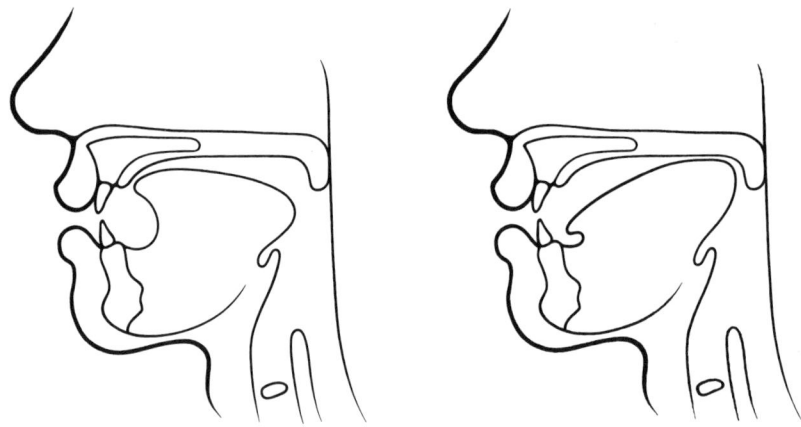

Figure 2.12 [s/z] + [x/ɣ]

2.9.3 Approximants

Rather than making contact between the articulators as in stops and fricatives, it is possible to narrow the opening through which the airstream is passing by putting them together (approximating them) without any contact, at least at the point of narrowing. (Some tongue approximants have side contact with the upper molars as in the obstruents.) In English [ɹ j w] are **approximants**. (An old-fashioned word for approximants that seems to have dropped out of use is **frictionless continuants**; this refers to the fact that the articulators are too far apart to produce local friction.)

Yet another term is sometimes used for some of the approximants: **semi-vowel** (see, e.g., Ladefoged [2006], pp. 227–229). This term is really a phonological one and is inappropriate (and unnecessary) in phonetic terminology. It is used to refer to those approximants which overlap with vowel articulations (see **vocoids** in the section 2.9.4), but which are used in the syllable margins (onset and coda), where consonants occur, like English [j w] in [jet] *yet* and [wet] *wet*, respectively. However, 'semi-vowel' is not a phonetic definition and its use often begs the question as to whether the sounds so designated are consonants or vowels. If we look at French, the definition of consonants and vowels has to be made on a functional, phonological basis, not on phonetic characteristics. [j ɥ w] all occur in word-initial position in French; they are all short versions of the vowel (vocoid) articulations [i y u], respectively. Before a word like [wazo] *oiseau* 'bird', the definite article has no vowel: *l'oiseau*; before a word like [wat] *ouate* 'cotton wool', the definite article has a vowel: *la ouate*; similarly we find [ləwiski] *le whiskey*. In all these and similar cases we find the article with or without a vowel, and this is the defining criterion for consonants and vowels in French: *le/la* + consonant, *l'* + vowel. We have just presented a phonological analysis for this bit of French, not a phonetic description. The term **glide** is also used in such cases. I shall not use the terms 'semi-vowel' or 'glide' as technical, phonetic terms in this book; see section 2.11.

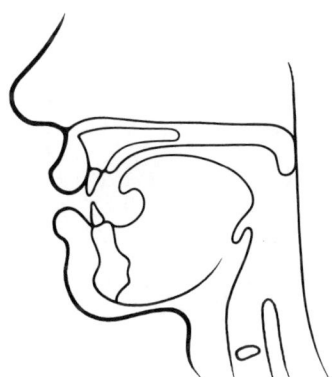

Figure 2.13 [j]

To keep phonetic and phonological terms completely apart, it is possible to retain the terms **contoid/vocoid** for phonetic descriptions and **consonant/vowel** for phonological classifications of the kind we looked at in French above, but not many linguists subscribe to this practice. (See, however, Lodge [to appear].)

2.9.4 Vocoids

So far I have used the term 'vowel' when describing this set of sounds, but now I want to introduce a phonetically more specific term: **vocoid**. This is a term which includes the approximants that we have just been discussung as well as what are typically referred to as vowels. None of the members of this set have any contact between the articulators, and most of the vowels do not even have lateral contact. Those articulations which depend on some contact between the articulators can be termed **contoids**.

The vocoids I want to discuss here are the subset produced by moving the body of the tongue into various positions beneath the roof of the mouth. If we consider the shape of this area, it is somewhat ovoid, as indicated in Figure 2.14.

In the tradition of the IPA this area is regularized to a trapezoid shape representing the extremes of the area beyond which contact with some articulator would be made, as in Figure 2.15. The vertical axis represents the height of the main bulk of the tongue from the floor of the mouth up towards the roof, and the horizontal axis the front-back dimension. The four corners of the diagram thus represent (1) the highest point, furthest to the front that a vocoid can be produced; (8) the highest, furthest back; (4) the lowest, furthest front; and

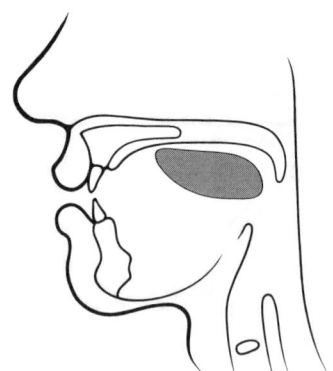

Figure 2.14 Vocoid area in the oral cavity.

(5) the lowest, furthest back. (The reason for these particular numbers will become clear shortly.)

Note that the lowest vowels are produced by lowering the lower jaw, which pulls the body of the tongue further away from the roof of the mouth. These represent ideals of vocoid articulation, whereas actual vocoids can be produced anywhere within this area. We shall come back to this point later, but for now we should concentrate on this idealized schema as a starting point. The vocoid articulations of this idealized set are known as the **cardinal vowels**, proposed by the British phonetician, Daniel Jones, in the early 20th century and incorporated into the Principles of the IPA (IPA [1949]). They are reference points from which one can plot actual vocoid occurrences, in rather the same way as one can plot directions and points on maps using the points of the compass, north, south, east, west, and so on. Since four reference points are insufficient to measure from, further intermediate points of articulation have been included, as in Figure 2.16.

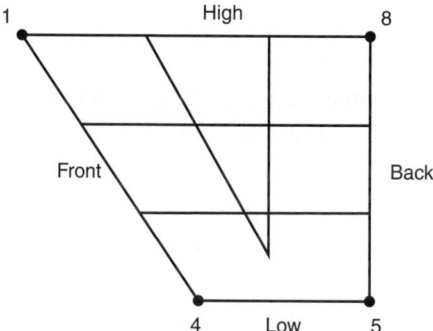

Figure 2.15 The vowel diagram.

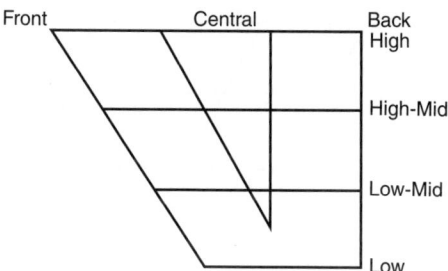

Figure 2.16 The vowel diagram with intermediate positions.

Note that the IPA uses the labels **close** rather than [high] and **open** rather than [low]. Whichever you choose to use, be consistent.

One further distinguishing feature of vocoid articulations is the position of the lips (see section 2.7). It must be emphasized that lip-rounding or spreading is not just a feature of vocoid articulations; it applies equally to contoids, and is often a feature of whole syllables. We shall return to this matter in Chapter Seven. For now we shall follow the conventions of the IPA and focus on the rôle of the lips in vocoid articulation.

As we noted in section 2.7, the lips can be spread or rounded from the position of rest (neutral). If we position the tongue for a high, front vocoid, we can have the lips in any of the three positions. In fact, since positions of the lips are not circumscribed as discrete areas, rounding and spreading are better thought of as extreme points of a continuum of possible lip positions, for which there are diacritics on the IPA chart. For our present purposes we just need the features [rounded] and [spread]. So, with the tongue in the high front position we can produce two vocoids which sound very different: [i y]. (When presenting such pairs, it is the normal convention to put the spread one on the left.) We can do this at each of the cardinal positions in Figure 2.16, and the result is the pairs given in Figure 2.17.

[Œ] is included to complete the full set of reference vowels, but it is a very awkward articulation to produce (and don't forget, speech is not intended to be awkward). Many speakers find it virtually impossible to lower the lower jaw to its full extent and to round the lips around the aperture of the mouth.

Each separate cardinal vowel is numbered by IPA convention, as follows: 1 [i]; 2 [e]; 3 [ɛ]; 4 [a]; 5 [ɑ]; 6 [ɔ]; 7 [o]; 8 [u], so each can be referred to in a short-hand way, for example, Cardinal Vowel (CV) 4. Note that these eight, called the primary set, do not all have the same lip-position. The other eight, with the opposite lip-position, are numbered 9 to 16, respectively, so [y] is 9 and [ɤ] is 15.

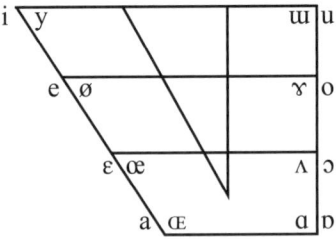

Figure 2.17

Articulation 41

There is an original recording of the cardinal vowels by Daniel Jones that is available from the IPA (or you can search for it using Google). It is important to hear them, memorize them as auditory reference points, and, if possible, learn to produce them.

The IPA vowel chart has more points of articulation and symbols on it, and is reproduced here as Figure 2.18.

In the middle of the chart is the symbol [ə], which represents the sound made with the tongue in the position of rest. It is often referred to as **schwa** [ʃwɑ]. In most native varieties of English it is used in unstressed syllables, but never in stressed ones; consider the following British English examples: [fɑðə] *father*, [əbaʊt] *about*, [fɑməsɪ] *pharmacy*, [fətɒɡɹəfə] *photographer*. In English the lip-position is usually neutral; on the other hand, in French, where it occurs less often, but is likewise always unstressed, the lips are often rounded: [løpɛʁ] *le père* 'the father', [ʒøpɑ̃s] *je pense* 'I think', [bwalø] *bois-le* 'drink it'.

Notice in one of the French examples there is a tilde [˜] above one of the vowel symbols: [ɑ̃]. This represents a nasal version of the vowel symbolized [ɑ] above. It is important to remember that although we are focusing on the position of the tongue and lips in this section, the rest of the speech production mechanism that we looked at in the previous sections is not doing nothing. What we have presented so far in this section has assumed articulations that are voiced and oral. This does not mean that other combinations are not possible. We can have voiced nasal vocoids: [ɑ̃ ɛ̃ õ ũ]; voiceless oral vocoids: [ɑ̯ ɛ̯ o̯ u̯]; or voiceless nasal vocoids: [ɑ̰̃ ɛ̰̃ õ̯ ṵ̃]. We shall return to

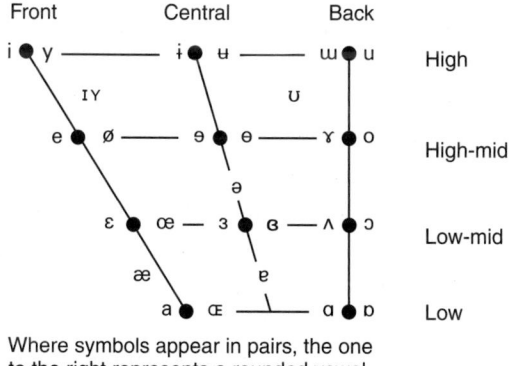

Figure 2.18 The IPA vowel chart.

these when we consider the possible combinations of the different parameters in the Chapter Three. Note that to symbolize them we need to use diacritics.

We shall see in Chapter Nine that acoustic analysis gives us an alternative to the articulation-based system of description discussed above. From an acoustic point of view it can be argued that the neat idealized set of articulations, especially in relation to the back vocoids is rather too far away from what actually goes on in speech. Ladefoged ([2006], p. 189) gives a pertinent quotation from G. O. Russell, who studied x-rays of vowel positions: 'Phoneticians are thinking in terms of acoustic fact, and using physiological fantasy to express the idea.' (See also Ladefoged's treatment of the cardinal vowels, [2006], pp. 211–218.) As long as we bear this caution in mind, the traditional, less accurate articulation-based labels work well enough, and are used extensively in both phonetics and phonology.

2.9.4.1 Moving vocoids

Another assumption that is made in relation to the vocoids that have been discussed so far in this section is that they are produced with the tongue in one position. Such steady-state vocoids are called **monophthongs** [mɒnəfθɒŋz]. (We shall need to return to the notion of a steady state in articulation when we consider acoustic displays of continuous speech.)

However, since the tongue is not crucially in contact with another articulator, as in the case of obstruents, for example, it can move around the vowel space while the airstream is being expelled. In theory it is possible to make as many movements as can be produced in one expulsion of breath, but in actual languages there seems to be an upper limit of two movements in any one syllable. Consecutive movements beyond this limit would be viewed as a sequence of (vowel-only) syllables. If a vocoid involves one movement, it is called a **diphthong** [dɪfθɒŋ] (literally 'two sounds'); if two movements are involved, it is referred to as a **triphthong** [tɹɪfθɒŋ] ('three sounds'). These traditional names for the moving vocoid articulations come from the segmental tradition, and the two or three symbols used to represent them are counted as segments. But it is important to think of them as movements, so on a vowel diagram it is usual to indicate diphthongs with an arrow joining the starting point and the finishing point, as in Figure 2.19; triphthongs are indicated by two straight lines or a curved one, as in Figure 2.20.

When there is movement in a vocoid articulation, it is usual for part of the articulation to be more prominent and longer than the rest. If the first part is more prominent, as in English [aɪ] and [oʊ], then we speak of **falling**

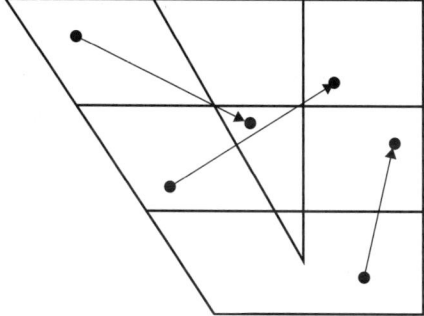

Figure 2.19 Diphthongs.

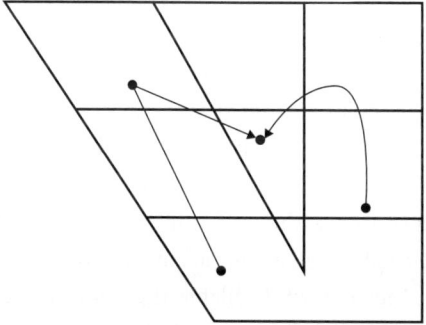

Figure 2.20 Triphthongs.

diphthongs; if the second part is more prominent, as in French [ua] and [ie], they are called **rising** diphthongs. It is possible for there to be no particular greater prominence or duration throughout the movement. How these vocoid movements are interpreted in particular phonologies varies from one proposed analysis to the next, and we need not be concerned with the details here, but we discussed one such possible analysis of French above in section 2.9.3. When there is equal prominence in a vocoid movement, this is usually interpreted as two syllables in most languages, for example, French [pei] *pays* 'country'; compare this with monosyllabic English [peɪ] *pay* with a falling diphthong. It should be pointed out here that the term syllable is an abstract, phonological notion with no reliable phonetic markers. I shall return to the issue in section 6.4.

Languages vary in the number of moving vowels they use. Some, such as Japanese and Turkish, do not use any; others, such as English, use quite a large number along with monophthongs. So, all languages have monophthongal vocoid articulations, only some use diphthongs and triphthongs.

For the most part we have so far been dealing with the identification and description of a set of idealized articulations and have said nothing about how we describe and transcribe actually occurring vocoid articulations in various languages, including English, though note that in some of the transcriptions of English used so far symbols not included in the vowel diagrams presented in this section have been used. We will return to this in Chapter Four.

2.9.4.2 Resonance

One final aspect of vocoid articulation needs separate consideration, as it relates to the majority of contoid articulations as well. The positioning of the body of the tongue on the front-back dimension, which involves the bulk of the tongue being positioned under the palate or the velum produces a features that is sometimes referred to as **resonance**. Not only is it a major feature of vocoids, but in any articulation that allows parts of the tongue to move about while the obstruction to airflow is maintained, the position of the rest of the tongue makes an acoustic and auditory difference. One of the most commonly described instances of this is the variation found in English lateral articulations. In standard British English laterals at the onset of a syllable have front resonance, while in the coda of a syllable they have back resonance: [lʲ] and [lˠ], respectively, as in [lʲʌlˠ] *lull*. There is, in fact, considerable variation across different accents of English, and so you may not follow this pattern in your own speech. Many American and Scottish speakers have [lˠʌlˠ], for example; [lʲʌlʲ] is also possible, though less common, for example, in rural Norfolk amongst old speakers. (See further section 8.4.3.) The back resonance is often referred to as **velarization**, as the back of the tongue is raised towards the velum; there is even an alternative symbol for the velarized lateral: [ɫ]. If the back resonance is produced by a back tongue position and further pharyngeal narrowing, it is referred to as **pharyngealization**, for which [ˁ] is placed after the appropriate letter-symbol. (See Chapter Three for a discussion of the so-called **emphatics** of Arabic.)

However, it is important to remember that other contoid articulations can vary according to tongue position besides the English laterals. Try alternating the tongue position of [l] in a continuous stream: [lʲlˠlʲlˠlʲlˠ]. Once you can do this in a controlled way, do the same tongue movements with [m]: [mʲmˠmʲmˠmʲmˠmʲmˠ]. Variation of resonance of [m], for example, occurs in Scots Gaelic. Another point to remember that we will take up again later is that resonance is very often a feature of a number of sounds at a time, for example, a whole syllable (see Kelly and Local [1989]).

2.9.5 Laterals

We now move on to a number of manners of articulation which are restricted to only some of the places of articulation. The first has already been mentioned in our discussions so far: laterals. Such sounds are produced by letting the egressive air flow out of the mouth round the sides of the tongue. (Laterals may be released down only one side of the tongue, or down both sides.) As mentioned in section 2.9.1, English stops in words like *bottle, hospital, middle, model*, when there is no vowel phase in the second, unstressed syllable, have a lateral release phase: [-tɬ], [-dɬ]. Say these words in this way and try to feel the sides of the tongue move away from the upper molars. The complete contact at the alveolar ridge is maintained.

There are two types of lateral: one in which the distance between the sides of the tongue and the side teeth is great enough to allow the air to pass freely, as in English [l]; these are called **lateral approximants**. The other type has close, but not complete contact with the teeth, resulting in **lateral fricatives**: [ɬ ɮ], both of which are found in Zulu, and the first one (voiceless) in Welsh: [ɬan] *llan* 'church'. This manner of articulation is restricted to points of contact from the teeth to the palate, though the fricatives are even more restricted to dental and alveolar places of contact. (The IPA chart also gives a velar lateral approximant, but I have never heard one and find it extremely difficult to produce because of the relatively small amount of the back of the tongue to lower at the sides.)

2.9.6 Taps and trills

Taps (sometimes called **flaps**) are produced by a rapid gesture of the tip of the tongue against the teeth, alveolar ridge or front of the palate (for retroflex sounds). The contact is like that for a stop, but very short. (Ladefoged [2006], pp. 170–172, prefers to distinguish between taps and flaps in terms of direction of tongue-tip movement.) Many American speakers use taps (oral and nasal) between vowels, as in [beɾi] *Betty*, [beɾɪŋ] *bedding*, [pẽɾi] *penny*. English speakers from the West Midlands also use it between vowels and after onset consonants, as in [veɾi] *very*, [fɾɪi] *free*, but not in the words the Americans use it in.

From an auditory point of view, **trills** are made up of a series of taps, but the articulatory mechanism is different. In alveolar trills the tongue-tip is put in a position behind the teeth-ridge so that it bangs repeatedly against it in the egressive airstream. The tension of the tongue is such that it moves back and forth in the expelled air at the right rate to produce the trilling effect. In theory trills can be extended for as long as the breath can be exhaled, but in practice languages with trills restrict the number of individual taps of the tongue tip to no more than three in normal conversational speech. Besides the alveolar trill, [r], it is possible to produce trills with both lips or with the uvular on the back of the tongue. The bilabial trill, symbolized [ʙ], is used by English speakers to indicate that they are feeling cold. Uvular trills are used by some German speakers in onsets, for example, [ʀaɪn] *rein* 'pure', and intervocalically taps are often used rather than a trill, for example, [eːʀ̆ə] *Ehre* 'honour'. (Note that there is no separate symbol in the IPA chart for a uvular tap, so I have put the shortness diacritic [̆] underneath the trill symbol.)

Two even more restricted articulatory possibilities are, firstly, trills accompanied by friction, as in Czech [r̝ɛk] *řek* 'rivers', [pr̝st] *přst* 'for'. Again, as there is no separate symbol for this, the diacritic for closer articulation (in this case causing friction) [̝] is used. The second sound is the labiodental flap used in the Nigerian language, Margi, in which the lower lip is flicked across the lower surface of the top teeth. There was no IPA symbol for this sound until 2005 because of its very restricted occurrence; again, we could invent a representation by using the brevity diacritic: [v̆]. (See Ladefoged [2006], pp. 171–173.)

2.10 Non-pulmonic airstreams

We must now consider the more restricted sets of sounds produced with air that is not simply breathed out from the lungs.

2.10.1 Implosives

As we have already seen, the vocal cords can be closed completely across the airflow, thereby stopping the pulmonic air from escaping. If a closure is also made at some point above the glottis in the oral cavity, then the air between the two closures is trapped. Note that for this to happen the nasal passages must be closed off, too, so the velum is closed; otherwise the air would escape through the nose. This means that the option [nasal]/[oral] (see section 2.5) is not available for these sounds. The larynx can be moved slightly up or down in the throat; if it is moved downwards while the air is trapped in the way that has just been described, then the air pressure in the oral cavity is reduced.

Under these circumstances the release of the supraglottal closure will draw air from outside into the mouth, producing what are referred to as implosives.

In speech, during the lowering of the larynx, the glottal closure is slightly relaxed, allowing vibration of the vocal cords in the air being pushed up from the lungs in readiness for the following sound (usually a vowel). For this reason the implosives are labelled [voiced] on the IPA chart, but a few voiceless implosives have been recorded.

The supraglottal closure can be made in a number of places: at the lips, at the alveolar ridge, at the velum, and so on. These all have a separate symbol on the chart: [ɓ ɗ ʄ ɠ ʛ]. Voiceless versions would be represented by the egressive stop symbol plus a hook on top, e.g. [ƥ ƭ ƙ].

2.10.2 Ejectives

With the same starting point as for implosives it is possible to raise the larynx, in which case the trapped air is compressed. The build-up of pressure behind the supraglottal closure leads to its release, propelling the trapped air out of the mouth. Sounds produced in this way are called ejectives. Once again we must note that ejectives are neither voiced nor voiceless, and cannot be nasal. Although such sounds are usually stops, it is possible to release the complete closure slowly by removing the articulator only slightly so that local friction is produced, so we can have ejective stops and ejective fricatives. These are all indicated with the symbol for an egressive pulmonic voiceless sound for the appropriate place of articulation followed by an apostrophe: [p' t' c' k' q' f' s']. (Note that many British English speakers, when they want to swear, stop themselves, and produce a labiodental ejective fricative [f'] instead.)

2.10.3 Clicks

The other way of trapping air in the mouth is called velaric. With the back of the tongue against the velum and a closure made somewhere in advance of this obstruction the air from outside can be drawn into the intervening space by first depressing the centre of the tongue to reduce the air-pressure in the remaining cavity and then removing the outer closure, producing a click sound. (It is also possible to expel the air out of the oral cavity with the click mechanism by raising the centre of the tongue to compress the air, but this does not seem to be used linguistically; see Ladefoged [2006], p. 139.) In this case the closure can be made at a number of points in advance of the front of the hard palate. So they can be produced at the lips, the teeth, the alveolar ridge, or on the alveolar ridge and the front part of the hard palate together; it is also possible to close the airstream centrally at the alveolar ridge and allow the air to be sucked in at the side of the tongue (laterally, either on one side only or on both sides). The symbols are: [ʘ ǀ ǃ ǂ ǁ]. (These are the latest recommended symbols (2005) for the clicks; they look very little like letters and two of them could be confused with the symbols some linguists use for stress-group and tone-group divisions that we discuss briefly in Chapter Six. The older versions for [ǀ ǃ ǁ] are [ʇ C ʖ], respectively.)

For British English speakers most of these clicks, or something very like them, are used for paralinguistic purposes, that is, they represent a conventional meaning but are not considered (parts of) words. The bilabial click is used to indicate a kiss; the dental and alveolar ones are used to indicate disapproval ('tut-tut'); the palatoalveolar one may be used to mimic knocking on a hard surface; the lateral one is used to encourage horses to go faster ('gee up').

The release of the clicks described above assumes that the velum remains closed, shutting off the nasal cavities. However, it is possible to release the velic closure as well, giving nasality to the release phase. This type of click is usually represented by a combination of the click symbol and the velar nasal stop symbol: [ʘŋ], [Cŋ], [ʖŋ]. Furthermore, the release of the velar closure may be accompanied by voiceless or voiced egressive pulmonic air, depending on the position of the vocal cords. These should be written with joint symbols as with the nasal ones above: [ʘk], [Cg], [ʖg]. (Ladefoged [2006], pp. 139–141, puts the symbols the other way round.)

It is very difficult to speak with ingressive air for very long; consider trying to talk after you have run quickly and are out of breath, breathing in and out in rapid succession. Therefore, speakers of languages that use implosives, for instance, only use ingressive air for a single syllable place, and the rest of the syllable uses egressive air. The Indian language, Sindhi, has [ɓ ɗ ʄ ɠ], as in the words [ɓani] 'field', [dʰəɠʊ] 'bull' (see Ladefoged [2006], p. 138).

2.11 Some pseudo-phonetic terms

Some terms that look like phonetic descriptive labels are used frequently by phonologists, but have no real articulatory equivalent. For the most part they have developed as a result of the mismatch between phonetics and phonology. We have already come across **advanced/retracted tongue root** (section 2.6) and **semivowel/glide** (section 2.9.3). Other common terms are as follows.

Liquid, 'a cover term for the [English - KRL] consonants /l, r/' (Ladefoged [2006], p. 73). (We can tell this is a phonological statement because of the phonemic slant lines round the IPA symbols.)

Guttural, a term that refers to the range of consonants produced at the uvular, the pharynx, the larynx, and those with pharyngeal back resonance in particular in Semitic languages (see, e.g., Zawaydeh [2003]). Just like [ATR], this is not a description of a simple phonetic phenomenon. (It is also used by (English) non-specialists to refer, often disparagingly, to any language that has non-English consonants from the velum backwards.)

Tense/lax, two terms used by phonologists for various purposes, but specifically in relation to the English vowel system. Latinate vocabulary, in particular, has pairs of related words with different vowels, as underlined in the orthographic examples: s*a*ne/s*a*nity, ser*e*ne/ser*e*nity, div*i*ne/div*i*nity, which are supposedly tense and lax respectively. This is not the place to go further into this bogus phonetic feature, but there is an excellent critique of what he calls 'the Emperor's New Feature' in Lass (1976).

None of these terms will be used in this book to refer to phonetic characteristics of sounds.

There is one other pair that deserves mention: **fortis/lenis**, which are also used by phonologists to describe contrasts. These terms refer to a complex of phonetic features, which may vary from language to language, but typically include degree of articulatory energy, muscular tension of the articulators, duration and phonation type. The phonetic attributes and distribution of what are sometimes called the fortis and lenis stops of, say, English, German and Icelandic are not the same. I will not use these terms in the book.

2.12 Further reading and advice

A more detailed account of the physiology of the vocal apparatus is given in Clark and Yallop (1995), and they give follow-up references, too. An extensive treatment of articulation is presented in Laver (1994).

Web searches can supply useful moving images for some of the articulators, for example, the vocal cords or an x-ray film of an utterance. There is a range of technological aids to help phoneticians examine human articulation; these include magnetic resonance imaging (MRI), ultrasound images, palatography and laryngeoscopy. Such topics go beyond the scope of this book, but there is an excellent introduction to some of the techniques used in Hewlett and Beck (2006).

The Articulators in Combination 3

Chapter outline

3.1 A descriptive framework	52
3.2 A re-presentation of the IPA chart	54
3.3 Oversimplification – a warning	55
3.4 Non-obstruents	57
3.5 Vocoids and lip-position	58
3.6 Types of resonance	62
3.7 Non-pulmonic air	63
3.8 Parametric representations	64
3.9 Further reading and exercises	66

In Chapter Two all the articulatory parameters were presented separately. We now need to consider how they are combined in various ways when we speak. In looking at the range of combinations it is important to distinguish between those that are possible and those that are found commonly in the world's languages. We have already seen in Chapter Two that some combinations and types are really quite rare, for example, the Margi labiodental flap or the Pirahã labio-lingual flick, whereas others such as voiceless stops appear to occur in all languages. But, however interesting and important the relative frequencies may be, not just for the phonetician but for the phonologist, too, this chapter is intended to consider all sounds equally, though we will note where aerodynamic considerations and audibility seem to affect frequency of occurrence. It is important to emphasize that my starting point is: what linguistic sounds can human beings make? It is not, for instance, what sounds do we need to describe standard British English phonological contrasts? In any case, if we look carefully at actual spoken language, we can find all kinds of interesting articulations used in all languages. Furthermore, if we are phoneticians interested in language pathology, then even more possibilities open up. (We shall not be dealing with commonly occurring abnormalities of speech production in this book, but see, for example, Ball [1993], which contains the specially extended IPA chart on page x and Ball and Lowry [2001].)

3.1 A descriptive framework

We need to provide a descriptive framework to reflect the contribution each articulatory mechanism makes in the production of a sound. The resultant description should be capable of defining the sound intended in an objective way. However, we must note that at this stage of phonetic description we are dealing with small segments of sound, not anything like continuous speech. Despite my misgivings about segmentation, which are presented in Chapter Five in particular, when learning about how to apply the descriptive labels it is necessary to start with small articulatory events and then move on to larger time spans (Chapter Seven). Provided we are aware of the limitations of the application of these somewhat idealized and phonologically orientated descriptions of individual sounds to describing actual speech events, then no harm has been done.

The starting point of such combined descriptions is the IPA chart reproduced on page x. But I have already mentioned some problems with the way in which the classifications are presented, for example, the use of the feature [plosive] rather than [stop] as a generic label for the mechanism, and the pretence that nasality is a manner of articulation rather than a completely separate mechanism relating to velic activity. So in what follows I intend to revise and re-present parts of the chart, so that a clearer, more consistent set of classificatory labels can be displayed.

Let us start with four independent mechanisms: phonation, velic activity, place of articulation and manner of articulation. These are the four categories most commonly used in describing articulation. We shall have to expand on the basic four quite considerably, but they are a generally agreed basic set. Each mechanism has a number of subsumed labels, which represent positions of the articulators within that mechanism, as indicated in Table 3.1. (Note that the labels are not in any particular order.)

We must note that the manner [lateral] can be combined with [approximant] or [fricative], and under place combinations are possible, such as

The Articulators in Combination

Table 3.1 Basic descriptors

Phonation:	[closed glottis], [voiceless], [voiced], [murmur], [creak]
Velic activity:	[oral], [nasal]
Place:	[bilabial], [labiodental], [alveolar], [retroflex], [palatoalveolar], [alveolo-palatal], [palatal], [velar], [uvular], [pharyngeal]
Manner:	[stop], [fricative], [lateral], [tap], [trill], [approximant], [vocoid]

Table 3.2 Sample descriptions

[b]: voiced, oral, bilabial stop
[ɸ]: voiceless, oral, bilabial fricative
[n̥]: voiceless, nasal, alveolar stop
[N]: voiced, nasal, uvular stop
[ɻ]: voiced, oral, retroflex approximant
[ɬ]: voiceless, oral, alveolar, lateral fricative
[ɫ]: voiced, oral, velarized, alveolar, lateral approximant
[ç]: voiceless, oral, palatal fricative
[ʋ]: voiced, oral, labiodental approximant
[j̃]: voiced, nasal, palatal approximant
[h]: voiceless, oral, pharyngeal fricative
[ʃ]: voiceless, oral, palatoalveolar fricative

[bilabial] + [velar] to give [labiovelar] articulations such as [w] or [ĝb], where the liaison diacritic [͡] indicates simultaneous contact involving two separate places of articulation.

If we combine (usually) one of each of the label sets, we can provide a good basic phonetic description of the articulation involved. Table 3.2 gives a number of possibilities with an appropriate symbol. I have omitted the square brackets round the labels, as these are really only necessary in the main text; the order of the labels is conventional.

It is important to realize that these descriptions say nothing specific about any of the other features of articulation that we discussed in Chapter Two. All the above are assumed to be made with an egressive pulmonic airstream. Because it is the major source of air in speech, it is treated as the default mechanism and not referred to explicitly. When a non-pulmonic airstream is used, it is referred to in the appropriate labels, as we shall see below. Another implicit feature in most of the above descriptions is in the non-lateral sounds; central articulations are those made with side contact in place. Since, again, this applies to the majority of contoids, it is left implicit, whereas [lateral] is used explicitly. Also, there is no reference to lip-position. In section 3.5 I shall present vocoid descriptions, which will involve expanding on the descriptive labels used in Table 3.2.

3.2 A re-presentation of the IPA chart

On the basis of the descriptions so far, I want to revise the IPA chart on the following lines: the manner of articulation is given at the top of each set of cells; the place is given along the top of each subset of cells; of the four symbols the top left is [voiceless, oral], top right [voiced, oral], bottom left [voiceless, nasal], and bottom right [voiced, nasal]. I have given four places of articulation; try to provide symbols for all the other places of articulation.

Table 3.3 Extended IPA chart (i)

Manner: stop								
Place:	bilabial		labiodental		dental		alveolar	
	p	b	p̪	b̪	t̪	d̪	t	d
	m̥	m	m̥̪	m̪	n̥̪	n̪	n̥	n

Manner: fricative								
	ɸ	β	f	v	θ	ð	s	z
	ɸ̃	β̃	f̃	ṽ	θ̃	ð̃	s̃	z̃

Some of these combinations are less common than others; this is to some extent reflected in the use of diacritics for the less common ones, rather than having separate letter-symbols for them. Both voiceless nasal stops and any nasal fricatives, especially voiceless ones, lack audibility. There are aerodynamic reasons for this. If the air is passing out through the nose, it is reducing the amount of air that can be directed through or around any kind of oral obstruction, so, for instance the amount of friction in [s̃] or [z̃] is much lower than in their oral counterparts. Voiceless nasals are used as distinctive sounds in some languages, for example, Burmese, where they combine with voiced sounds in syllables, which helps their audibility, and most English children use

Table 3.4 Extended IPA chart (ii)

Manner: stop
Place: bilabial   alveolar   retroflex   uvular

b̥	b̤
m̥	m̤

d̥	d̤
n̥	n̤

ɖ̥	ɖ̤
ɳ̥	ɳ̤

ɢ̥	ɢ̤
ɴ̥	ɴ̤

Manner: fricative

β̥	β̤
β̰	β̰̤

z̥	z̤
z̰	z̰̤

ʐ̥	ʐ̤
ʐ̰	ʐ̰̤

ʁ̥	ʁ̤
ʁ̰	ʁ̰̤

them in the early stages of acquisition for the adult sequences [sm-] and [sn-], as in [m̥ɔö] for adult [smɔɫ] *small*. (The significance of the two dots over [o] will be explained in section 3.5.) Nasal fricatives can be heard variably in conversational English, where in other circumstances a nasal stop would occur, for example, [tez̃z] alternating with [tenz] (see section 7.2.1).

Table 3.3 only covers two phonation types, voiceless and voiced. For each of the others we will need further charts of symbols with the appropriate diacritics or combination of symbols. In Table 3.4 I give similar sets of symbols for the phonation types, murmur and creak. I give four places of articulation; you produce symbols for the others. (Note that hand-writing the symbols enables you to put multiple diacritics under a letter-symbol, something that is difficult on a computer.)

If a glottal closure is used in combination with a supraglottal one, the glottal stop symbol is used, raised and in front of the equivalent voiceless symbol: [ʔp ʔc ʔq]. Whereas it is possible to hand-write these symbols one on top of the other: [p̓ ɋ], it would require the creation of new symbols to do this in print. Note that the timing of the two releases is crucial to distinguish glottally reinforced articulations from ejectives: if the oral closure is released in a glottally reinforced stop, then the glottal closure is released first; an ejective releases the two closures simultaneously. Furthermore, glottally reinforced stops use egressive pulmonic air, whereas ejectives use an egressive glottalic airstream.

3.3 Oversimplification – a warning

At this point it would be useful to consider the issue of oversimplification even in the descriptions of these small speech events, and recapitulate some of the aspects of stop poduction discussed in section 2.9.1. The stop symbols in

Tables 3.3 and 3.4 give no information about the interplay of the stop mechanism and the vocal cord activity, nor the type of release involved, if any. I give below the possible timing relationships between the onset and cessation of voice with reference to the closure and release of a bilabial stop mechanism. The vocal cords can start to vibrate at any time after the start of the utterance. If we take bilabial closure and release followed by a vocoid, this gives (at least) the following possibilities:

    Onset of voicing
- (i) [pa̦] = no vibration at all;
- (ii) [pʰa] = vibration starts after the lips are opened;
- (iii) [pa] = vibration starts as the lips are opened;
- (iv) [ˬba] = vibration starts after the lips are closed, but before they are opened;
- (v) [ba] = vibration starts as the lips are closed.

At the end of a syllable a mirror-image of the options in (i)–(v) applies, given as (vi)–(x).

    Cessation of voicing
- (vi) [a̦p] = no vibration at all;
- (vii) [aʰp] = vibration stops before the lips are closed;
- (viii) [ap] = vibration stops as the lips are closed;
- (ix) [ab̥] = vibration stops after the lips are closed, but before they are opened;
- (x) [ab] = vibration stops as the lips are opened.

The symbolization of each of these is different, so the detail of the interaction can be given in a transcription. Whereas I have given five possibilities at each end of the syllable, if we want to know exactly when voicing stops or starts, it can be measured in milliseconds from the start of the utterance without reference to any of the five types. This is a matter of **gradient** (timing in milliseconds) versus **categorical** (classification according to one of the five possibilities) interpretation of the phenomena. On their own the symbols [p b] can give no indication of these more subtle differences. It is possible to represent these timing relations without using letter-shape symbols; I shall discuss this in section 3.8. Different types of detail in transcription are dealt with in Chapter Four, and we discuss the issue of segmentation with reference to these possibilities of onset and cessation of voicing in section 5.3.

    The above possibilities relate to a change from voicelessness to voice, or voice to voicelessness, but we also noted that there could be different kinds of phonatory change, such as closed glottis to voice, or creak to glottal closure. In many northern English varieties the glottal stop is used as the definite article, so an utterance-initial stop may start with glottal closure and change to being voiceless or voiced before release, as we saw in the following examples from section 2.2.1: [ʔpʊb] *the pub*, [ʔtɹeːn] *the train*, [ʔkʊkə] *the cooker*, [ʔbʊs] *the bus*, [ʔdɹeːn] *the drain*, [ʔgeːm] *the game*. In these cases the glottal and supraglottal closures are simultaneous, but the glottal release precedes the oral one. Similarly, some speakers of English have creaky voice on a vowel preceding glottally reinforced stops, as a slow transition from full voicing to glottal closure, as in [kæʔp̚] *cap*, [kæʔt̚] *cat*, [kɹʔk̚] *kick*. Details of the interplay between the articulators will be considered further in Chapter Seven; for the time being we just remind ourselves of the simplification of the symbolizations of combined mechanisms, and continue our present survey.

3.4 Non-obstruents

The presentation of the approximants, laterals, taps and trills can be done along the same lines as the obstruent articulations above. Table 3.5 gives a selection of approximants. Again, add as many more possibilities as you can. (The bilabial lateral approximant cells are meant to be empty.)

We should note that in the IPA conventions the sound usually transcribed [w] is described as a voiced, oral, labial-velar approximant. The feature [labial-velar] is used to refer to the lip-rounding (see below, towards the end of section 3.5); similarly, [ɥ] is a labial-palatal approximant. The voiceless [ʍ] may or may not have friction; if it has, it can equally well be transcribed as [ɸʷ].

The lateral fricatives are restricted to just dental and alveolar places of articulation. Table 3.6 gives the alveolar options; the dental ones would be the same except for the added diacritic [̪].

Table 3.5 Extended IPA chart (iii)

Manner:	approximant					
Place:	bilabial		alveolar		palatal	
	ɸ̞̥	β̞	ɹ̥	ɹ	j̊	j
	ɸ̞̃	β̞̃	ɹ̥̃	ɹ̃	j̊̃	j̃
Manner:	lateral approximant					
			l̥	l	ʎ̥	ʎ
			l̥̃	l̃	ʎ̥̃	ʎ̃

Table 3.6 Lateral fricatives

Manner: lateral fricative

ɬ	ɮ
ɬ̃	ɮ̃

Table 3.7 Taps and trills

Manner: tap

Place:	bilabial	alveolar		retroflex		uvular	
		ɾ̥	ɾ	ɽ̥	ɽ	ʀ̥	ʀ̝
		ɾ̥̃	ɾ̃	ɽ̥̃	ɽ̃	ʀ̥̃	ʀ̝̃

Manner: trill

ʙ̥	ʙ			r̥	r			ʀ̥	ʀ
ʙ̥̃	ʙ̃			r̥̃	r̃			ʀ̥̃	ʀ̃

The representation of the taps and trills works on the same principles, as in Table 3.7.

The nasal trills are quite awkward to produce because the open nasal cavities divert air away from the trill mechanism.

3.5 Vocoids and lip-position

The vocoids do not have a point of contact to use under the heading of place of articulation. Instead the place descriptor is replaced by the three other types of feature discussed in section 2.9.4. Two describe the orientation of the main body of the tongue, one on the high-low axis, the other on the front-back axis; the other is the position of the lips. I reproduce the IPA vowel chart again here as Figure 3.1 for convenience.

In Table 3.8 I give a sample of all the possible combinations of the different parameters for vocoids. Do not confuse [central] that is used in vocoid descriptions with the term we referred to above meaning non-lateral; the latter is not normally used in descriptions, anyway. As pointed out in Chapter Two, in the IPA conventions the terms **close** and **open** are used where I have used **high** and **low**, respectively. Note that there are no symbols to denote neutral lip-position.

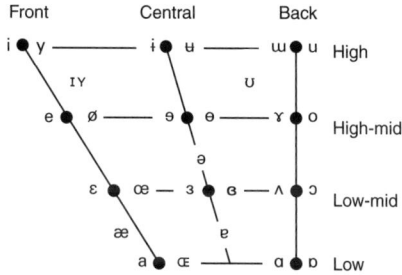

Where symbols appear in pairs, the one to the right represents a rounded vowel.

Figure 3.1 The IPA vowel chart.

Table 3.8 Sample vocoid descriptions

[i]:	voiced, oral, high, front, spread vocoid
[e̥]:	voiceless, oral, high-mid, front, spread vocoid
[ɛ̃]:	voiced, nasal, low-mid, front, spread vocoid
[ø̃]:	voiced, nasal, high-mid, front, rounded vocoid
[ḁ̃]:	voiceless, nasal, low, front, spread vocoid
[ʉ]:	voiced, oral, high, central, rounded vocoid
[o̤]:	murmured, oral, high-mid, back, rounded vocoid
[ɔ̰]:	creaky, oral, low-mid, back, rounded vocoid
[ɑ̃]:	voiced, nasal, low, back, spread vocoid
[ɯ̃]:	voiced, nasal, high, back, spread vocoid
[ɘ̥]:	voiceless, oral, high-mid, central, rounded vocoid
[y]:	voiced, oral, high, front, rounded vocoid.

It is possible to represent it by using, say, the symbol for a rounded vocoid and put the diacritic that indicates less rounded underneath it, for example, [ɔ̜], [ʉ̜], [ø̜].

We have still only given symbols for the cardinal vowels and a few intermediate positions, but we have already noted that vocoid articulations can be made anywhere within the vowel area. So how do we describe and symbolize these other intermediate positions? If a vocoid is produced with the tongue pulled away from the extreme front of the vowel area towards the centre, it is referred to as **retracted** and symbolized with a subscript diacritic [̱]. If a vocoid is produced with the tongue away from the extreme back of the vowel area, it is **advanced** symbolized [̟]. (Don't get these terms the wrong way round: advanced front vocoids and retracted back ones are somewhat tricky!) If the bulk of the tongue approaches the edge of the central area, some phoneticians describe such articulations as **centralized**, and denote it with the

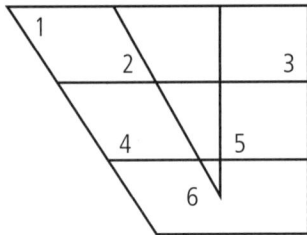

Figure 3.2 Sample vocoid positions.

Table 3.9 Descriptions

1 [i]: voiced, oral, high, retracted, spread vocoid
2 [ë]: voiced, oral, high-mid, centralized, spread vocoid
3 [o̟]: voiced, oral, high-mid, advanced, rounded vocoid
4 [œ̠]: voiced, oral, low-mid, retracted, rounded vocoid
5 [ä]: voiced, oral, low-mid, centralized, spread vocoid
6 [ä]: voiced, oral, low, centralized, spread vocoid

diacritic [¨]. Figure 3.2 gives a sample of positions with a reference number and the descriptions and symbols follow in Table 3.9. Number 6 is often symbolized [ɐ], the nearest symbol on the IPA chart.

Then there is the matter of raising and lowering the tongue from the lines of the cardinal vowels: such articulations are **raised** [˔] and **lowered** [˕], respectively. Figure 3.3 gives further sample intermediate positions, with symbols and descriptions in Table 3.10. Where two subscript diacritics are required, one, the plus or minus sign, has been placed after the symbol instead.

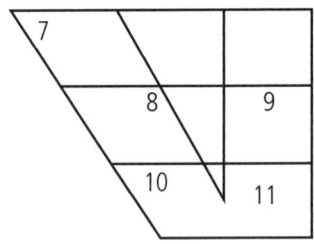

Figure 3.3 Sample vocoid positions.

Table 3.10 Descriptions

7	[i̞-]:	voiced, oral, high, lowered, retracted, spread vocoid
8	[e̞]:	voiced, oral, high-mid, lowered, centralized, spread vocoid
9	[o̞+]:	voiced, oral, high-mid, lowered, advanced, rounded vocoid
10	[ɛ̞-]:	voiced, oral, low-mid, lowered, retracted, spread vocoid
11	[a̝+]:	voiced, oral, low, raised, advanced, spread vocoid

Some of the intermediate positions can equally well be described as raised rather than lowered; for example, 8 could be [low-mid, raised] and 10 could be [low, raised]. Some of the intermediate positions have their own symbol, reflecting common occurrence in several languages (originally European ones), for example, [ɪ ʏ ʊ æ], which we will return to in Chapter Four.

I now want to look at the matter of lip-position in a little more detail. We have already mentioned above that the variability of lip-position is not restricted to vocoid articulations. In fact, in many languages whole syllables have either spread or rounded lips throughout, for example, in German *Tier* 'animal' exemplifies a spread syllable, whereas *Tür* 'door' is a rounded syllable. (For some speakers the syllable coda may involve a slackening of the lips to neutral.) Similarly, the stressed syllables in *Biene* 'bee' and *Bühne* 'stage' are spread and rounded, respectively, with the lips moving to neutral during the nasal and the unstressed schwa. Also, some sounds other than vocoids have rounded lips all the time. For many speakers of English [ʃ ʒ] and sometimes [ɹ] have rounded lips in all positions, so [ʃuut] *shoot* will have lip-rounding throughout, whereas [ʃiit] *sheet* will only have lip-rounding in the onset. For a discussion of lip-rounding in the Turkish harmony system, see section 7.2.1.

When lip-rounding occurs with contoid articulations, it is often referred to as **labialization**, and is represented by [ʷ] after the main symbol, for example, [ɸʷ bʷ θʷ]. Spread or neutral lips is not usually indicated in these circumstances, so English *two* can be transcribed [tʷʰuu] and *tea* [tʰɪi]. The former stop can be described as a voiceless, oral, rounded (or labialized), alveolar (aspirated) stop. Note that there is an assumption here that rounded lips are in some way unusual (**marked** is the term phonologists often use), since there is no diacritic for spread, but this is misleading. The position of rest is neutral, and both rounding and spreading represent divergence from this position.

One final aspect of vocoid articulation requires further discussion. In Table 3.8 I gave some examples of voiceless vocoids. These are represented with a subscript circle [̥]. These occur in English as a voiceless onset to a following vowel, for example, [ɪ̥ɪd] *hid*, [e̥ed] *head*, [ɑ̥ɑd] *hard*, [ɜ̥ɜd] *heard*. In most transcriptions of English these are all transcribed as [h]. This is simply a broad transcription based on a phonological analysis. The quality of the voiceless vocoid is always the same as the voiced phase, and so each quality is predictable. For this reason they are interpreted phonologically as variants of the same sound [h]. This is another good reason for keeping separate the terms contoid/vocoid and consonant/vowel, referred to in section 2.9.3. The fact that a vocoid articulation occurs in the syllable margins does not prevent it on phonetic grounds from being a consonant. Just as in the case of the French 'semivowels', it is patterns of behaviour that determine what is a consonant and what is a vowel in English. In English the forms of the definite and indefinite articles determine the classes of consonants and vowels: [ðə]/[ə] + consonant, [ðɪ]/[ən] + vowel, so it's [ðə/ə mæn] *the/a man*, [ðɪ/ən eg] *the/an egg*, and, importantly, [ðə/ə hæt] *the/a hat*. (In case you are wondering how to accommodate those few speakers who insist on pronouncing *an historical* with [ən hɪ . . .] rather than [ən ɪ . . .], consider them confused clever Dicks who think spelling has some kind of magical powers. They would not say *[ðɪ hɪ . . .], by the way.) Because many phonologists want consonantal-like terms for phonological consonants, the description 'glottal fricative' is used for [h], but any friction produced during such an articulation is usually what can be termed **cavity friction**, the slight amount of friction caused by air flowing over any object, in this case all the 'clutter' in the mouth. (See also the discussion in Ladefoged [2006], p. 265.)

The voiceless vocoid does not have to be the same as the voiced one from an articulatory point of view, though in all languages that I know of which have a phonological /h/ this is the case, but it is possible to change the vocoid quality as the phonation changes, for example, [ɔ̥ɑ], [i̥y], [ɜ̥u]. It is also the case that in some languages a voiceless vocoid can be a vowel; for example, in Japanese high vowels are voiceless between or, in final position, following vocieless obstruents: [ki̥sen] 'steamship', [katsɯ̥] 'win' (see Tsujimura [1996]). In the suggested broad transcription for English presented in Chapter Four I will use [h].

3.6 Types of resonance

In section 2.9.4.2 we discussed the parameter of resonance and noted that it, too, could be syllable-length. In fact, it can extend even further than one syllable in some languages, including English (see the discussion in Kelly and Local

[1986] of frontness and backness in /l/ and /r/ in a number of English accents). The part of the tongue that is not being used to produce an obstruction can be bunched into a number of positions to produce variation in the resonant quality of a contoid or approximant articulation. Three are differentiated by the IPA symbols: [mʲ bˠ θˤ]. The first represents frontness or **palatalization**; the second backness or **velarization**; and the third **pharyngealization**, where the root of the tongue is pulled back into the pharynx, thereby narrowing it. There is further possible shaping of the tongue; for instance, in many Arabic dialects the so-called emphatic stops (which are usually simply referred to as pharyngealized) are produced with the tip of the tongue on the back of the top teeth and gums, the blade on the alveolar ridge and the rest of the tongue flattened and extended sideways between the side teeth. The root is pulled back into the pharynx. The point of contact for the fricatives varies from dental to alveolar. (This detailed description was given to me in a private discussion many years ago at Leeds University by T.F. Mitchell, one of J.R. Firth's former colleagues.) A description of [dˤ] using the conventional labels would be a voiced, oral, pharyngealized, denti-alveolar stop.

In Irish and Scots Gaelic front and back resonance variation is quite marked, sometimes extending over whole words, for example, [mʲagʲ] *meaig* 'magpie', [mˠaːdˠərˠə] *madra* 'dog', sometimes affecting just the rhyme of the final syllable, with a grammatical function, as in [kilʲaːnˠ] *coileán* 'pup' (nominative) and [kilʲaːnʲ] *coileáin* (genitive). (For further details, see Gussmann [2002], p. 7–11.)

3.7 Non-pulmonic air

All the previous sections have dealt with sounds made with an egressive pulmonic airstream. We now have to consider the possible combinations for implosives, ejectives and clicks. We noted in chapter two that these are much more restricted than the egressive pulmonic sounds. To start with, the nasal/oral option is not available to implosives and ejectives; if the velum were lowered in such cases, the air would simply escape through the nose. So, as the velum has to be closed, we do not need to mention that parameter specifically. Also, whereas implosives may be voiceless (rarely) or voiced, ejectives are neither. As the larynx is raised in a piston-like action to compress the trapped air, the vocal cords remain shut, so the term [ejective] covers the phonation type. The clicks can be combined with velar stops, as was described in section 2.10.3. The feature choices [voiceless/voiced] and [oral/nasal] refer to the

Table 3.11 Sample descriptions of non-pulmonic sounds

[ɓ]: voiced, bilabial implosive
[ʛ]: voiceless, velar implosive
[t']: alveolar ejective stop
[s']: alveolar ejective fricative
[ʘ]: bilabial click
[ǀk]: alveolar click with voiceless velar plosive
[ǂɡ]: palatoalveolar click with voiced velar plosive
[ǁŋ]: lateral click with voiced nasal velar stop

velar stop mechanism, not the clicks themselves. Table 3.11 gives a selection of descriptions of non-pulmonic sounds.

3.8 Parametric representations

If we want to indicate some of the timing relationships between the operation of the individual articulators, as in the discussion of voice onset and voice offset in section 3.3, we can use representations that do not rely simply on letter-symbols. There is no standard form that parametric representations take; the way in which individual articulatory mechanisms are represented often depends on what features are being discussed. If we consider voice onset time in relation to stop closure, hold and release, instead of the verbal descriptions in (i) to (v) in section 3.3, we can use diagrams such as those in Figures 3.4–3.8, respectively, with the symbol transcription added for comparison. Phonation is represented simply as nothing for voicelessness and a horizontal line for voicing; the lips are represented as closed with the line at the top of the area marked 'lips' and open at the bottom.

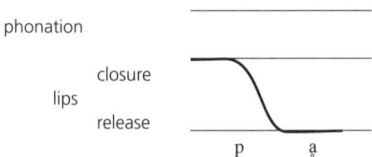

Figure 3.4

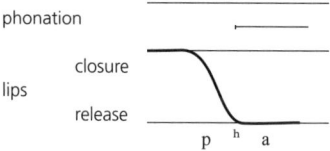

Figure 3.5

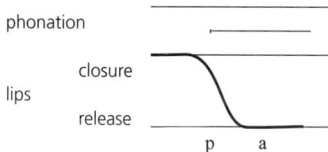

Figure 3.6

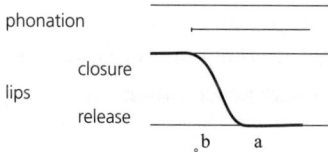

Figure 3.7

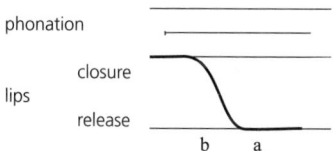

Figure 3.8

Voice offset time can be represented in a similar way; Figure 3.9 represents [ab̥]. Draw parametric representations for the other offset options given above.

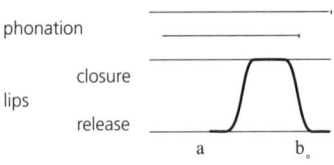

Figure 3.9

I shall return to parametric representations in Chapters Five and Seven.

3.9 Further reading and exercises

There is an excellent introduction to parametric representations in Tench (1978). Pike (1943) pp. 107–120, Laver (1994) pp. 101–118 and Ball and Lowry (2001) pp. 81–89 also discuss parametric views of speech.

Take one parameter, for example, phonation or velic activity, and plot it against a transcription of the English words *satisfy* [sætɪsfaɪ], *attention* [ətenʃn], *mounting* [maʊntɪŋ]. Look at Tench (1978), as well as Figures 3.4–3.9 above, to get an idea of what your representations should look like. Then try plotting two parameters against each other.

4 Transcription

Chapter Outline

4.1 Transcribing Standard British English (SBE)	70
4.2 General American	81
4.3 French	83
4.4 German	86
4.5 Modern Greek	89
4.6 Malay	91
4.7 Practice	94
4.8 Further reading	95

Now that we have reviewed the basics of articulation and the possible combinations of the various parameters, we need to consider further the issue of transcription, which has been dealt with on a rather ad hoc basis so far, though some kind of consistent system was presented in Chapter Three. We need to consider the various reasons for transcribing speech and the influence each has on the resulting form of the transcription. A fundamental question that has been in the background so far, and it relates to some extent to the issue of segmentation, is: how much detail do we want to indicate in our transcriptions? The general answer is: it all depends on the transcriber's reasons for transcribing.

Let us start with various possible transcriptions of the English word *cab* in (4.1).

(4.1) [kæb]
[k^{h}æb]

[kʰæb̥]
[kʰæːb̥]
[kʰæːb̚]

Each of these is slightly different and gives more information in each case, though the last two may represent different types of articulation: the fourth one may be used to indicate final (voiceless) release of the bilabial stop, whereas the last one specifically indicates that the final stop is unreleased. We can do the same thing with transcriptions of the word *dart* in (4.2).

(4.2) [dɑːt]
[dɑt]
[˳dɑt]
[˳dɑʔt]
[˳dɑʔt̚]

The point I am trying to make here is that the transcriptions in (4.1) and (4.2) are alternatives for representing the same phonetic event, not necessarily variant pronunciations of the same word. This will be dealt with in detail in Chapter Eight in relation to English. However, as an example of variant forms of the same word by different speakers, consider variants of *dart* in (4.3) with some of the details of (4.2) omitted.

(4.3) [dɑt]
[dɑɹt]
[dɑɻt]
[dɑɻt̺]
[dɒɻt̺]
[dɑɹʔt̚]
[dɑrt]
[daːt]
[dɑː ʔ]
[daː ʔ]

Such pronunciations could all be found in the British Isles.

So, to start with, we need to make a clear distinction between variant pronunciations and variant transcriptions. For the purposes of this chapter we will concentrate on the latter, and fix on a general purpose transcription for standard British English and one for General American. (Don't forget, neither of these will necessarily be your accent. In this chapter, SBE refers to standard British English pronunciation, and GA to General American.) After a discussion of two standard varieties of English we will move on to a consideration of other European languages, and then consider aspects of training in transcription with suggestions for appropriate exercises.

Within variant transcriptions there is a distinction to be made between those that represent a lot of phonetic detail, called **narrow** transcriptions, and those that give little detail, called **broad** transcriptions. Our general purpose transcriptions will be relatively broad. The choice of transcription is usually based on the transcriber's needs and aims (and competence). If the focus is on fine phonetic detail, as would be required in assessing speech production difficulties or in the investigation of fine-grained sociolinguistic variation, then as narrow a transcription as possible would be needed. For instance, in either case, we might want to investigate the onset on voicing in word-initial stops. (Of course, some of the fine distinctions are very difficult to represent in IPA symbols, so a set of measurements of voice onset time in milliseconds would be preferable to transcription.) On the other hand, if we want to represent the spoken output in the context of some other discussion, say, a syntactic analysis, or a general comparison of English and French in a language-learning manual, then a broader transcription is usually adequate. It is also the case that many phonologists are not interested in what they would consider 'low-level' features of pronunciation, and therefore only use broad transcriptions, sometimes appearing to treat them as unanalysed data. Certainly, many of the broadest transcriptions are determined by a desire to represent only phonological contrasts rather than phonetic information beyond that. To take a simple example, let us consider the two types of lateral articulation in English, one velarized, the other not (see section 2.9.4.2). If we wish to indicate the difference between the two, we use two different symbols: [lɪtɫ] *little*, but since the occurrence of the two varieties of lateral (its **allophones**, as they would be called in phonological analysis; see, for instance, Davenport and Hannahs [2005]) is predictable, it is only necessary to indicate the phonological unit with one symbol: [lɪtl]. If we know this is English, and we know the rules of the allophonic distribution for this distinctive sound, then we know that the first lateral is not velarized and the second one is.

One of the uses of broad transcription is in dictionaries, but consider how unhelpful it would be for a foreign learner if details such as those given for the English lateral above were ignored, and only the broadest transcription, [lɪtl], were given. An even more problematic transcriptional convention occurs in German dictionaries. What is considered to be a phonological unit in standard German, /r/ (to represent which we put the symbol between phonological slant lines), is pronounced in some positions as a voiced, uvular trill or fricative, [ʀ] or [ʁ]. However, in syllable codas, especially after long vowels, it is pronounced as a centralized (sometimes lowered) low-mid vocoid, [ɐ̈] (also transcribed [ɐ]). If a broad transcription is used, using [r], then a word like *Spur* 'trace' will appear as /ʃpuːr/, whereas a foreign learner needs to know that it is pronounced [ʃpuːɐ̈]. The *Oxford Duden German Dictionary* does actually use the symbol [ɐ] after long vowels, but uses slant lines, that is, phonological representations, for the transcriptions. (It also transcribes *little* as /lɪtl/, without the detail for foreign learners.) So dictionary entries, especially those aimed at non-native learners, need a suitable compromise between no detail and too much detail for the learner.

The upshot of all this is that you will come across very many different types of transcription, all claiming to represent the same accent. This may seem very confusing to start with, but the trick is to learn the conventions of the transcriber (sometimes these are made explicit) and treat each book you look at afresh. If you find two or more books using the same transcriptional conventions, then that is a bonus. To make matters worse, however, many American linguistics books do not use the IPA system of transcription, but have their own, sometimes called the American Phonetic Alphabet (APA). Odden (2005) provides an excellent comparison of the two systems of symbols. Problems can arise when the same symbol is used to represent different sounds, for example, IPA [j] = APA [y], whereas IPA [y] = APA [ü]. Also you must not forget that when American linguists refer to English, they usually mean some kind of American variety. So, don't say you haven't been warned – and keep your wits about you!

4.1 Transcribing Standard British English (SBE)

In what follows we shall look at both narrow and broad transcriptions, and settle on a broad one to practice with until you gain confidence. You may well have come across the term 'received pronunciation' (RP) referring to a standard British pronunciation. Firstly, we may note that the term originates in the late Victorian period as a value-laden label for how one should speak in the best ('received') social circles. To some extent this (unacceptable) evaluation is avoided by the common practice of just using the initials 'RP'. Secondly, we may note that an estimate from the 1970s (Trudgill [1974]) suggested that between 2 to 3 percent of the population of Britain used this type of pronunciation. This means that in any phonetics class in Britain there are going to be very few such speakers, if any. In addition the accent has been disappearing off the radio and television over the past twenty-five years, so the estimate of 2 to 3 percent is possibly on the high side. Thirdly, we may note that since the standard textbooks on RP were published and widely used (e.g. Jones [1956], Gimson [1962]), several changes have taken place in the pronunciation habits of standard speakers, so that the kind of RP presented as a model to foreign learners is often old-fashioned and dying out. Fourthly, we must note that accents and dialects are not neatly and discretely cut off from one another; they form a continuum that can be investigated by sociolinguists. So, it is perfectly possible to find speakers who speak with most of the characteristics of RP with a few local London features, or a speaker from the Midlands who fluctuates between northern and southern forms. Taking all this into account, I have chosen to refer somewhat vaguely to SBE in this book. My description and suggested transcription will take into account the more recent developments in pronunciation that have taken place.

The consonants of most varieties of British English need the following symbols in a broad transcription:

[p t k b d g tʃ dʒ m n ŋ f θ s ʃ v ð z ʒ w l ɹ j h].

These will be exemplified in transcriptions below, after we have considered the vowels. As we have seen in transcriptions of English I have used so far, we could indicate more of the articulatory detail. So, we could use [pʰ tʰ kʰ] in onset position of a stressed syllable, or [ʔp ʔt ʔk] in coda position, or indicate lack of release in final stops. And there is always the possibility of representing both [l] and [ɫ], as in [lɪtɫ]. When learning to transcribe, it is probably better to start with the broad transcription, and add details as and when you feel confident. (I always encourage the students I teach to be as adventurous as they feel able, but have to warn them that a wrong transcription is wrong. We don't want glottally reinforced voiced stops in codas, e.g., *[lɪʔd] *lid*, or unreleased fricatives, e.g., *[s̚], where the asterisk indicates a wrong transcription.)

The representation of the vowel system of English needs a more detailed discussion. This is because most English vowels are not in cardinal positions or on the periphery of the vowel area at all. I shall deal with them in groups, so that the accompanying vowel diagrams are not cluttered. Sections 4.1.1–4.1.5 deal with vowels in stressed syllables (see section 4.1.6). Sample transcriptions of whole words are given in section 4.1.7.

4.1.1 Monophthongs

As can be seen from the positions on the chart, most of these vowels are either retracted or advanced, and even central. In narrow transcriptions in which subtle differences of position are focussed on as important, for example, sociolinguistic investigations, it would be possible to use the diacritics given in section 3.5 (Tables 3.9 and 3.10), but in broader transcriptions the convention is to use the nearest cardinal vowel symbol or one of the distinctive intermediate symbols [ɪ æ ʊ].

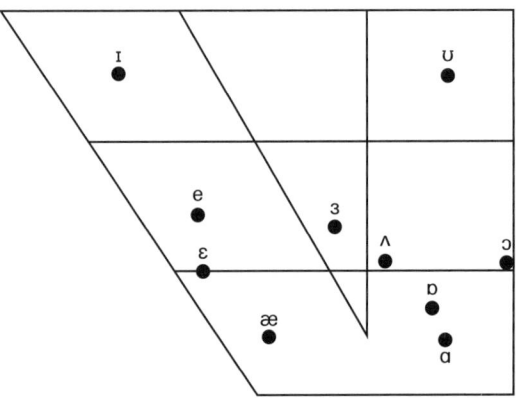

Figure 4.1 Vowel chart containing [ɪ e æ ɒ ʌ ʊ ɛ ɜ ɔ ɑ].

One symbol in particular needs further comment: [ɛ] is the monophthong used by most SBE speakers today in words like *fair, bear, bare, bared*. In earlier forms of RP these words would have had a centring diphthong [ɛə] (see section 4.1.4). Since the articulation is nearly always in the region of a front low-mid vocoid, I have chosen to use the symbol [ɛ] to represent it and use [e] for the vowel in *pen, said, friend, dead*. (Compare this with transcriptions for these vowels, Ladefoged [2006], p. 39, Table 2.2.)

Some variation is apparent even in SBE: [ɪ e æ] may be relatively close, as indicated by the positions in Figure 4.1, or relatively more open (so [æ] could be transcribed [a]), and [ʊ] may be centralized (along with [uu], as described in section 4.1.3). [ɜ] is slightly further forward and/or more open for some young speakers: [ɛ̈]. Note that the lip-rounding represented by the symbols for the back vowels is often missing (except in [ɔ]), speakers using neutral lip-position instead for [ʊ] and [ɒ]. Note, too, that despite being a centralized vowel close to [ɐ] the vowel of SBE *cup, come*, is transcribed with its traditional symbol [ʌ].

4.1.2 Front-closing diphthongs

In the case of diphthongs the starting point and the direction of the movement of the tongue is indicated. The end point may be quite varied, but in a broad transcription it is not necessary to indicate more than the general direction; thus, a movement such as [aɛ] can be transcribed as [aɪ], and [ɛi] as [ɛɪ]. Of course, the starting point may also vary, quite considerably in the case of some English vowels, so there is variation even in SBE between [aɪ] and [ɑɪ], and [ɛɪ] and [eɪ]. In a broad transcription I suggest using the symbols on Figure 4.2. Note the change in lip-position in [ɔɪ].

One of these diphthongs, [ɪi], is often represented as a (long) monophthong, with or without a length mark: [i(ː)] (see, e.g., Gimson [1962], and Ladefoged [2006]). Since most speakers of SBE, and many of the local varieties, use a diphthongal movement, I choose to indicate that in the transcription. It is a relatively small movement, but is very clear in spectrographic representations (see Chapter Nine) in comparison with true monophthongal high front vocoid articulations. Incidentally, there are languages with such monophthongal high front vowels, for example, French and German, so it is a visual reminder to foreign learners of English that the English articulation is (and sounds) different from their own native one; for instance, the difference is clear, if one compares a native pronunciation of the German word *bieten* 'to offer' with English *beaten*.

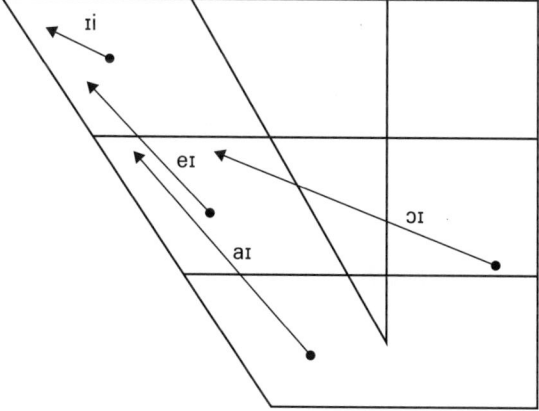

Figure 4.2 Vowel chart containing [ɪi eɪ aɪ ɔɪ].

4.1.3 Back-closing diphthongs

Again, the starting point of all these can vary. [aʊ] varies with [ɑʊ] in words such as *sound, cow, plough,* the latter being rather conservative and less common today; [oʊ] varies with [əʊ] in words such as *stone, folk, though,* the latter being less common now; the second transcriptions and articulations are recommended by Gimson (1962) in each case, whereas Ladefoged (2006) uses the first two of each alternative. The sequence [jʉu], as in *use,* goes from front to back, so the intermediate central position can be indicated, but in a broad transcription [jʊu] is sufficient. [ʊu] is often transcribed [u(ː)], and I have the same reasons for my preferred transcription as I had for [ɪi] above. At this point a word of warning is necessary. Many speakers of SBE up to the age of about 50, and in particular women, use a much more centralized articulation for this English vowel, that is, [ʉː], sometimes monophthongal, sometimes slightly diphthongal. This again can be clearly seen on a spectrogram. So, whichever variety you use, take careful note of the other common articulations and keep them distinct in your mental sound archive.

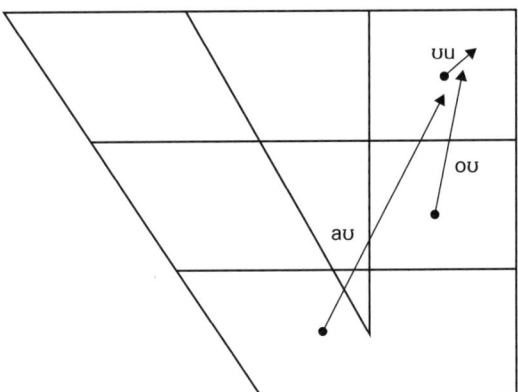

Figure 4.3 Vowel chart containing [aʊ oʊ ʊu].

4.1.4 Centring diphthongs

This type of diphthong, where the tongue moves from a relatively peripheral position towards the centre of the vowel area, is one that is on the decrease

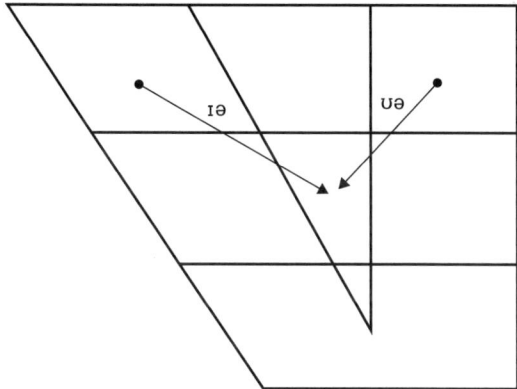

Figure 4.4 Centring diphthongs with just [ɪə] and [ʊə].

in modern SBE. Some speakers only have one: [ɪə], as in [fɪə] *fear*, [bɪəd] *beard*, [aɪdɪə] *idea*. The others, that are given in Gimson (1962), are [ʊə] in *poor*, [ɔə] in *board* and [ɛə] in *bear* and *bare*. The second of these was disappearing even when Gimson's book was first published, and now the other two have as well in SBE (though not in some regional varieties). A few SBE speakers may still differentiate between *poor* with [ʊə], *pore* with [ɔə] and *paw* with [ɔ], but the vast majority of British speakers today no longer use the diphthongal articulations, but use [ɔ] instead for all three words (and others like them, e.g., *sure*, *shore*, *Shaw*). Of course, in terms of transcription from speech it depends what the speaker actually says that determines whether you write [ʊə] or [ɔ] in any given word. The final one, [ɛə], is rarely heard now, having been replaced by the monophthong [ɛ], given in Figure 4.1.

4.1.5 Triphthongs

The diphthongs [aɪ aʊ eɪ ɔɪ oʊ] can all combine with schwa ([ə]) to produce triphthongs: [aɪə] as in *fire*, [aʊə] as in *shower*, [eɪə] as in *player*, [ɔɪə] as in *coir* and [oʊə] as in *mower*, as in Figure 4.5.

However, some speakers may use diphthongs for some of these or even monophthongs: [aə] in *fire*, and [ɑə] or [ɑ] in *shower*. (In my own speech, which is SBE with northern English features such as [æ]/[a] in *last, bath, master*, I make a distinction between [aʊə] *hour* and [ɑ] *our*.)

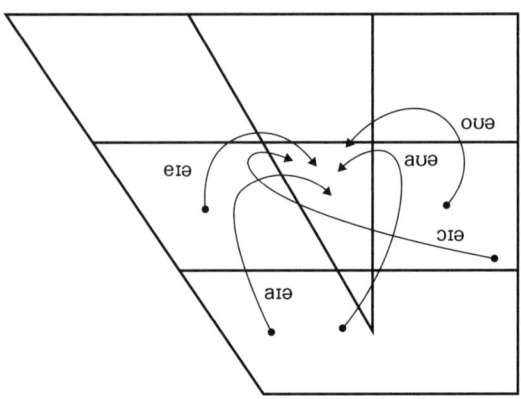

Figure 4.5 Triphthongs.

4.1.6 Unstressed vowels

We have not yet discussed stress as a feature of speech. It will be looked at in more detail in Chapter Six along with its interactions with pitch, vocoid quality and duration, and in Chapter Seven in connected speech, but for now we just need to note that in English a stressed syllable is produced with more muscular energy, making it stand out from the unstressed ones around it. From the hearer's point of view a stressed syllable will be more prominent than unstressed ones. Many English words of more than one syllable have just one stress; say the words *father, about, festival, elephant, astonish, photographer,* and see if you can pick out the stressed syllable in each one. On the other hand, some words have more than one stress; do the same with the following: *photograph, elephantine, opportunistic, parliamentarian, referee*. Even words with just two syllables, if they are compounds, can have two stresses: *blackbird, armchair, dashboard*. However, even when there is more than one stressed syllable, one will stand out more than the others; this is referred to as the main stress of the word.

In SBE there are vowels which only occur in unstressed syllables: [ə] and [i]. The first list of words in the preceding paragraph can be transcribed as follows, the stressed syllable being marked by a preceding [']: ['fɑðə], [ə'baʊt], ['festɪvl], ['elɪfnt], [ə'stɒnɪʃ], [fə'tɒgɹəfə]. The other vowel, [i], is found at the end of words such as *city, happy, calamity, photography*. The pronunciation of this final unstressed vowel is somewhat variable: older forms of SBE (and many northern English varieties) have [ɪ] and varieties from the South East and recent forms of SBE have a brief diphthongal movement: [ii]. When listening to actual speech, see if you can detect which variant is being used; see also if there is any kind of pattern or variation in the speaker's usage. Finally, see which kind of articulation you use.

Besides [ə], [ɪ] is the other vocoid that is found in non-word-final unstressed syllables and final syllables ending in a consonant, for example, in [dɪˈzɒlv] *dissolve*, [bɪˈfɔ] *before*, [ɪˈɹædɪkeɪt] *eradicate*, [ɪkˈstɜmɪneɪt] *exterminate*, [ˈwɒntɪd] *wanted*, [ˈteɪkɪŋ] *taking*, [ɪˈlæstɪk] *elastic*. Over the past fifty years or so there has been a gradual increase in the use of [ə] in syllables which once had [ɪ]. For example, words like *before* and *enough* may have schwa in the first syllable, and maybe even words like *dissolve* and *dissent*. Some speakers make no distinction between *except* and *accept*, pronouncing both as [əksept] rather than [ɪksept] and [əksept], respectively. For some speakers the past tense marker, written -*ed*, is [əd] rather than [ɪd]. On the other hand, the present participle marker, written -*ing*, always has [ɪ], and the word-final syllables spelled -*y* are never [ə]. (In any case English speakers need to distinguish, e.g., *photography* and *photographer*.) Forms such as [pɹɒblɪm] *problem* and [sɪstɪm] *system* are probably no longer current except amongst the oldest RP speakers.

Some speakers use other vowels in unstressed initial syllables, for example, [elekˈtɹɪsətɪ] *electricity*, [kɒnˈsɪdəɹət] *considerate*, and may distinguish between [ekˈsept] *except* and [ækˈsept] *accept*. These non-schwa vowels (often referred to as **unreduced**, as opposed to the **reduced** vowel, schwa) are unstressed but have vocoid qualities that are not those associated with the position of rest. They may be considered to have a secondary stress like the words *photograph* and *elephantine* above, but we should note the warning in Ladefoged ([2006], pp. 111–114) regarding the difference between the stress and intonation pattern of polysyllabic words spoken in isolation and the same words spoken in whole sentences, which we shall discuss in section 6.2.

If you look at the transcriptions of *festival* and *elephant*, you will see that there is no schwa symbol in their final syllables. This is because no vocoid articulation occurs; the transition from one consonant to the next can take place without moving the tongue into (roughly) the position of rest and back again. Think about this in relation to the movements required to go from [v] to [ɫ] and [f] to [n]. The lateral and nasals in English can all act as syllable nuclei, so we hear [bɒtɫ] *bottle*, [kɒtn] *cotton*, [ɹɪðm] *rhythm*, [hɪdn] *hidden*. Many dictionary entries put a schwa symbol in all such words, for example, [hɒspɪtəl] *hospital*, [sædən] *sadden*, but this is misleading. However, many young speakers from the South East of England are indeed using a schwa in such words, which may be a regional London and south-eastern feature spreading into SBE. The syllabic laterals and nasals are, nevertheless, still widespread. Even those speakers who regularly use syllabic laterals and nasals may not use them in all words; if there is a consonant cluster or a nasal before the final unstressed syllable ending in a nasal, then schwa may well occur, for example, [lʌndən] *London* (though [lʌndn] is possible) and [pɜmənənt] *permanent*. In a very few cases a lexical distinction can be made between, for example, [bɪtn] *bitten* and [bɪtən] *bittern* (a rare bird that breeds in East Anglia – and, therefore, a rare word for anyone who is not an ornithologist). The syllabic consonants can be written with a subscript diacritic to indicate the syllabicity, for example, [l̩], [n̩]. In a broad transcription of English, however, it is not necessary to do so in most cases, as the consonantal sequences involved, such as [-tl], [-zn] can never belong to the same syllable as a coda.

4.1.7 Sample transcriptions

There now follows a list of SBE pronunciations of individual words in the broad transcription I have proposed (Table 4.1). Once again I must emphasize that these may well not represent your own pronunciation of these words. You must also be aware of the difference between variation in the phonetic realizations of words (which may be regionally determined to some extent) and the variation in what is known as **lexical incidence** in the same accent. In the first case, one speaker may say [skɒʔlənd] *Scotland* and another [skɒtlənd]. On the other hand, lexical incidence is the technical term for which vowel is used in which words (it usually deals with vowels in English, though it could be consonantal distribution as well). So, it is a question of whether speakers of SBE say [ɹikənɒmɪks] or [ekənɒmɪks] *economics*, [plæstɪk] or [plɑstɪk] *plastic*. The former case would not need to be indicated in a broad transcription, but the second case would. I give some alternative SBE pronunciations in what follows. The rows across contain words which have the same stressed vowel. Alternative pronunciations are indicated with brackets around optional sounds, where two alternatives are possible.

I have deliberately omitted the centring diphthongs other than [ɪə] because of their gradual disappearance. A speaker using the system of pronunciation represented in Table 4.1 would use [ɛ] in all the words given [ɛə] in a dictionary, e.g. [skwɛlɪ] *squarely*, [debənɛ] *debonair*, and [ɔ] in words given [ʊə], for example, [pjɔ] *pure*, [pɔ] *pour, pore, poor* (as well as *paw*, which has [ɔ] for all speakers), [əbskjɔ] *obscure*, [əzjɔ]/[əʒjɔ] *azure*, [ɪnʃɔɹəbl] *insurable*.

In the case of the words which vary in terms of number of syllables or occurrence of schwa, say the words in (4.4) and see how many syllables you

Transcription

Table 4.1 Standard British English (SBE)

[tɪn] tin	[sɪti] city	[ɪdɪət] idiot
[ten] ten	[meni] many	[estɪmət] estimate
[tæn] tan	[hæmə] hammer	[sætədɪ] Saturday
[kɒd] cod	[hɒli] holly	[kɒnf(ə)ɹəns] conference
[kʌd] cud	[θʌndə] thunder	[pɹədʌkʃn] production
[kʊd] could	[pʊli] pulley	[pʊlmənɹɪ] pulmonary [pʌlmənɹɪ]
[bɛ] bear, bare	[fɛlɪ] fairly	[kɛflnəs] carefulness
[fɑm] farm	[pɑtɪ] party	[vɪɹagoʊ] virago
[fɜn] fern	[sɜvnt] servant	[kənvɜʃn] conversion
[tɔn] torn	[nɔtɪ] naughty	[ɔdɪbl] audible
[siin] seen, scene	[kɹiitʃə] creature	[gæɹəntii] guarantee
[tɹeɪn] train	[feɪljə] failure	[hjʊmeɪn] humane
[daɪn] dine	[haɪtn] heighten	[haɪpəmɑkɪt] hypermarket
[kɔɪn] coin	[lɔɪtə] loiter	[ɪndʒɔɪmənt] enjoyment
[saʊnd] sound	[aʊtə] outer	[əkaʊnt(ə)nsɪ] accountancy
[goʊt] goat	[əloʊn] alone	[foʊtəgɹæf] photograph [foʊtəgɹɑf]
[flʊʊt] flute	[lʊʊnɪ] looney	[kɹʊʊʃl] crucial
[bɪəd] beard	[ɒstɪə] austere [ɔstɪə]	[ɒkʃ(ə)nɪə] auctioneer [ɔkʃ(ə)nɪə]

use in each case. You will probably find that you do not treat each word in the same way, for example, [hɪstɹɪ] with no schwa, [mɪzəɹɪ] with one. Note that there are other possible stress patterns in some of the words, for example, *secretary* may be pronounced [ˈsekɹəˈteɹɪ] with two stresses rather than one. If there are American and British speakers in your class, see what differences there are in the words below.

(4.4)
history	secretary	camera	laboratory
cutlery	natural	boundary	conservatory
seperate	misery	desolate	especially
miserable	surgery	finally	elaborate
every	century	javelin	temperature
pedalling	factory	family	comfortable
licorice	marginal	nursery	treasury
decimal	chocolate	general	quandary
company	prisoner	mystery	vegetable
definite	personal	awfully	national
reference	brightening	opener	parliamentary

4.1.8 'Long' and 'short' vowels

In the above description of SBE vowels I have not used the terms 'long' and 'short', which are often found in books on English phonetics and phonology. This is because they are phonological terms, and, as far as English is concerned, do not refer directly to duration. Whereas under some circumstances it may well be that [ɪ] is shorter than [ii], or [ɒ] is shorter than [ɔ], when we look at continuous speech we find that the duration of English vowels is determined by the phonation of the following consonant and/or the stress pattern of the sentence. For example, under the same stress conditions the [ɒ] of *pot* is shorter than in *pod*. When a voiced consonant follows the vowel, the vocoid phase is longer than before a voiceless sound. When nothing follows, there is greater vocoid duration, too, for example, [sɔt] *sort*, [sɔd] *sword*, [sɔ] *saw*. The stress and rhythm of a sentence also has an effect on duration. If we call our friend John by name using a high-fall + low-rise intonation pattern, the vocoid articulation [ɒ] would be far longer than a so-called long vowel in a longer utterance, whether the word containing it carried the main stress or not, for example, *Joan* ([dʒoʊn]) *went to the cinema yesterday*. In other words the duration of English vocoid articulations is very variable. So, why do linguists use 'long' and 'short' when referring to English vowels? One reason is tradition: it is assumed that in Middle English (c.1100–1450) there were pairs of long and short vowels, so their descendants (with a few changes of category) can be considered in the same way. The other reason is that there is a phonological distinction between the two sets, but it has nothing to do with duration. The 'short' vowels must be followed by a consonant in a stressed syllable, so [tɪn], [tæp] and [tʌn] are good English words, but *[tɪ], *[tæ] and *[tʌ] are not, and never could be, unless the phonological structure of English words changes dramatically in the future. The 'long' vowels, on the other hand, are not subject to this restriction and can occur without a following consonant, so [seɪ] *say*, [sii] *see*, [sɔ] *saw* and [saɪ] *sigh* are fine. These sets could equally well be referred to as **checked** and **unchecked** vowels, respectively, according to the syllable type they occur in. Checked syllables are usually called **closed**, unchecked ones **open**. (Do not confuse these terms with the alternative labels for vocoids, **close** (high) and **open** (low).) We shall consider duration further in Chapters Six and Seven, but the definition of vowel length in English is another good example of phonological behaviour not being dependent on phonetics. So strong is the desire on the part of phonologists to have a unitary feature to describe somewhat disparate phonetic phenomena, that if one label proves insufficient for some reason, other labels are found and applied to the same phonological phenomenon. Both 'tense' and 'lax' and '+ATR' and '−ATR' have been applied to English vowels (see, for instance, Davenport and Hannahs [2005], p. 112, and Kenstowicz [1994]).

4.2 General American

There are two consonantal differences between SBE and GA that need to be discussed: the alveolar tap [ɾ] and the occurrence of coda [ɹ]. Many speakers of American English use a tap articulation in intervocalic position where English speakers use [t d n]. (A few SBE speakers use this occasionally in mimicry of the American norm, but it is lexically restricted, e.g., to commonly occurring words such as *got to* [gɒɾə].) American examples are: [beɾi] *Betty*, [nɔɾi] *naughty*, [kwɑləɾi] *quality*, [dæɾi] *daddy*, [hɑləɾeɪ] *holiday*, [sʌ̃ɾi] *sunny*, [seɹəməɾi] *ceremony*. The tap is not used if the position of the sound is before a stressed vowel, as in [əteɪn] *attain*, [ədɔɹ] *adore*, [ənɔɪ] *annoy*. Where British speakers have [nt] in the same circumstances, many Americans have either just a nasal stop [n] or a nasal tap [ɾ̃]: [twẽɾ̃i] *twenty*.

The occurrence of [ɹ] in the coda of English words, e.g., *cart, card, car, carter,* is known as **rhoticity**, and is a major distinguishing feature of accents of English (see Chapter Eight). General American is rhotic, SBE is non-rhotic. So in GA the first three words can be transcribed [kɑɹt], [kɑɹd], [kɑɹ], respectively. But it is not simply a question of putting [ɹ] after all the vowels of the system; it is only a restricted number of them that can occur before it. (For surveys of various kinds of rhotic English accent, see Wells [1982] and Harris [1994] and Chapter Eight.) The GA vowel + [ɹ] sequences are included in Table 4.3, after we have discussed the vowel system.

In GA there are two vocoid articulations that are often referred to as **rhotacized**: [ɜ˞] and [ə˞], which occur in stressed and unstressed syllables, respectively. Ladefoged (2006), pp. 224–226 describes three different tongue positions for these, but since we are dealing with a broad transcription, we can symbolize them all in the same way. The tongue positions are related to those of the retroflex sounds discussed in section 2.8.5, and the approximant [ɻ] can be regarded as their consonantal equivalent, in the way that [j ɥ w ɰ] were paired with [i y u ɯ], respectively. Table 4.2 gives a number of examples of GA pronunciations with [ɜ˞] and [ə˞].

Note that the words with [ə˞] could also be transcribed with [ɻ] instead, and we could interpret it as a syllabic consonant along with the lateral and nasals: [fɑðɻ̩], [beɹɻ̩], [fɻ̩get]. For many speakers the last word *terrorist* may

Table 4.2 General American (GA)

[bɝd] *bird*	[kɝɫ] *curl*	[fɝɾɫ] *fertile*
[fɑðɚ] *father*	[lɪɾɚ] *litre*	[sɛnəɾɚ] *senator*
[bɛɾɚ] *better*	[fɑɹmɚ] *farmer*	[ɪ̃ɾɚvjuu] *interview*
[fɚment] *ferment*	[pɚsweɪd] *persuade*	[tɛɹəɹɪst] *terrorist*

have a relatively long phase of retroflex approximation: [tɛɹ(ɹ)ɹɪst]; note, too, that I have used two or three symbols to represent the long duration, but this cannot be considered an accurate representation of any particular duration.

The GA vowels are different in certain respects from those of SBE, and their distribution in the lexicon is also different. For instance, there is no distinction between [ɒ] as in SBE *pot* and [ɑ] as in SBE *father*; in GA both words have [ɑ], which is usually shorter than the SBE articulation in roughly the same area of the vowel diagram, and which is pronounced with either spread or neutral lips. It is, however, a member of the unchecked ('long') set of vowels, since it can occur without a following consonant, unlike English [ɒ]. The diphthongs [eɪ] and [oʊ] can vary with monophthongal variants [e] and [o], respectively. (Note that if you are transcribing a speaker with monophthongal variants in these two cases, it will be necessary to use [ɛ] for words like *ten, bed, leather, friend,* and so on, to keep the two front vowel symbols distinct.) The other vowels are more or less the same, though there is a greater tendency for Americans to nasalize all vowels before nasal consonants than is found in British speakers. Table 4.3 gives a number of examples, including vowel + [ɹ] sequences, some of which indicate the different lexical incidence in GA from that found in SBE; common alternatives are also indicated.

As we noted above, fewer vowels can occur before coda [ɹ] than before any of the other consonants. In phonological terms this means that there are fewer vowel contrasts. A proper phonological analysis of this restriction is not our concern here, but we need to note that, for example, [ii] and [ɪ] do not contrast in this position. From a phonetic point of view it means that the articulatory position within the high, front area is greater when there is no contrast, so speakers vary in tongue height from [i] to [ɪ], for instance, in words like *beer*. It is certainly the case that many American speakers have the relatively lower tongue position for the high and the mid vowels before [ɹ], for example, [bɪɹ] *beer*, [bɛɹ] *bear, bare*, [pʊɹ] *poor*, [fɔɹ] *four, fore, for*, and this even applies before intervocalic [ɹ] as well, so we may find [mɛɹi] *merry, Mary* or [mæɹi] *marry, Mary*, and variation between [pɛɹənt] and [pæɹənt] *parent*.

Table 4.3 General American (GA)

[nɪɹ] near	[bɪd] beard	[ʌɫtɪɹɪɚ] ulterior
[bæθ] bath	[bæd] bad	[pæɹɑri] parity
[beɹ] bear	[bɑɹ] bar	[fɑɹm] farm
[kɔɹn] corn	[bɔɹ] bore, boar*	[pʊɹ] poor
[lɑŋ] long [lɔŋ]	[klɔθ] cloth	[bɑɾm] bottom
[fɑðɚ] father	[bɹɑ] bra	[kjʊɹ] cure

*Some speakers make a distinction here and pronounce *boar* [boʊɹ].

It is now important to go beyond English, though we will return to a more detailed investigation of varieties you may have come across which may or may not be your own in Chapter Eight. I will look at three other European languages, though not in the same detail as we considered English, and an Asian language from a different language family, Malay.

4.3 French

To a native speaker of English, French sounds very different. This is not just a question of not understanding it, because even for those who have learnt it, its pronunciation still holds a challenge. The structure of the whole sound system of French is quite different from that of English. (Many of the differences may well relate to the fact that English is a Germanic language, whereas French is a Romance language, that is one derived from Latin.)

If we start with the consonants and their symbols in a broad transcription, the system can look very similar to English.

[p t k b d g m n ɲ ŋ f s ʃ v z ʒ w l j ʁ]

However, the differences in the stops are obscured by the broadness of the transcription. [t d] are, in fact, dental in French, so should be written [t̪ d̪], and the voiceless stops are unaspirated, that is, conform to option (iii) in the list in section 3.3. (Do not forget, in onset position of stressed syllables in English voiceless stops are aspirated and [t d] are alveolar.) [l] may be alveolar or dental, and there is no velarized lateral in codas: compare English [tʰeɫ] *tell* with French [t̪ɛl] *tel(le)* 'such'. The extra nasal [ɲ] is palatal and [ʁ] is a uvular fricative. Although conventionally it is written as though it were always voiced in broad transcriptions, it is voiceless, [χ], when it follows voiceless obstruents, for example, [tχɛ̃] *train* 'train', [dʁɛ̃] *drain* 'drain', [mɛtχ] *mettre* 'to put', [pudʁ̥] *poudre* 'powder'.

The vowels of standard Parisian French are quite different from those of English. They are nearly all peripheral to the vowel area. Figure 4.6 gives the monophthongs.

The mid central vowel only occurs in unstressed syllables, like schwa in English; in some phonological analyses it is treated as a variant of and transcribed as [œ]. (It is also sometimes transcribed as [ə] with no indication of the lip-rounding; see section 2.9.4.) Most speakers of standard Parisian French no longer distinguish between [a] as in *la* 'the (feminine)', *patte* 'paw', and [ɑ] as in *las* 'tired', *pâte* 'paste' (often still prescribed for foreign learners); [a] is used for both sets of words, making the pairs **homophonous** (= sound the same).

There are three nasal vowels, low-mid and low, as in Figure 4.7.

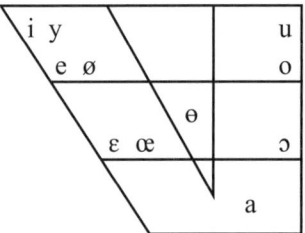

Figure 4.6 French vowels.

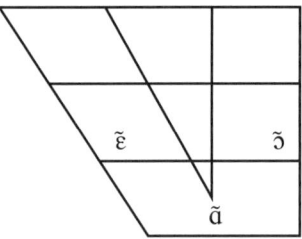

Figure 4.7 French nasal vowels.

Again there is an older type of pronunciation which includes a rounded counterpart of [ɛ̃]: [œ̃], as in *brun* 'brown', *un* 'a' (masculine), but today most standard speakers say [bʁɛ̃], making it homophonous with *brin* 'blade (of grass)', and [ɛ̃], respectively.

French has no falling diphthongs like those in English, but there are vowels within one syllable where the more prominent, longer phase is the latter part, that is, rising diphthongs. These include: [ua ie iɛ iɛ̃ iɔ̃ ui uɛ yi]. Many of these, which only occur word-internally, are interpreted as a sequence of 'glide + vowel. This is a phonological analysis; use of the term 'glide' indicates indecision between classifying the sound as a consonant or a vowel. Whatever the arguments for and against any particular analysis may be, in a broad transcription use of [w j ɥ] to indicate the starting point of the movement has the advantage of showing that these are rising diphthongs; the above transcriptions would thus be replaced respectively by [wa je jɛ jɛ̃ jɔ̃ wi wɛ ɥi].

Sample transcriptions are given in Table 4.4; each monophthong is in (i) a monosyllable, (ii) a non-final syllable of a polysyllabic word, and (iii) the final syllable of a polysyllabic word. I have omitted the dental diacritic for simplicity.

Table 4.4 French

[li] *lit* (bed)	[sitχɔ̃] *citron* (lemon)	[vɑ̃dʁədi] *vendredi* (Friday)
[le] *les* (the, plural)	[eʁo] *héros* (hero)	[epe] *épée* (sword)
[lɛ] *lait* (milk)	[lety] *laitue* (lettuce)	[etɛ] *était* (was)
[la] *la* (the)	[savɔ̃] *savon* (soap)	[matla] *matelas* (mattress)
[ly] *lu* (read)	[kyʁjø] *curieux* (curious)	[ɑ̃tɑ̃dy] *entendu* (heard)
[pø] *peu* (little)	[kχøze] *creuser* (to excavate)	[nəvø] *neveu* (nephew)
[sœl] *seul* (alone)	[flœʁi] *fleuri* (flowery)	[fymœʁ] *fumeur* (smoker)
[lu] *loup* (wolf)	[guvɛʁn] *gouverne* (guidance)	[ʒalu] *jaloux* (jealous)
[po] *peau* (skin)	[ʃofaʒ] *chauffage* (heating)	[mɔʁso] *morceau* (bit)
[kɔk] *coque* (shell)	[sɔlɛj] *soleil* (sun)	[ekɔl] *école* (school)
[fɛ̃] *fin* (end)	[sɛ̃sɛʁ] *sincère* (sincere)	[ɑ̃fɛ̃] *enfin* (at last)
[bɔ̃] *bon* (good)	[ɑ̃fɔ̃se] *enfoncer* (to thrust)	[balɔ̃] *ballon* (balloon)
[dɑ̃] *dans* (in)	[dɑ̃se] *dancer* (to dance)	[ɑ̃fɑ̃] *enfant* (child)

Stress is always on the final syllable of polysyllabic words spoken in isolation, which tends to lengthen the syllable. The quality of the mid vowels preceding the stressed syllable can vary from speaker to speaker, and not all speakers distinguish between [e ø o] on the one hand and [ɛ œ ɔ] on the other in non-stressed syllables. [œ] and [ɔ] have to be followed by a consonant in the same syllable. Certain consonants, [v z ʒ ʁ] and for some speakers [l], lengthen a preceding vowel, as in [pasaːʒ] *passage* 'passage', [œːvʁ] *œuvre* 'work', [ʁoːz] *rose* 'rose'. The rhythm of French sentences will be discussed in section 6.5.

4.4 German

The consonantal system of German is as follows:

[p t k b d g pf ts m n ŋ f s ç ʃ x v z ʒ l j ʀ h].

[ç] and [x] are normally considered variants of the same sound, but for practising transcription can be used in the appropriate circumstances: [ç] occurs after front vowels and consonants, and at the beginning of morphemes, [x] occurs after central and back vowels. [ʀ], the uvular trill, is the prescribed articulation in standard German, but many speakers use a fricative instead: [ʁ]. At the beginning of this chapter we noted that [ʀ] or [ʁ] only occur before vowels within a word, whereas in codas we find a vocoid articulation [ʌ] (for simplicity I will omit the centralization diacritic), especially after long vowels. (Many speakers today use [ʌ] after all vowels.) [ʒ] is only found in words borrowed from other languages, especially French, and some speakers replace it with [ʃ], in particular in word-initial position.

There is a restriction in German on the occurrence of voiced obstruents: they cannot occur in syllable-final position. Speakers of standard German apply this restriction very rigorously, even in words borrowed from, for example, English (even when the speaker can speak English well), so *Trend* is [tʀɛnt], plural *Trends* [tʀɛnts], and *Kid/Kids* are [kɪt]/[kɪts]. (Compare these pronunciations with SBE [tɹend(z)] and [kɪd(z)].) Note that this restriction applies within words, too, for example, [vɛkgeən] *weggehen* 'to go away', [ʃupladə] *Schublade* 'drawer'.

Unlike French, but like English, [t d] are alveolar, and [p t k] are aspirated in the onset of stressed syllables. However, glottal reinforcement and no release only occurs before another consonant, not utterance-finally; [haʔt̚ gəmaxt] *hat gemacht* 'has made' is possible, but the final [t] of *gemacht* will be released. Glottal reinforcement and no release are used less by German speakers than English speakers use them in English, so the final [t] in *hat* could also be released. (Interestingly, in another Germanic language, Swedish, it is normal to release two (voiceless or voiced) stops in succession, e.g., in *köpte* 'bought' and *byggde* 'built'; see Ringen and Helgason [2004].)

The vowels of standard German are different from both English and French. Like French, several of them are peripheral; like English, there are also non-peripheral articulations. There is also a distinction of length, which in most cases accompanies a distinction in vocoid quality. The long vowels are accompanied by relatively short consonantal phases in the same syllable, and short vowels have relatively longer consonantal phases. We could represent this correlation somewhat crudely by using the 'half-length' diacritic, as follows: CV·C versus C·VC·, as in [bɑn] *Bahn* 'way' versus [ban] *Bann* 'spell' (see Chapter Six). Note that in the broad transcription I propose below, there are no length marks, but different vowel symbols. This is partly because the long vowels can occur with less duration when they are in pre-stress position; this applies, in particular, to loanwords from Latin and Ancient Greek (see the examples that follow). One vowel I have omitted: [ɛː], as is prescribed for the orthographic long *ä(h)*, as in *Käse* 'cheese', *käme* 'come (subjunctive II)', *Schädel* 'skull', *wählen* 'to choose'. This sound is artificially imposed by prescription and is not used consistently by many German speakers (see Boase-Beier and Lodge [2003], pp. 129–130, and references). Schwa occurs in unstressed syllables only.

I give the vowel diagram for the long monophthongs in Figure 4.8, for the short monophthongs and schwa in Figure 4.9, and for the falling diphthongs in Figure 4.10.

[ɑ] may be articulated in the same place as [a] (see Figure 4.9), or slightly further back, as indicated in Figure 4.8.

As in English, the short vowels only occur in closed stressed syllables, for example, [man] *Mann* 'man', [dʏn] *dünn* 'thin', [gɔt] *Gott* 'god'; monosyllables such as *[gʏ], *[fɛ], *[bʊ] are not possible.

The stress system in German is similar to that of English in that it has a heavy stress not fixed to any one syllable in words (unlike French, where it is

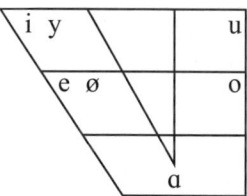

Figure 4.8 German long vowels.

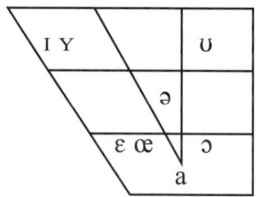

Figure 4.9 German short vowels.

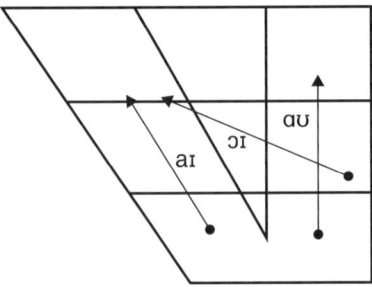

Figure 4.10 German diphthongs.

always word-final), and polysyllabic words can have more than one stress. On the other hand, the range of vowels that can occur before the main stress in polysyllabic words (**pre-tonic** position) is much greater than in English: compare the two equivalents [fəˈtɒɡɹəfɪ] *photography* and [fotoɡʀaˈfi] *Fotografie*. In **post-tonic** position (after the main stress) [ɪ a ʊ ə] can occur, as in [ˈhøflɪç] *höflich* 'polite', [ˈfʀɔɪntʃaft] *Freundschft* 'friendship', [ˈhɔfnʊŋ] *Hoffnung* 'hope', [ˈɛndə] *Ende* 'end'.

Sample transcriptions are given in Table 4.5; each vowel is given in (i) an initial stressed syllable or monosyllable, (ii) pre-tonic position in a polysyllabic word, and (iii) in a final stressed syllable.

Table 4.5 German monophthongs

[bitn] *bieten* (to offer)	[piˈkant] *pikant* (spicy)	[ʒeˈni] *Genie* (genius)
[vytn] *wüten* (to rage)	[hyˈbʀit] *hybrid* (hybrid)	[paʌˈfym] *Parfüm* (perfume)
[bux] *Buch* (book)	[tuˈʀɪst] *Tourist* (tourist)	[naˈtuʌ] *Natur* (nature)
[ɡebən] *geben* (to give)	[leˈɡɛndə] *Legende* (legend)	[ɡəˈbet] *Gebet* (prayer)
[ʃøn] *schön* (beautiful)	[føˈtal] *fötal* (foetal)	[fʀiˈzøʌ] *Friseur* (hairdresser)
[zon] *Sohn* (son)	[koˈlɔnə] *Kolonne* (column)	[naˈtsjon] *Nation* (nation)
[ban] *Bahn* ((rail)way)	[maləˈʀaɪ] *Malerei* (painting)	[zaˈlat] *Salat* (salad)
[bɪtn] *bitten* (to ask for)	[kʀɪsˈtal] *Kristall* (crystal)	[kɔmpoˈnɪst] *Komponist* (composer)
[hypʃ] *hübsch* (pretty)	[hʏsteˈʀi] *Hysterie* (hysteria)	[no example]
[mʊnt] *Mund* (mouth)	[mʊskuˈløs] *muskulös* (muscular)	[kataˈpʊlt] *Katapult* (catapult)
[hɛl] *hell* (bright)	[ʀɛstoˈʀant] *Restaurant* (restaurant)	[doˈtsɛnt] *Dozent* (lecturer)
[hœlə] *Hölle* (hell)	[œstʀoˈɡen] *Östrogen* (oestrogen)	[paʌˈfœŋ] *Parfum* (perfume)
[zɔnə] *Sonne* (sun)	[kɔˈleɡə] *Kollege* (colleague)	[ɔʌtoˈdɔks] *orthodox* (orthodox)
[hat] *hat* (has)	[aˈle] *Allee* (avenue)	[muziˈkant] *Musikant* (musician)

The diphthongs do not pattern in the same way; sample words are [baɪn] *Bein* 'leg', [baʊm] *Baum* 'tree', [lɔɪtə] *Leute* 'people'. In Table 4.5 there are alternatives for 'perfume', both in spelling and in pronunciation in this case. It is quite usual for loanwords to have a number of pronunciations (though not always spellings as well). The word [eleˈfant] *Elefant* 'elephant' can also be pronounced [ɛləˈfant], which is partly Germanized in having a schwa and a different first vowel. Also words from French with nasal vowels have been borrowed, and some speakers use (a version of) the French vowel, whereas others use a vowel + [n] or vowel + [ŋ], so *Pension* 'guest house' or 'pension' can be pronounced [pãˈsjɔ̃] (more or less the French pronunciation, but probably with an aspirated initial stop), [pãˈzjon], [pɛnˈzjon], and even [paŋkˈsjon]; similarly *Restaurant* may be [ʀɛstoˈʀã], [ʀɛstoˈʀant] or [ʀɛstoˈʀaŋ].

4.5 Modern Greek

Next we can take a brief look at a European language which is much more distantly related to English, French and German than they are to each other, Modern Greek. The consonants are as follows.

[p t k b d g m n ŋ f θ s ç x v ð z j ȷ̊ l r]

[t d] are dental; the voiceless stops are not aspirated; [s] is usually lamino-alveolar (though some speakers have [ʃ] instead). [ç] and [x] are considered variants of the same phonological unit (as in German); some speakers do not have the fricative [ȷ̊], only [j].

The vowel system is much smaller than that of English, French or German, and there is no unstressed schwa-type articulation. There are just five vowels, as in Figure 4.11.

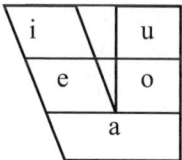

Figure 4.11 Modern Greek vowels.

There are no diphthongs either, though two vowels can occur in sequence, interpreted as two syllables.

Sample transcriptions are given in Table 4.6; I have not given the Greek orthography, just a gloss. Each consonant is given (i) in word-initial position,

Table 4.6 Modern Greek

[pi'yame] *we went*	['vlepo] *I see*	[pso'mi] *bread*
[ta'verna] *tavern*	['spiti] *house*	['tsai] *tea*
[ka'fes] *coffee*	['ðeka] *ten*	['ksero] *I know*
[bo'ro] *I can*	[ka'bana] *bell*	[em'bros] *in front*
[du'lapi] *cupboard*	[ado'çi] *endurance*	[dza'mi] *mosque*
[gar'son] *waiter*	[a'gaθi] *thorn*	[gri'njazo] *I complain*
['filos] *friend*	[a'fu] *since*	['ftano] *I arrive*
['θelo] *I want*	[va'θis] *deep*	['θlipsi] *grief*
[si'kono] *I lift*	['isos] *perhaps*	[ste'nos] *narrow*
['çeri] *hand*	['eçi] *he has*	[sçe'ðon] *almost*
['xorepses] *you danced*	['exun] *they have*	['xronos] *year*
['vurtsa] *brush*	[fo'vate] *he fears*	['vyazo] *I take out*
['ðipsasa] *I got thirsty*	[ði'ðasko] *I teach*	['ðrama] *play*
[zo'i] *life*	[spu'ðazo] *I study*	['zvino] *I extinguish*
[ya'lazjos] *blue*	[ayo'ra] *market*	['yðinome] *I get undressed*
[ji'rizo] *I turn*	[pi'jeno] *I go*	['vjeno] *I go out*
['miti] *nose*	['yrama] *letter*	['mnimi] *memory*
['naftis] *sailor*	['ine] *he/she/it is*	['njata] *youth*
	[sfuŋ'gari] *sponge*	
[li'mani] *harbour*	[ro'loi] *clock*	['pleno] *I wash*
['ruxa] *clothes*	['ora] *hour*	['vraði] *evening*

(ii) word-internally and (iii) as the first member of a consonant cluster. Option (iii) is only possible with the obstruents and nasals; [ŋ] only occurs before velar obstruents, and [ç j/ʝ] only occur after other consonants, not before them. [l r] in clusters, too, only occur after consonants.

Note that the possible combinations of the obstruents are quite different from those of English, French and German (though the last two have imported some of them in loans from Ancient Greek). Loanwords typically have various possible pronunciations and have rarer occurrences of some sounds, for example, intervocalic voiced stops; for instance, the word for 'champagne', a loanword from French into Greek, has the possible pronunciations: [ʃam'panja] (the most like French), [sam'panja], [sam'banja] and [sa'banja], which is the most nativized.

4.6 Malay

Finally, we can consider a language unrelated to any European language, Malay, a member of the Malayo-Polynesian family. The variety described here is that of Petaling Jaya, Kuala Lumpur, and is based on a description in Hashim and

Lodge (1988). The consonants are as follows; [t d] are dental [n] varies between dental and alveolar.

[p t k b d g tʃ dʒ m n ɲ ŋ s ɣ r l j w h ʔ]

However, in a country which is essentially Muslim, Malay has borrowed a lot of vocabulary from Arabic and with it some of the Arabic consonants. Not all speakers use these imported consonants and they are often replaced by the nearest equivalent from the native Malay system. The borrowed consonants are: [f v θ ð z ʃ x ɣ]. Examples of the replacements are given in Table 4.7; [z] is not subject to replacement in standard Malay.

Table 4.7 Loan and replacement consonants in Malay

[fitnah]	[pitnah]	to slander
[junivəsiti]	[junibəsiti]	university
[θabet]	[sabet]	to prove
[reða]	[reda]	willing
[ʃabas]	[sabas]	excellent
[baxel]	[bakel]	mean
[ɣaʔep]	[gaʔep]	to vanish

[s] alternates with [h] in final position in some common words, for example, [kipas] 'fan' may also be [kipah], but [waɣas] 'healthy' is considered formal and does not have an alternative form. [r] and [ɣ] are alternatives except in word-final position. Note that this [ɣ] is never replaced by [g] in the way the loan consonant is in Table 4.7.

(4.5)	[rasə]	[ɣasə]	to feel
	[pəreʔsə]	[pəɣeʔsə]	to examine
	[sərboʔ]	[səɣboʔ]	powder

In syllable-final position [r] can alternate with zero, as in (4.6).

(4.6)	[bəsar]	[bəsa]		big
	[subor]	[subo]		fertile
	[kərtas]	[kəɣtas]	[kətas]	paper
	[ʔarnap]	[ʔaɣnap]	[ʔanap]	rabbit
	[sərboʔ]	[səɣboʔ]	[səboʔ]	

The stops [p t k] are glottally reinforced morpheme-finally, even when a vowel follows. When a consonant or nothing follows, they are unreleased as well.

(4.7) [hadaʔpˀ]   front
     [hadaʔpan]   to face
     [mənhadaʔpˀkan]   to cause to place in front
     [dihadaʔpi]   to cause to be placed in front
     [dapaʔtˀ]   to get
     [pəndapaʔtan]   income
     [galaʔkan]   encouragement

The consonants given at the start of this section are to be found in onset or intervocalic position. In codas there is a much more restricted set:

[p t m n ŋ s r l h ʔ].

There are six monophthongs in the vowel system, as in Figure 4.12.

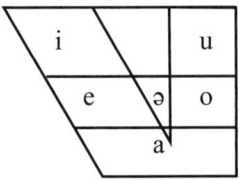

Figure 4.12 Malay vowels.

Note that they may all be stressed or unstressed, even [ə]. There is a restriction on the vowels that occur in the final syllable: [i ə u] occur in open syllables, [e a o] in closed syllables, as exemplified in (4.8). When no other consonant occurs in the onset of a syllable, [ʔ] occurs.

(4.8) [tari]   dance   [kames]   Thursday
     [ʔitu]   that   [landʒot] detailed
     [ʔapə]   what?   [ʔanaʔ]   child

Some loanwords are exceptions to this regularity, for example, [kɣitiʔ] *critic* from English and [daʔip] *weak* from Arabic. [ə] may alternate with zero provided it is not in the stressed syllable; a word like *besar* 'big' can, therefore, be [bəsar], [bəsa], [bsar], or [bsa]. (Note that there is no assimilation of phonation in the resultant sequence [bs-].)

Nasality is a feature of whole syllables in Malay. A nasal stop is followed by a nasal vocoid and nasality continues through the word until an oral obstruent occurs. Consider the examples in (4.9).

(4.9) [nãnti] to wait
[mẽdʒə] table
[mãhã̄l] expensive
[gunõŋ] mountain
[mã̄ʔãp] to forgive

There are three diphthongs: [ai au oi], which are never followed by a consonant in the same syllable. There are also sequences of two such vowels but they are separated by a glottal stop (as a default onset, see above) and are counted as two separate syllables, for example, [disukaʔi] 'to cause to be liked'. In many speakers the glottal onset to vowels is shorter than the coda glottal stop, as in [galaʔ] 'to encourage', [pəɣeʔsə], [ʔanaʔ].

Table 4.8 Malay

[pakai] to wear	[dapaʔt] to get	[hadaʔp] front
[topeŋ] mask	[batu] stone	[ulaʔt] insect
[kəsaʔt] to wipe	[pokoʔ] tree	[galaʔkan] encouragement
[bəsar] big	[subor] fertile	[lambaʔt] late
[dukə] sad	[hidoŋ] nose	[mãndi] to bathe
[gunõŋ]mountain	[mã̄gah] proud	[mãŋgə] mango
[tʃintʃen] ring	[kutʃeŋ] cat	[mãntʃoŋ] high
[dʒomlãh] total	[mẽdʒə] table	[pandʒaʔt] to climb
[riboʔt] storm	[bəras] rice	[gəmãr] to like
[ɣiboʔt]	[bəɣas]	[gəmã]
[jaken] to believe	[mã̄jãʔt] corpse	
[waras] healthy	[mã̄wã̄r] rose	
[hantu] ghost	[tahu] to know	[buʔah] fruit
[ʔitu] that	[mã̄ʔãʔp] to forgive	[əmpoʔ] soft

In Table 4.8 I give relatively broad transcriptions with the consonants in the positions they can occur in, and examples of all the vowels. I have not included the loan consonants. Most roots, that is, basic morphemes, are disyllabic, but may take affixes of various kinds. The phonological analysis is not straightforward because of a number of regular alternations, for example, [galaʔ]/[galaʔkan], so, although the transcriptions are broad, they do not necessarily reflect phonological relationships. For instance, onset [ʔ] and coda [ʔ] are not phonologically related to one another.

4.7 Practice

The question now is: how should you practice transcription? To start with practice writing down transcriptions of isolated words from English (SBE or GA), and try reading transcriptions out loud, so you learn to use and read them. I firmly believe that it is best to do this from actual spoken words (phonetics teacher, tape, CD), but if this is not always possible, then use any written material as a basis. Once you have gained confidence with English, move on to French or German (or Modern Greek), if you know them, or any other foreign language you know.

However, to make things a little more difficult, by taking away your ability to recognize actual lexical items, you should move on to English nonsense words, that is words that follow the phonological rules of English, but do not happen to exist. Then move on to complete nonsense, that is sequences of any sounds not just English ones, that do not belong to any language (as far as I know). Below I give some examples of each type. Try reading them aloud, but spread the practice out over a number of weeks. Don't expect to be able to do all this at once. I have put all these exercises at the end of this chapter because this is the one that deals primarily with transcription, but transcription skills need continuous and incremental development over a period of time, and so should be practised every week throughout your course – the longer, the better. Don't be put off by your mistakes; try to understand them and why you make them.

> (British) English nonsense:
> [ˈglabə] [ˈpɑθnlɪ] [tɹekəˈɹeɪʃn] [məˈskɹiːl] [soʊgəˈfɪnθ] [ˈfɹaɪgblʊust]
> [ˈstɹandʒɪiθ] [ˈbʌðəɹeŋk] [kəˈpleɪzoʊfiːzd] [pʊtɹəˈsklam] [ˈɜspədɪŋgə]
> [keɹəˈnoʊfledʒ] [hɑθəˈkæpəmoʊð] [fɹɪsˈtʊukənblaɪðd] [ˈɹʌntʃɒŋk]
>
> Complete nonsense:
> [ɔ̃jatˈɛ] [ʔafχitupʼ] [ŋaɔʎy] [βiɮɔ] [ʏrskɹoɛ] [føʒne] [m̥ekʼyɸ] [kn̥ɛɓã]
> [oŋãvɯ] [txɔĩɛ] [ʒmaiɬɔ] [psu̟ɽɴ] [yqɒvɹ̟ə] [ɹɪsbaṭeɢubrɑʔ]

4.8 Further reading

There are numerous book on the phonetics of English. Whenever you look at books on the pronunciation details of a language, always remember that it will be a description of an idealized speaker of the standard language, unless it specifically states otherwise. Also remember that the variety of English being described (usually SBE or GA) will not be an exact guide to your own speech or that of many of the people you know. Although the reference I have given to Gimson (1962) is to the first edition of the work, it should be pointed out that there are six editions altogether. The most recent, Cruttenden (2001), has been revised in many places but the same basic approach in terms of segmental phonetics and phonology is maintained.

For further details of French phonetics, see Tranel (1987). For a brief discussion of German phonetics, see Boase-Beier and Lodge (2003); for a much more detailed account, see Kohler (1995). Introductory accounts of Modern Greek are few and far between, but try Pring (1950). Malay is described by Hashim and Lodge (1988) and Maris (1980).

For a discussion of how much phonetic detail is relevant to phonological analysis, see Kelly and Local (1989); Docherty and Foulkes (2000); Scobbie (2005); Silverman (2006).

5 Segmentation

Chapter outline

5.1 A parametric view of speech	98
5.2 Overlap and timing variation	101
5.3 The timing of vocal cord activity	104
5.4 Long-domain features	107
5.5 Further reading	109

As suggested in section 1.5, the idea that words are made up of segments at both the phonological and the phonetic levels needs to be discussed in some detail. Now that I have introduced the basic descriptive apparatus of articulation and presented techniques of broad transcription, this is a suitable point at which to consider the issue. Standard textbooks often introduce the notion of a phonetic segment ('phone') without any attempt to justify it; for instance, Gussenhoven and Jacobs ([2005], p. 1) tell us, 'A phonetic symbol stands for a particular speech sound or **segment**, which is defined independently of any language' (original emphasis), and there is no further discussion of the concept. Segmental phonetics enables and justifies the establishment of segmental phonology, but does not necessarily capture many of the interesting and crucial aspects of real speech. In other words, the requirements of the segmental phonologist determine how the phonetics is presented and described, but, for instance, a speech therapist working with the real-world problems of poor articulatory skills (developmental or acquired) may well have little need for such an approach. Even phonologists might do well to examine their segmental assumptions, as suggested, for example, by Silverman (2006), especially Chapter Seven, and Lodge (to appear).

Segmentation is also supported by the long tradition of alphabetic writing in many languages, and indeed transcriptions in the IPA alphabet, which we have introduced in the preceding chapters. It provides easily readable approximations of what the spoken language sounds like. However, in most cases a lot of invaluable detail is missing and therefore lost to the reader/interpreter of the transcriptions. So in this chapter I want to consider a number of instances where an insistence on segmentation obscures the nature of articulation. In so doing, I shall elaborate on some of the articulatory descriptions, which were introduced in Chapters Two and Three, and I shall return to these issues in later chapters, too, in particular Chapter Seven, where we shall look at continuous speech in detail.

If we take a simple example, [bed], a representation of the English word *bed*, looks as though it is made up of three 'things' strung together. We can describe it in these terms by using the descriptive labels in the way we used them in Chapter Three to describe individual sounds: a voiced, oral, bilabial plosive, followed by a voiced, oral, front, mid, spread vocoid, followed by a voiced oral alveolar stop. However, what such a transcription and verbal description fail to indicate, amongst other things, is that (i) the position of the tongue for the vowel [e] is taken up at the same time as the lips are put together for the [b], or very slightly afterwards, but certainly before the lips part for the release of [b]; in other words [b] and [e] overlap to some extent; (ii) the vocal cords do not start to vibrate for [b] until after the lips are put together; and (iii) the vocal cords cease to vibrate before the tongue is taken away from the alveolar ridge in the release of the [d]. We saw in Chapter Four that we can accommodate some of this detail in letter-shape transcriptions, though some aspects, for example, overlap, are much more difficult, if not impossible to represent with letters.

Whatever arguments there may be for a phonological analysis of the speech continuum in terms of concatenated segments (see the brief discussion and the references given in Chapter One), we need to be clear from the outset that in phonetic terms segmentation is at best only a convenient way of conceptualizing speech for further phonological analysis. Of course, it has to be stressed that, in fact, a lot of what purports to be the representation of actual speech forms is a preliminary analysis for further refinement (see Archangeli and Pulleyblank [1994], pp. 159–161, for a discussion of this issue). In other words, a lot of phonological analyses are carried out on already idealized data represented by relatively broad transcriptions.

5.1 A parametric view of speech

How, then, should we view the phonetic structure of real speech? If we think of speech as being rather like a piece of orchestral music, the individual organs of speech (vocal cords, tongue, lips, etc.) can be seen to contribute to the overall effect of utterances in the same way as the individual musical instruments contribute to the performance of the music. The analogy is not entirely water-tight in that each musical instrument can play its part on its own, whereas some of the contributory articulators cannot operate without the others doing something. For example, it is not possible to extricate voicing and perform it on its own without anything else. Of course, this is a consequence of the nature of the human vocal apparatus: it is all part of one human being. Musical instruments are all separate entities. However, it is possible to appreciate the contributions each of the articulators makes in any given utterance. This non-segmental view of speech focusses on the interplay, overlap and duration of the individual components of articulation (often referred to as **parameters**) and I introduced it in section 3.8. As was pointed out, there is no standard way of presenting parametric analyses. Besides the relatively simple examples in section 3.8, they can be represented visually in diagrams such as Figure 5.1 from Silverman (2006, p. 54), a schematized and simplified representation of the word *looney* without the initial consonant.

Each parameter is given on the left of the diagram, and the lines indicate the change in configuration of the articulators as indicated on the right. Even in

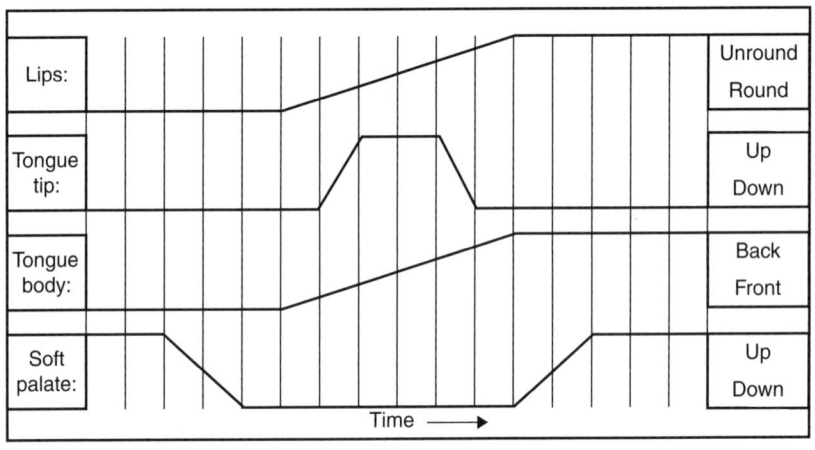

Figure 5.1 A parameterized representation of [uni].

this simplified representation the interplay of the lips, tongue and soft palate can clearly be seen and any attempt to segment these movements by slicing neatly across all the parameters with vertical cuts would not give us anything resembling an equivalent to the three segments (of four) in the transcription [uni]. (This is Silverman's transcription of an American pronunciation; compare this with my proposed transcription for a British English pronunciation in Table 4.1.)

I have referred to the parametric approach as non-segmental, but, strictly speaking, it involves cutting up the speech continuum just as much as the cross-parametric slicing of an approach based on sequentially ordered discrete segments. The important difference is the direction in which the slicing occurs. In a parametric approach the slicing is along the temporal axis rather than across it at particular points. Laver (1994, pp. 101–118) discusses these two approaches in some detail. Despite stressing the importance of the parametric view in phonetics (101–106), he still chooses a segmental view of phonology. Parametric representations of speech and the discussion of the validity of segmentation in phonetics are not new; Pike (1943, pp. 90–106) presents a number of parametric descriptions and representations in his discussion of various articulatory mechanisms and their interaction. He then goes on to discuss segmentation (Pike [1943], pp. 107–120) which he defines as being based on a peak or a trough of constriction during the passage of air through the articulators. These peaks and troughs are defined as the centres of segments, which have indefinite borders. Such parametric analyses of speech have informed the phonological theories of J. R. Firth and his colleagues (see, for instance, Palmer [1970]), and Browman and Goldstein (1986, 1989).

The notion of vertical segmentation and its tenacity even in phonetics is importantly related to our system of writing with the Roman or other related alphabets (see Morais et al. [1979], Bertelson et al. [1985], Mann [1986], Morais et al. [1986], Read et al. [1986] and Morais [1991] on segmentation and literacy); its influence on phonological theory is discussed in Silverman (2006, pp. 11–13, pp. 202–215) and Lodge (to appear). There is a crucial interplay between phonetics and phonology and the status of the segment in that relationship is a focus of recent debate (Ogden [1999], Lodge [2003, 2007], Local and Lodge [2004], Scobbie [2005], Silverman [2006]), but this is not the place for an extended discussion of the issue. Let us simply note here that the focus of the research of Morais and his associates listed above is the relationship between a putative naturally developing ability to segment speech into phoneme-like units and the teaching and learning of reading and writing skills.

Two important groups of people provide crucial information in this regard: illiterates and those who have non-alphabetic writing systems, such as that employed for Chinese. On the basis of an investigation of Portuguese literate and illiterate adults Morais and his co-workers found that the latter did not have the concept of initial consonant or onset, the term used in phonology for all initial consonants in a syllable. (See section 6.4 for a discussion of the syllable.) The results of the experiments reported on in *Cognition* 24 (1986, referred to above) all point to the fact that it is only after alphabetic writing is learned that people may develop their segmentation abilities. On the basis of informal observations over 30 years of teaching phonetics and phonology, the present author would suggest that even literates do not all develop the segmentation skill to the same level. Many educated people have no sense of segments in speech, even if they clearly do have in writing; whereas *bed* may be seen to have three segments, *rhythm* produces a wide range of responses to the question 'How many sounds are there in.......?', some related to spelling, that is, 'six', some to syllable count, that is, 'two' (*rhy - thm*). Clearly, this is an area deserving further careful investigation.

The assumption of segmentation in the earliest stages of acquisition (see, e.g., Macken [1995], pp. 688–689) makes it a complicated matter to explain some phenomena which are explicable in terms of timing of the individual parameters of articulation. In Lodge (1983) I give an example from a $3¾$-year-old boy, represented as [-ɬ-] for the adult target /lzs/ in *Mrs Neal's selling her house*. Rather than attempt the difficult timing and overlap of the features of laterality, friction and phonation involved in the adult realization as [-ɬz̥s-], the child simply uses the three features laterality, friction and voicelessness (rather than alternating between voiced and voiceless) all together for the duration of the consonantal phase, along with alveolar contact, which is consistent over this phase in the adult version, too. If we take these four parameters in the adult sequence, we can represent the feature durations as in Figure 5.2.

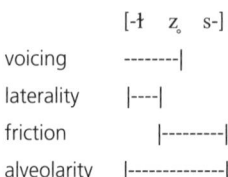

Figure 5.2

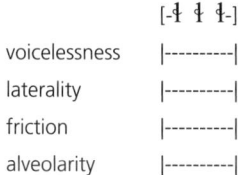

Figure 5.3

In the case of the child's utterance, he has not attempted the articulatory overlap and changes in what is at this stage a complex phonetic sequence (I assume he has recognized it as three consonants), but gives the four parameters equal duration. In the case of vocal cord activity he chooses voicelessness, resulting in what I have transcribed as [-ɬɬɬ-], as represented in Figure 5.3. The 'segment' that is of relevance here is the sequence of three consonants, two in the coda of one syllable and one in the onset of the next one.

5.2 Overlap and timing variation

Silverman (2006) gives a number of examples of the relative timing of phonetic features in various different languages. For instance, in Trique, an Otomanguean language from southern Mexico, there are voiceless-voiced stop pairs with a three-way distinction of place. The velar stops have extended back resonance and lip-rounding when a preceding lip-rounded vocoid articulation occurs, for example, [nukwah] 'strong', [rugwi] 'peach'. This extended duration of these features is not found with other consonants, for example, [rune] 'large black beans', [uta] 'to gather'. This has led to a situation where in Trique there are no sequences such as *[uka] or *[uga]. In these circumstances [w] can be interpreted not as a segment, as suggested by the transcription, but as an overlap phenomenon; in historical terms lip-rounding has been extended vis-à-vis the other parameters. (For details, see Silverman [2006], pp. 135–143.)

In a standard segmental view of phonetics and phonology there are many cases of so-called deletion and insertion of sounds. In English (and many other languages) such phenomena are often variable in connected speech, so, in other words, a speaker may articulate the sequence of words in one way on one occasion and in another in other circumstances. Examples would be 'reduced' realizations of a word like *hand-rail* as [hænɹeɪɫ], where the [d] at the end of *hand* appears to be missing. Such 'deletions' in English only affect the middle of three consonants under circumstances that will be demonstrated in section 7.2.4. It can occur in words like *find, old, post, lift, ask*, when another consonant follows, but not in words like *sent, salt, milk* under the same circumstances, so it can occur in *postman* but not in *milkman*. This 'deletion' is optional, so there is variation in the actual pronunciation of words like *hand-rail* and *postman*. But it is not just a question of deletion or non-deletion, since in many instances of such sequences the duration of the articulation (= 3 consonants) is maintained, because the timing of the relevant articulatory movements varies. So in a case such as [hændɹeɪɫ] *hand-rail*, the change from [n] to [d] is achieved simply by raising the velum to shut off the nasal cavities, changing the articulation from a nasal one to an oral one (see section 2.5). In other instances the velum is often simply not raised, so the resultant articulation could be transcribed [-nnɹ], where the two [n]-symbols represent a longer period of nasal articulation than in [hændɹeɪɫ]. So *hand-rail* could be pronounced [hændɹeɪɫ], [hænɹeɪɫ] or [hænnɹeɪɫ], depending on how long and in what timing relation the velic articulation and the stop mechanism in the mouth happen to be. It is, therefore, inappropriate to interpret lack of velic closure as segment deletion in all cases.

It is equally inappropriate to interpret variation in the timing of velic closure and the cessation of vocal cord vibration in words like *dense* as segment insertion in all cases. In the case of nasal-fricative sequences, such as [-ns] in *dense*, a delayed onset of frication, caused by the slight opening of the articulators at the alveolar ridge, gives a period of voiceless closure. Figure 5.4 is a representation of the timing differences in the manner parameter.

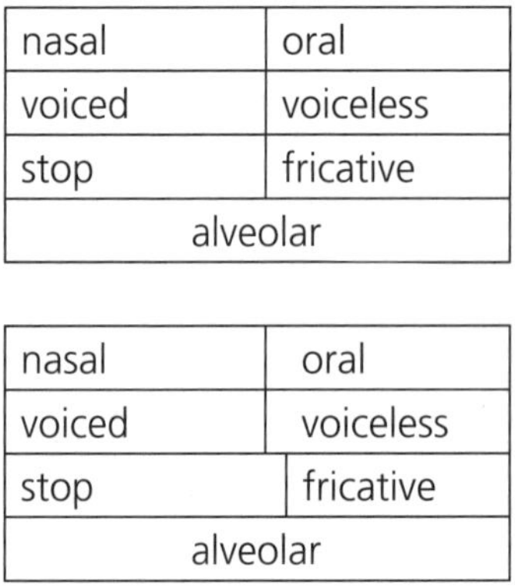

nasal	oral
voiced	voiceless
stop	fricative
alveolar	

nasal	oral
voiced	voiceless
stop	fricative
alveolar	

Figure 5.4

Segmentation **103**

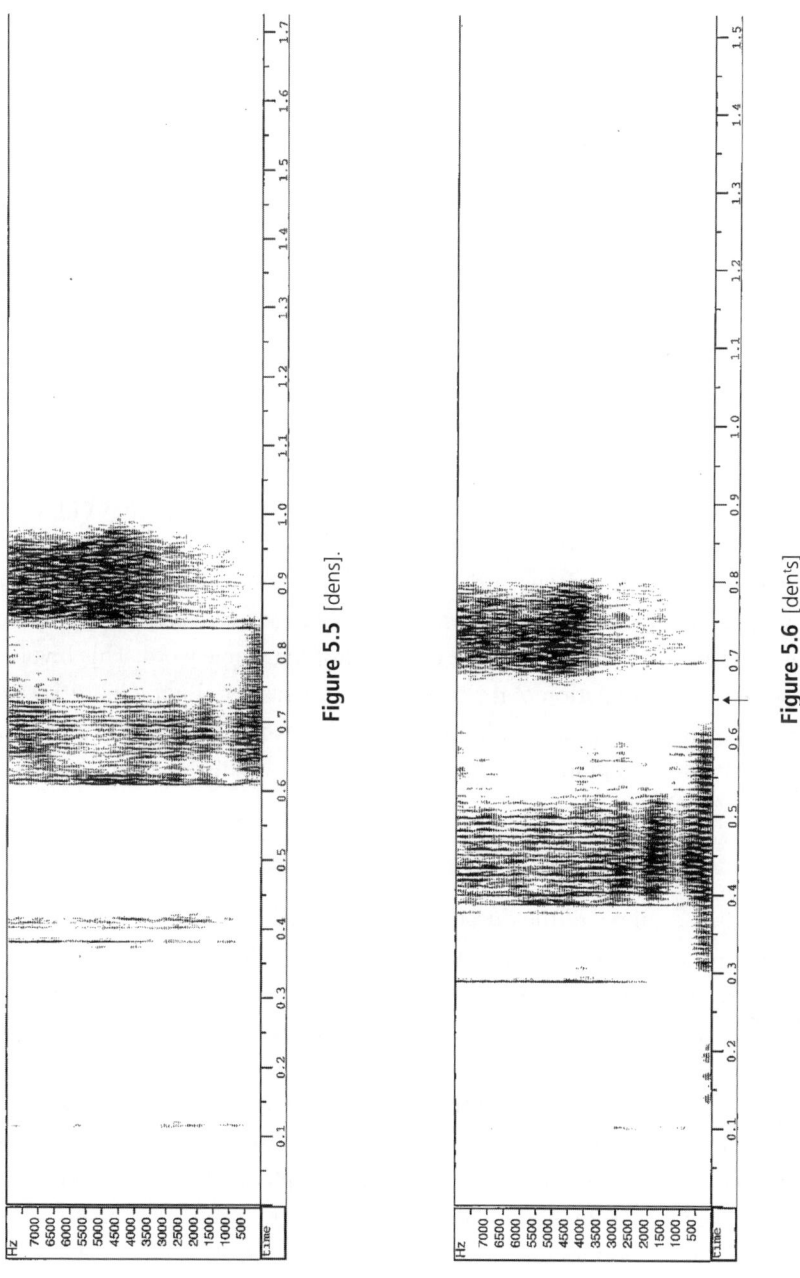

Figure 5.5 [dens].

Figure 5.6 [den's]

(Manner, don't forget, refers to the type of obstruction in the oral cavity, complete, close approximation, and so on.) The vertical lines indicate the point at which the articulator changes position, for example, the velum goes from open to closed, so the top figure represents [dens] and the bottom one what is often transcribed as [dents]. Even representations such as Figure 5.4 give a somewhat incorrect impression in that the vertical lines suggest an abrupt change rather than a gradual one.

This is often referred to as [t]-epenthesis or [t]-insertion (see, e.g., Gussenhoven and Jacobs [2005], pp. 119–120). The delay in the change of manner of articulation causes a [t]-phase of variable duration in some instances. If we want to transcribe this in letter-shape symbols, then we have to use a [t], though it can be made a superscript so that its short duration is indicated: [denᵗs]. But it is important to remember that it is only the transcription which leads us to describe this phenomenon as insertion rather than a delay in the change of articulatory position of the tongue vis-à-vis the other articulators that are involved. Note too that because this is a matter of relative timing, we might also describe it as an early change of velic and vocal cord activity rather than a delay in the change from stop to fricative. In fact, we would actually measure in milliseconds the change-over times of each parameter in relation to the start of the utterance of the whole word. This involves an acoustic representation of the utterance (see Chapter Nine). Figure 5.5 and Figure 5.6 are spectrograms of [dens] and [denᵗs] respectively; the break in the acoustic record in Figure 5.6 indicated by the arrow is the [t]-phase.

5.3 The timing of vocal cord activity

As an initial example of the duration of vocal cord activity over both a vowel and a consonant, we can take glottal activity in Chong (Silverman [2006], pp. 79–80). In root-final position there is a contrast between two types of stop articulation. Both sets are unreleased, but one set has open vocal cords, for example, [kəkɛːp̚] 'to cut with scissors', [lɛːk̚] 'chicken', while the other set has creak, caused by the slow, intermittent vibration of the vocal cords, indicated by [̰] below the vowel symbol, on the final part of the preceding vowel phase, for example, [kəsṵːt̚] 'to come off', [kənɔ̰ːc̚] 'nipple'. So here, too, we have feature overlap; complete glottal closure cannot overlap the articulation of the vowel, since it would totally obscure it, so glottal creak is used instead, maintaining the appropriate quality of the vowel. Rather than a sudden transition from vibrating vocal cords to a complete glottal closure, we have a slow transition causing a slow-down in the rate of vibration during the vocoid phase. We noted in section 3.3 that some English speakers do this, too.

Similar timing phenomena relating to vocal cord activity, such as postaspiration (= delay of voice onset time until after the obstruction in the mouth is removed) and preaspiration (= the early onset of voicelessness during vocoid articulations) are suitably considered under this heading.

What is usually referred to as aspiration is really one of a number of possible onsets of voicing in a syllable. The vocal cords can start to vibrate at any time after the start of the utterance. As we saw in section 3.3, if we take bilabial closure and release followed by a vocoid, this gives (at least) the following possibilities:

(i) [pḁ] = no vibration at all;
(ii) [pʰa] = vibration starts after the lips are opened;
(iii) [pa] = vibration starts as the lips are opened;
(iv) [ˌba] = vibration starts after the lips are closed, but before they are opened;
(v) [ba] = vibration starts as the lips are closed.

(ii) is what is referred to as aspiration, indicated by the superscript [ʰ]. Clearly it is a matter of a timing relationship between no vibration of the vocal cords and vibration. (Gussenhoven and Jacobs [2005], pp. 3–4, for instance, define aspiration in terms of voice onset time.) With this definition there must be voicelessness followed by voice to identify aspiration. The small circle underneath a symbol indicates that the sound represented is voiceless; option (i) is not usually found as a syllable type. When the circle is placed before the symbol as in (iv), it means that the sound represented by a symbol that would otherwise indicate voicing, such as [b d g m n v z l] is voiceless to start with. This is typical of utterance-initial voice onset for English [b d g]; note that utterance-initial means at the very start of an utterance; internal to an utterance, such as *the bed*, where [b] is surrounded by voicing, it would be fully voiced throughout, as indicated in (v).

At the end of a syllable a mirror-image of the options in (i)–(v) applies, given as (vi) to (x).

(vi) [ap̥] = no vibration at all;
(vii) [aʰp] = vibration stops before the lips are closed;
(viii) [ap] = vibration stops as the lips are closed;
(ix) [abˌ] = vibration stops after the lips are closed, but before they are opened;
(x) [ab] = vibration stops as the lips are opened.

(vii) is usually referred to as preaspiration; (viii) applies to most varieties of English, though typically the glottis is closed at the same time, which gives a different kind of phonation, glottal reinforcement, that we referred to in section 2.2.1: [kæʔp] *cap*, [kæʔt], *cat*, [kɪʔk] *kick*. In English these stops are also typically unreleased, like the Chong examples above. (ix) occurs in utterance-final position in English (with or without release of a stop) and often before a voiceless sound, as in *cab-size, good food, big curtain*. Before another vocied sound (x) occurs, that is, voicing is maintained throughout, as in *good dog, goodnight*.

Gimson ([1962], pp. 146–148) furnishes a good example of how a phonetic description of this kind can be turned into a segmental interpretation without any justification, specifically in relation to aspiration. We are told that /p t k/ in the onset of a stressed syllable are 'usually accompanied by aspiration, i.e. there is a voiceless interval consisting of strongly expelled breath between the release of the plosive and the onset of the following vowel' ([1962], p. 146). As a description of the interrelationships of the various articulatory parameters involved, that we have just been looking at, this is already a misrepresentation: to describe delayed onset time as an 'interval' that occurs 'between' a consonant and a vowel, as opposed to a voiceless onset to the articulation of the vowel, sets the scene for segmentation whereby the aspiration is interpreted as part of the stop segment; for example, in initial position of a stressed syllable [p] is 'voiceless fortis aspirated' ([1962], p. 148), so not only does delayed voice onset time belong to the [p] segment, but the phonation is aligned exclusively with bilabiality, full closure and orality (even though non-native learners of English are warned 'to pay particular attention to the aspiration', ibid.). Furthermore, if we treat aspiration as a transition from a consonant to a vowel, its status is downgraded along with all other 'transitions' between 'segments'. Thus, in connected speech there are 'segments', the focus of phonological analysis, and 'transitions' which glue the important bits together, but are not the focus of attention. If such an approach is appropriate, it has to be argued for and not taken for granted at the outset. On the other hand, Ohala (1992) argues that it is the transitions that give speakers the cues to what is being said, and so they should be focussed on equally.

A similar situation obtains with Gimson's treatment of the so-called voicing contrast in English coda obstruents ([1962], pp. 90–91, p. 147). The duration of the preceding **nuclear** vowel goes together with differences in the duration of voicing and yet 'length' is attached to the vowel segments and 'voicing' to the coda consonants. ('Nucleus' refers to the vowel of a syllable, considered to be its core component in phonology; see section 6.4.) It is only an insistence on segments that forces analysts to make such arbitrary decisions. So what we find is pairs of words that are distinguished by the duration of the nuclear vowel and the duration of coda voicing, as in *cat - cad*; *cart - card*; *cot - cod*; *caught - cord*. (Remember that, despite what the spelling suggests, none of these words has a coda *r*-sound in most English English accents; the situation is different in many American, Scottish and Irish accents, along with those of the West Country in England. We shall consider varieties of English and their transcription in Chapter Eight.)

One final example of anisomorphism, that is the lack of a one-to-one relationship between vocal cord activity and other articulations is furnished by the Liverpool accent. In word-final position what would be voiceless stops in most accents of English are typically voiceless fricatives at the same place of articulation, for example, [sɪɸ] *sip*, [sas] *sat*, [sax] *sack*. (Although I have written [s] twice in *sat*, for many speakers they would not be articulated in quite the same way, but that detail need not concern us here.) The coda voicelessness varies considerably in duration, so that it is possible for it to 'overhang' the coda consonant, as in [kˣaʰsʰ] *cat*. We can see from this example how clumsily the IPA alphabet deals with relationships of the parameters involved. The voicelessness can start part way through the preceding vocoid and continue to the end of the utterance; the contact for the alveolar friction is much shorter than the voicelessness, as indicated in Figure 5.7.

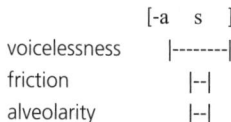

Figure 5.7

5.4 Long-domain features

Many of the features we looked at in Chapters Two and Three can be seen as extending through the speech chain: phonation types, nasality, lip-position, resonance are all features that typically extend beyond the individual bits of sound we have been looking at so far. But even other features, which are conventionally associated with individual consonants or vowels, such as place or manner, can extend over quite a long domain in any utterance, and this has consequences for our appreciation of how articulation works in connected speech, as we shall see in Chapter Seven. We can see in Figure 5.2, for example, that alveolar contact is maintained over the three consonants. Consider the extent of alveolarity in [wɒnts stɒpɪŋ] *wants stopping*. Many of the examples of assimilation that we will discuss in detail in section 7.2.1 have long-domain place and/or manner features, for example, velar contact in [kʊgŋʔkˈget] *couldn't get*, and alveolar friction in [kɒsssssɪkspəns] *costs sixpence*. Far from being the exception, long-domain features are normal in connected speech.

In section 3.5 we noted that lip-position is very often a feature of a syllable rather than just of a vowel or a consonant. In German, where lip-position is phonologically distinctive and normally associated with the vowels, a form like *heben* 'to raise', in broad transcription [hebən], can be transcribed more narrowly [e̜ebən] with lips changing from spread to neutral during the intervocalic bilabial stop. On the other hand, *höben*, a form from the subjunctive II paradigm of the same verb, can be transcribed [øøʷbən]. I have put the lip-rounding superscript before the [b] to indicate that the stop starts with rounded lips but the lips have changed to neutral by the time of its release. We should note that many phonologists would consider this to be low-level detail and an 'obvious' transition, that is to say a natural consequence of the way articulation works, but, in fact, the point at which lips change their position is not preordained by universals of articulation. In a vowel-harmony language like Turkish (see section 7.2.1) syllables are either rounded or spread and transitions take place earlier than in the case of the intervocalic consonant(s) in German. The word *tütüncü* 'tobacconist' is rounded throughout: [tʷytʷynʷdʒʷy]; the final syllable of *tütüncüde* 'at the tobacconist's' is spread, which I leave unmarked: [tʷytʷynʷdʒʷyde] with the lip-change at the closure of the alveolar stop. Conventional segmentation ignores such fine distinctions. They may, of course, turn out to be irrelevant to the phonological systems of the languages concerned, but how do we know, if we cannot investigate them and rule them out of account? Notice, too, how awkward the conventions of the IPA alphabet are in writing down such long-domain features. It would be better to have one superscript symbol and a line extending for the duration of the feature over the top of the letters, for example, [ʷt̄ȳt̄ȳn̄d̄ʒ̄ȳ].

We will look at more examples in Chapter Seven. In particular, we will look at resonance features (to be discussed further in our consideration of variation in English) and nasality. In respect of nasality, in at least one language, Terena, as described by Bendor-Samuel (1960), the feature has significance as a grammatical marker of first person singular. The examples in (5.1) are from Bendor-Samuel.

(5.1) [emoʔu] his word   [ẽmõʔũ] my word
     [ajo] his brother   [ãj̃õ] my brother

If we insist on cross-parametric slicing into discrete segments, consider the difficulties involved in making grammatical statements of the regularity at a phonetic level. This is largely a phonological issue, so don't spend too much effort on it in a phonetics course.

5.5 Further reading

If you want to pursue the issue of segmentation further, look at Silverman (2006, especially Chapter Seven). Kelly and Local (1989) present an approach to phonology that does not take the segment as the basic unit of analysis. Lodge ([2007] and [to appear]) also discusses this particular issue.

6 Prosodic Features

Chapter outline

6.1 Pitch	112
6.2 Stress	116
6.3 Duration	119
6.4 Syllables	121
6.5 Rhythm	130
6.6 Practice	134

In this chapter we shall look at those features of speech that affect whole utterances or large parts of them. In Chapter Five we looked at a number of features that had a considerable duration in the articulation of whole words. These can be referred to as **prosodic** features; they go syntagmatically through speech and their function often determines the relationships between different parts of an utterance. For instance, when we talk about stressed syllables in English, we are referring to the fact that one syllable (or more) stands out in relation to the surrounding ones, as in *cómfort, photógrapher, referée*, as we noted in section 4.1.6. The prosodic features I shall deal with in this chapter are pitch, stress, duration, syllables and rhythm.

The aspects of speech listed above are called **suprasegmental** features by those phoneticians and phonologists who consider segments to be the basic unit of observation and interpretation. They are seen to be aspects of speech which affect more than one segment in a particular utterance, or deal with the relationship between one segment and another. But such a distinction between what purport to be different characteristics of speech is at best misleading. We looked at a few examples of the difficulties with a segmental approach to speech in Chapter Five; many more could have been added. To take just two more, we can demonstrate that it is not just pitch, stress and duration that are discerned over considerable stretches of the speech continuum. Kelly and Local (1986) show that the phonetic feature of resonance associated with the phonological elements /l/ and /r/ in various accents of English stretch over several syllables. They are clues speakers can use in identifying lexical /l/ and /r/, and they go from the stressed syllable immediately preceding the /l/ or /r/ up to the next stressed syllable. The domains are marked with underlining in the examples in (6.1) from Kelly and Local ([1986], p. 305).

(6.1) 'Terry'll 'do it.
'Terry'll be 'able to 'do it.
'Terry'll be a'bout to'morrow.

Each accent they study has a contrast of front versus back resonance which is distributed phonetically as indicated by the underlining. The accents differ as to which resonance goes with which other articulation; Stockport, for example, has a front /r/ and a back /l/, Cullercoats a front /l/ and a back /r/. In the contrastive pair in (6.2) the whole of the underlined word is front or back.

(6.2) It's 'Terry.
It's 'Telly.

I will return to a consideration of the details of these resonance features in section 8.4.3.

The other example is nasality in Malay. In standard Malay a nasal stop triggers nasality over the next few syllables unless and until an obstruent or [r] intervenes. Thus the examples in (6.3) demonstrate that whole syllables, and indeed whole words, are nasal (not just the nasal 'segments').

(6.3) [nãnti] to wait   [mẽdʒə] table
      [mãhãl] expensive   [mãw̃ãr] rose
      [mãʔãp] to forgive   [gunõŋ] mountain
      [pərmãĩ] pretty   [mãŋga] mango
      [mãnẽs], [mãnẽh̃] sweet

The last example is given as two alternative forms of the word; note the difference between the extent of nasality in each case, depending on the occurrence of a fricative [s] or a voiceless vocoid, in broad transcription [h]. Note too that the glottal stop is not an oral stop.

Given the proviso that they are not the only prosodic features, we will now turn to the focus of this chapter: pitch, stress, duration, syllables and rhythm.

6.1 Pitch

Pitch is an auditory property of sounds; native speakers of different languages can place sounds on a scale from high to low. Changes in pitch produce the 'tune' of the words being spoken. There are basically two ways in which pitch is used in languages. It can be used to differentiate between individual words of a language; such languages are called **tone** languages, for instance, Mandarin Chinese. On the other hand, the pitch changes may be made over whole utterances and not be associated with particular words, as in English. Such patterns of pitch changes are referred to as **intonation**, which we looked at in section 1.3. We have already noted that it is the rate of vibration of the vocal cords that determines these pitch changes. The movement of the vocal cords together and apart during vibration produces a series of fluctuations in air pressure with relatively regular peaks and troughs. If we measure the rate at which the peaks occur in terms of numbers of complete opening and closing movements (cycles) per second, this gives us an indication of the pitch. This is known as the **frequency** of the sound and is measured in Hertz (Hz). (The older way of expressing this measurement was 'cycles per second' [cps].) A sound with 200 cycles of pressure change per second is said to have a frequency of 200 Hz. We shall return to how we can observe frequencies in Chapter Nine.

The frequencies used, whether in tone languages or intonation systems, vary across speakers, or even for one and the same speaker on different occasions. In other words, we cannot say that a high tone is always x Hz and a low tone always y Hz. What is important linguistically is the relationship between high and low, that is, they are relative terms. As observers, whether we distinguish between two (high, low) or three (high mid low), or even more levels of pitch, depends on how useful the resultant categories are in describing and analyzing the language we are investigating. Pitch levels are a continuum; the levels relevant to linguistic analysis are expected to be categorical. (Remember our discussion of gradient versus categorical phenomena in section 3.3.) As a clear indication of the relativity of pitch changes, consider the different pitch ranges that men, women and children typically use. All English speakers of the same community will have the same system of intonation, but the actual pitches at which it is realized will vary considerably. In general, men can go deeper in pitch than women (about 150 Hz for men, about 230 Hz for women), and both have deeper ranges than young children. At the top of the range the frequency is about 450 Hz for both men and women. However, it is important to remember that in addition to the differences between men and women in this regard caused by physiology, there is also an overlay of social convention as to which pitch range is considered appropriate for particular occasions. For instance, men in Britain often choose to use lower pitch ranges, but also use high pitches in certain circumstances, for example, when talking to their own young children, their pets or getting excited at a football match. Equally, women in authority roles in the West may choose to use the lower ranges of pitch; Margaret Thatcher was trained to lower her voice for some of her functions as Prime Minister.

Tone languages use differences of pitch to differentiate between lexical meanings. Mostly this is not a feature of European languages, but Ewe, Yoruba, Igbo, Xhosa, Zulu and Kalenjin are all African examples, and Thai, Vietnamese, Burmese, Mandarin Chinese and Cantonese are all Asian examples. As an exemplification of the kinds of tonal system that there are, we can take Mandarin Chinese. The tones, which are associated with the whole syllable, and the lexical meanings of the words are given in Table 6.1.

Table 6.1 Mandarin Chinese tones

Tone	word	meaning
high level	[ˉma]	mother
high rising	[ˊma]	hemp
fall-rise	[ˇma]	horse
high falling	[ˋma]	scold

There are many ways of symbolizing tonal differences; the above is just one way, using the IPA symbols. (For further discussion and exemplification of tone languages, see Ladefoged [2006], pp. 247–254.)

Most European languages use pitch changes in a different way. If we take English as our example, we saw in section 1.3 some of the uses to which pitch is put. Basically, there is syntactic information, for example, what constitutes a noun phrase in any particular instance (cf. *They are sailing ships* in section 1.3), or what might be called non-lexical information. The different pitch patterns of English, the components of which can be referred to as tones, without implying that English is a tone language, signal what is termed by some linguists **information structure**, conversational markers, and also the attitude or feelings of the speaker at the time of utterance. All these aspects of sentence/

utterance meaning are difficult to describe and are not fully understood. For English there are some generalities that can be established, but the more detailed implementation, such as in *You might have told me* discussed in section 1.3, does not seem to be subject to clearly generalizable rules of interpretation. The same intonation pattern may mean different things depending on the lexical items and syntactic structures chosen.

Information structure deals with the distribution of what the speaker considers to be old (given) and new information for the hearer. (Note that the speaker can get this wrong, and is usually corrected quite quickly by the hearer.) The main sentence stress, which is accompanied by a marked change of pitch, and is called the **tonic stress**, falls on the word of the sentence that is considered to be the focus of new information. If the word is a monosyllable, then the pitch changes on that; if it is polysyllabic, then the pitch change runs over the whole word (and sometimes over accompanying unstressed words as well), though the tonic stress still falls on the stressed syllable of the word. The examples in (6.4) show how the focus of the utterance, which otherwise has the same lexical content, can be moved to different lexical items. The tonic syllable is given in bold. Try saying each one of the possibilities and say what you think the difference in focus signifies. Note, too, that it is possible to split up what is one syntactic whole into two or more groups of syllables, known as **intonation groups** or **tone groups**, by having more than one tonic stress.

(6.4) There's a new couple coming to live at the **house** next door but one.
There's a new couple coming to live at the **house** next door but **one**.
There's a **new** couple coming to live at the house next door but one.
There's a new **couple** coming to live at the house next door but one.
There's a new couple coming to **live** at the house next door but one.
There's a **new** couple coming to live at the **house** next door but one.
There's a new **couple** coming to live at the house next door but **one**.
There's a **new** couple coming to live at the house next door but **one**.

(For a detailed introduction to information structure and the rôle of intonation in English, see Halliday [1967] and Brazil, Coulthard and Johns [1980].)

The cues that people use in interchanges to judge what is going on, for example, whose turn it is, what the communicative intentions of the speaker are, the assumed relationships between the interlocutors, are varied and cannot be discussed in detail in this book, but they include fairly simple markers of endings of turns and hesitation phenomena. In general, English, like many languages, uses a rising intonation to indicate a question or an intention to continue speaking, whereas a low fall at the end of an utterance indicates finality. To take a simple example, consider a list of items to be bought in a shop or at a market stall. That the list is continuing, even after a long silence, is indicated by a high rise; the end of the list by a low fall, as in (6.5).

    (6.5) I'd like some ´apples,´pears,´oranges, ba´nanas and ˎfigs.

A hesitation indicating uncertainty but an intention to hold the floor may be signalled by maintaining the articulation of a vowel or consonant much longer than usual, as in (6.6), where the speaker is demonstrating his/her uncertainty about the accuracy of the number of people involved. (The [m] in *ten* is an instance of **assimilation** and will be dealt with in detail in Chapter Seven.)

    (6.6) [teːmːːpɹipɫ] are coming to the party tomorrow night.

    The attitudinal significance of pitch variations is even more difficult to pin down, but in English the greater the gap between the highest and lowest pitch levels in an utterance, the more emotionally involved the speaker is assumed to be. Thus, a generally low pitch ending in a low fall tends to indicate lack of interest and/or boredom.

    (6.7) That was an ˌinteresting ˎevening.

On the other hand, a low rise followed by a jump in the pitch to high and then a fall indicates enthusiasm.

    (6.8) That was ˌreally ˋinteresting.

The emotional involvement may be of many different kinds, for instance, anger, enthusiasm, nervousness, surprise, happiness. Just think of the different ways you can *Hello* to someone you meet. If you use a high fall, that will indicate pleasure at seeing the other person, but perhaps that you have no time/reason/desire to talk at that moment. If, on the other hand, you use a fall-rise, which goes from near the top of your range to the bottom and up again, then it would be very odd to continue to walk past the addressee and not engage in a conversation. The use of the extreme pitch ranges in English to indicate personal involvement either with the addressee(s) and/or the subject matter explains why such tones are not used in, for example, news bulletins on the radio or television. Again, consider the ways in which the sentence in (6.9) could be delivered, and which you would expect to hear from a newsreader.

    (6.9) The Prime Minister, Margaret Thatcher, has resigned.

6.2 Stress

In section 4.1.6 we noted that a stressed syllable is produced with more muscular energy, making it stand out from the unstressed ones around it, and that from the hearer's point of view a stressed syllable will be more prominent than unstressed ones. So stress is relative: syllable σ is stressed in comparison with syllables α, β, γ in (6.10), where C = consonant and V = vowel.

(6.10)

This may represent one word or many. It could, for example, represent the English sentence *See Dad at home* [siː ˈdæd ət hoʊm]. The syllable and its structure will be discussed further in section 6.4; for now we only need to know that part of the speech continuum stands out in comparison with the surrounding sounds, and that the part is always identified as a syllable.

Ladefoged ([2006], p. 112) points out that there is a difference in English between polysyllabic words spoken in isolation and the same words in a sentence. So, the stress pattern for a word like *pharmacologist* is different in the two circumstances. Try saying the word on its own and then in sentence (6.11) with the tonic stress on *boss*. I have marked the stressed syllables simply with an acute accent over the vowel.

(6.11) The phármacólogist wént to see her bóss.

You should be able to perceive that on its own the word is given an intonation pattern similar to a full sentence of the syllabic pattern in (6.12).

(6.12) Carl was stopping it.

So both have the pattern indicated in (6.13).

(6.13) [ˌfɑməˈkɒlədʒɪst]
[ˌkɑɫwəzˈstɒpɪŋɪt]

The reason for this is simple: when uttering any sequence of syllables, a native speaker of English will automatically give them an intonation pattern. (British readers of this book should consider the dehumanizing effect of having no intonation pattern at all by listening to the Daleks speaking in the BBC science fiction programme *Dr Who*.) In the full sentence (6.11) *pharmacologist* is in stressed, but pre-tonic position, so the levels of stress are more or less the same. Some phoneticians distinguish varying degrees of stress, usually up to four (see the discussion in Ladefoged [2006], p. 114), but in many cases in English polysyllabic words or sentences it is very difficult to measure or perceive relative degrees of stress. For instance, what are the relative stress levels of the unstressed, but unreduced diphthongs in the third and fourth syllables of a word like [ɪnˈdʌstɹɪəlaɪˈzeɪʃn] *industrialization*? And is the first syllable reduced or not, since [ɪ] can occur in both stressed and reduced syllables in most varieties of English?

The main point to note in all this is that stressed syllables can usually be perceived by native speakers of languages that use different levels of stress in their lexical items. In English a few words are differentiated only by their stress pattern, for example, [ˈɪntɹɪig], [ɪnˈtɹɪig] *intrigue*, [ˈdɪspjuut], [dɪsˈpjuut] *dispute*, [ˈbɪloʊ] *billow*, [bɪˈloʊ] *below*. (In the last pair this is not the case for those speakers who have schwa in the first syllable of *below*.) Mostly, however, differences in stress pattern, for example between nouns and verbs, is accompanied by changes in vocoid quality. Consider the pairs in Table 6.2, each member of which belongs to a different syntactic category (though not always nouns and verbs). Say each one, note the difference of stress pattern, and decide which category each belongs to. Note that in the case of *récord* in GA the second syllable is reduced (as well as rhotacized): [ˈɹekɚd].

Table 6.2 English stress patterns

[ˈdezət]	[dɪˈzɜt]
[ˈɹebl]	[ɹɪˈbel]
[ˈɒbdʒɪkt]	[əbˈdʒekt]
[ˈɔgəst]	[ɔˈgʌst]
[ˈpɜmɪt]	[pəˈmɪt]
[ˈpɹoʊsɪidz]	[pɹəˈsɪidz]
[ˈpɹoʊgɹes]	[pɹəˈgɹes]
[ˈɹekəd]	[ɹɪˈkɔd]

In section 1.3 we looked briefly at a function of stress in English which differentiates syntactic and/or lexical structure. In this case the distinctions drawn are between two words in sequence which belong to two different syntactic categories, for example, verb and noun, and a compound noun. The former structure takes the main stress on the second word, the noun; in the latter case the main stress falls on the first word, indicating a compound. Consider the two possible structures, and hence interpretations, of (6.14).

(6.14) They're playing cards.

Either this sentence refers to some people playing cards, or it refers to some objects, which are playing cards. (Note that in the latter case some writers use a hyphen: *playing-cards*.) Further examples involving other syntactic categories for the first word are given in (6.15). Say the pairs and decide which is which. (Note the difference made in the orthography to indicate the structural difference.)

(6.15)
black bird	blackbird
black board	blackboard
paste board	pasteboard
green fly	greenfly
high brow	highbrow
cross words	crosswords
four runners	forerunners
blue bottle	bluebottle
drawing pins	drawing-pins
light house	lighthouse

This could be extended to other cases where quite different lexical items are involved, such as *he'll support - heel support; we'll base - wheelbase; we'd kill her - weedkiller*.

There is a strange tendency amongst British radio and television newsreaders and reporters, who, of course, are reading out their texts, to stress the final syllable of a sentence or clause, irrespective of its structure (and meaning). This leads to very odd misinterpretations of what is said, in conflict with the given context. For example, I once heard an item about a threatened petrol crisis in East Anglia, which was soon going 'to hit the [fɔˈkɔts]'. This can only be understood as *four courts*, which, of course, is nonsense in this context; *forecourts* can only be [ˈfɔkɔts] in line with the examples in (6.15). I assume that this reflects poor training in reading aloud, and I would not expect the same people to speak like this in ordinary conversation.

Whereas English does not restrict the main stress to any particular syllable in all words, other languages do. We saw in Chapter Four that in French stress falls on the last syllable of any polysyllabic word. (In connected speech this can

Prosodic Features

Czech
x x x |x́ x x x |x́ x x x |x́ x x x |x́ x x x |x́ x x x |x́ x x x

Polish
x x x x x́ x |x x x́ x| x x x x́| x x x x́| x x x x́| x x x x́| x x

French
x x x x́ x́|x x x x́|x x x x́|x x x x́|x x x x́|x x x

Figure 6.1

be altered for certain specific effects of emphasis and argument.) Czech words, on the other hand, take the main stress on the first syllable, and Polish on the penultimate syllable. (Note that exceptions to these statements may be found in loanwords or minor word types, such as nursery talk.) Speakers of languages with fixed stress will usually divide up a sequence of beats at equal intervals of time with a heavier beat placed on every fourth one according to their linguistic stress rules. Figure 6.1 represents a sequence of beats (x) with the stressed ones indicated by an acute accent; the vertical lines are where a Czech (C), a Pole (P) and a French speaker (F) will normally hear a break in the sequence.

Other languages restrict the position of main stress in polysyllabic words or phrases of more than one word, but not just to one syllable; in Modern Greek, for example, the main stress has to fall on one of the last three syllables. (There are some sub-rules, which need not concern us here.) If a trisyllabic word is stressed on the first syllable, but has an unstressed syllable (**enclitic**) added to it, for example, an unstressed personal pronoun, then an extra stress has to be added to break up the four unstressed syllables, as in the examples in (6.16).

(6.16) ['afise] *let go*   ['afi'seme] *let me go*
      ['tonoma] *the name*   ['tono'mamu] *my name*

The loss of the vowel of the definite article [to] is normal elision when two vowels come together and one is unstressed.

6.3 Duration

So far we have used the terms **long** and **short** in a loose, relative way, or as a description of different phonological categories in some languages. So, if we are talking about French phonology, we can say that it does not have a long-short distinction, but we can also say that the vocalic nucleus of a stressed syllable is typically longer than the others in a polysyllabic word, without contradicting the former statement because the latter refers to one of the phonetic exponents of stress, not a phonological distinction. We can also say that the voiced fricatives in French lengthen any preceding vocoid articulation in a word-final syllable. Whereas the terms 'long' and 'short' may be used as phonological terms or as phonetic descriptions, it is preferable to distinguish between phonological **length** and phonetic **duration**. The former, which may or may not relate to duration (compare our discussion of the different definitions of length in English and in German in Chapter Four), has to be established in relation to the ways in which long and short partners behave in the language concerned, for example, what kind of syllable they can occur in. The latter is either based on an auditory judgment of relative duration, or is measured in milliseconds. If we want to check the claim that German has long consonants with short vowels and vice versa, then we record a number of native speakers saying the different possibilities (as naturally as possible, given the unnatural circumstances of recording) and measure each instance of them from spectrograms (see Simpson [1998]). This will give us ranges of actual duration in as many instances as we can get, so that we can see whether there is a clear differentiation between the two categories or not. (That there might be overlap between the categories is an issue beyond the scope of this book; see, however, Silverman [2006].) In the conventions of the IPA the length mark [ː] gives the impression that there is some kind of absolute measure of duration that can be captured by the presence or absence of the symbol. That impression is underlined even more by the notion that there is such a thing as 'half-length' [ˑ]. The use of these marks in transcriptions may be impressionistic in the narrow kind, but in broad transcriptions it is usually based on phonological considerations. For instance, in the transcription for RP proposed by Gimson (1962, and all later editions) the length mark is placed after all the single symbols representing vowels that can occur in both open and closed syllables (along with the diphthongs); the vowels that are restricted to closed syllables, and unstressed [ə] and [ɪ], do not have the length mark.

From time to time in what we have discussed so far there has been a suggestion that stressed vowels are longer than non-stressed ones. We shall consider below the interplay of stress, pitch and duration in continuous speech when we look at rhythm in the next section, but it is worth noting that so many factors affect duration that we need to be cautious making any general statements about it. For instance, if we look at a sentence of English, as represented in the spectrogram in Figure 6.2, it is clear that the stressed and unstressed full vowels are longer than schwa or unstressed [ɪ] in the early part of the sentence. But look at the relative duration of the final schwa.

If we examine similar instances with final schwa, we will find that in many cases they can be longer than a stressed vowel. This has to do with how we finish our utterances: if they are vowel-final, they tend to be longer than those that end in a consonant, voiceless ones ending the shortest syllables.

We can also demonstrate the claims I made in section 4.1.8 regarding the duration of vocoids in English under different circumstances. The spectrograms in Figures 6.3–6.5 represent the sentences given below them in phonetic transcription and orthography. The vocoid articulations are represented by the dark horizontal bars between the paler or blank portions, the contoid articulations. The horizontal axis of the spectrogram is the time-line, calibrated in 100 milliseconds. Measure each of the vowels and see if my claims hold true in these cases. (Note that measuring the vocoids in three utterances is no guarantee of generality, but you have to start somewhere.)

The [ɑ] in *heart* is approximately 300 milliseconds. long; in *hard* 320; in *car*, which is followed by a voiceless fricative, only 220. The [ɜ] in *surgery* is 170 milliseconds; in *surface* and *service* 130. Now try measuring some of the other vocoids. Also, record some simpler sentences yourself with similar vocoid articulations as the nucleus of the utterance-final stressed syllable and measure those, too. If you use the examples in (6.17), compare the measurements for these three vocoids with those of Figures 6.3–6.5.

(6.17) This is my cart.
This is my card.
This is my car.

6.4 Syllables

Another term we have used frequently in our discussions so far is **syllable**. From a purely phonetic (articulatory, acoustic or auditory) point of view there is no satisfactory definition of a syllable. (See Ladefoged [2006], pp. 237–242, for a discussion of various attempts to define it.) For this reason we shall consider phonological issues rather more than we have elsewhere in the book. However, this does not mean that it is therefore of no use to us. It seems as though it must be the basic unit of articulating linguistic meaning: any utterance that has meaning is at least a syllable in length, even very short ones.

122 A Critical Introduction to Phonetics

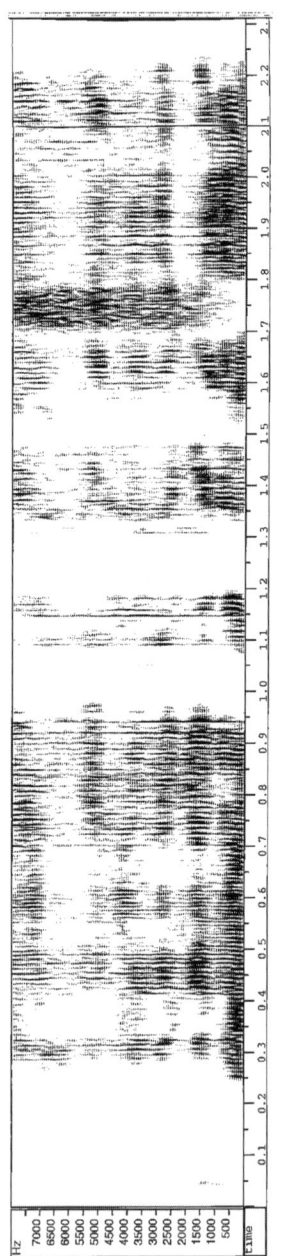

Figure 6.2 Spectrogram of *The man in the hat looked like my father.*

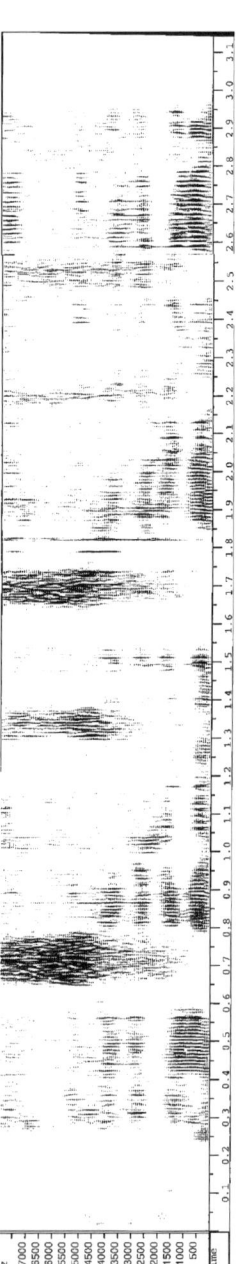

Figure 6.3 [ðə hɑt sədʒəɹi wəz ə bɪt skɛɹi fə maɪ fɑðə] The heart surgery was a bit scary for my father.

Prosodic Features

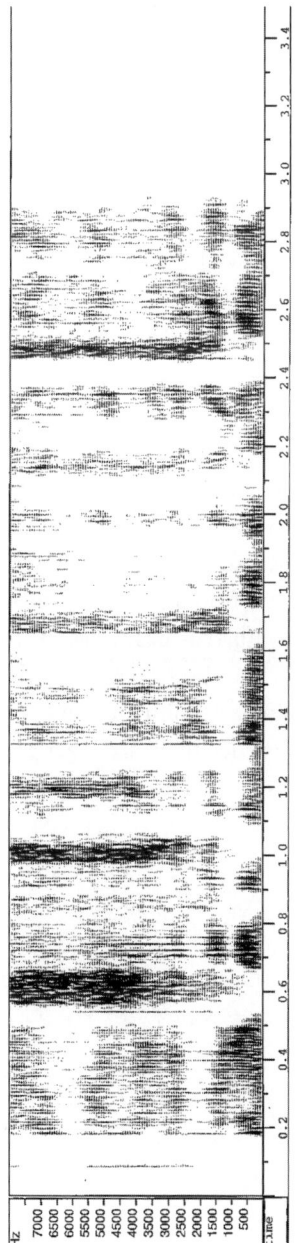

Figure 6.4 [ðə hɑd sɜfɪs wəz ə bɪɡ ɪmpɹuuvmənt fə maɪ tɹeɪlə] The hard surface was a big improvement for my trailer.

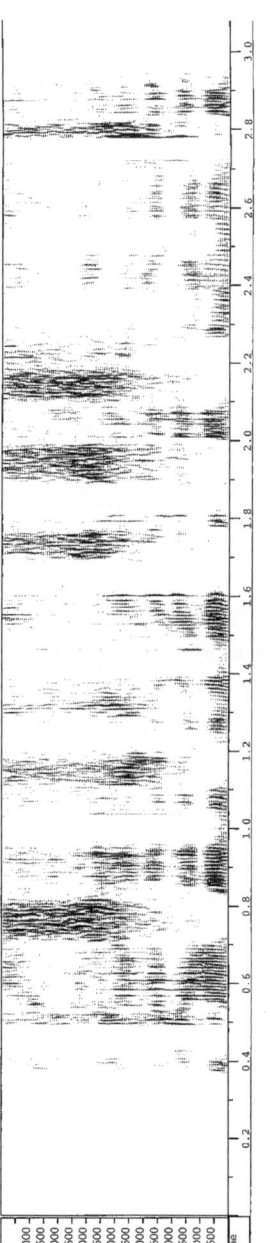

Figure 6.5 [ðə kɑ sɜvɪs wəz ə ɡɹeɪt səkses fə maɪ moʊtə] The car service was a great success for my motor.

(I am not including here false starts, which may be a single elongated contoid articulation, but they have no meaning.) In English we can utter a monosyllabic word in many contexts and convey an appropriate meaning: [aɪ] *eye, I*; [ii] *E*; [oʊ] *oh, O*; [goʊ] *go*; [lɪt] *lit*; [ten] *ten*. Any of these could be used as answers to questions, or in one case as an imperative (*Go!*). Note that some of them are just vowels. On the other hand, there are monosyllables that have a much more complex structure in terms of possible consonants (C) and vowels (V) that can go together, such as [twaɪs] *twice* (CCVC), [lɪst] *list* (CVCC), [stɹɪkt] *strict* (CCCVCC), [twelfθs] *twelfths* (CCVCCCC). The last example, with the maximum number of final consonants allowed in English, is morphologically complex: *twelve + th + s*.

So, we might want to define it as an organizing structure for both articulation and for the phonological system. Once again, we should be careful to perceive a difference in these two interpretations of the syllable. The latter interprets the speech continuum as discrete locations (**onset, rhyme, nucleus, coda**; see further below) where phonological behaviour can be described. This means that we assume native speakers process what they hear at the level of syllables. The former may involve overlap between the components of the syllable, for example, the delayed voice onset time from the initial consonant into the following vowel phase, and we will see further examples of feature overlap below.

The basic syllable structure from a phonological point of view is as in Figure 6.6. Since this is a theoretical, abstract construct, there are other proposals that have been put forward, but I do not intend to discuss them in this book.

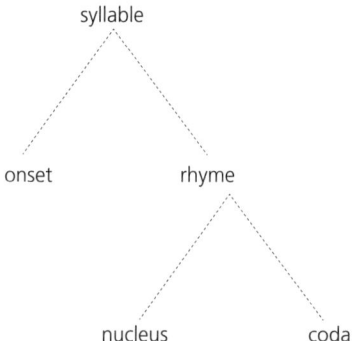

Figure 6.6 Syllable structure.

Not all the elements have to be realized in any particular syllable. In a previous paragraph we saw English examples with nucleus only; onset and nucleus; onset, nucleus and coda. We could also have nucleus and coda, as in [aɪl] *aisle*, *I'll*; [eɪm] *aim*; [ɪl] *ill*. We saw, too, that onsets and codas can be complex, that is, contain more than one consonant. (Whether diphthongs should be interpreted as V or VV I will not consider here.) It is assumed that usually all stressed syllables have to have a vocalic nucleus; unstressed syllables may have consonantal nuclei. We should note that these are phonological interpretations of speech and do not always take the phonetic reality as the basis of the interpretation. For instance, some phonologists will claim that all syllables have to have a vocalic nucleus by definition; since consonants are defined as occuring in the onset or coda, vowels occur only in the nucleus. So, a form such as [lɪtɫ] with a syllabic velarized lateral is interpreted phonologically as having a CVCVC structure: /lɪtəl/. This is the origin of many transcriptions in dictionaries – however misleading they may be from the point of view of actual pronunciation by native speakers. The relationship between this phonological representation and the pronunciations people use can be described in terms of a combination of the vowel, realized as the velarization, and the consonant, realized as the lateral articulation. In such a view two phonological segments are realized as one phonetic 'segment'.

So, once again, we have to be quite clear about which aspect of speech we are considering when describing syllabic structure, the phonological or the phonetic. There are indeed languages that have contoid nuclei, even in stressed syllables. We saw in section 2.9.6 that Czech has the word [pr̩st] 'for', which has no vocoid articulation in it. Even in English it is possible to have contoid realizations of a syllable nucleus even in stressed position. One of the possible pronunciations of *children* besides [ˈtʃɪɫdɹɪn] is [ˈtʃɫ̩dɹɪn] with no vocoid articulation at all. As we noted above in the interpretation of syllabic velarized laterals in English, the resonance component is associated with vocoid articulations in particular, so one can argue that both vowel and consonantal features overlap one another completely. It is also the case that the stressed lateral will be longer than the unstressed one in *little*.

This brings us back to duration. Assumed syllabicity in contoid articulations is also related to relative duration. This applies equally to unstressed syllables. If we consider two possible pronunciations of *can stain* and *can sustain*, we will find greater duration in the syllabic sibilant, as indicated in the transcriptions in (6.18).

(6.18) [kə̃z̃ˈsteɪn] *can stain*
[kə̃z̃sˈsteɪn] *can sustain*

(The occurrence of a nasalized fricative as the final consonant of *can* will be explained in Chapter Seven.) Some people would differentiate between the two in a broader transcription than those in (6.18) by using the syllabic mark [ˌ] in *sustain*, for example, [ˈsteɪn] versus [s̩ˈsteɪn]. Even in cases of contoid syllabic nuclei the type of resonance is relevant. In the case of *sustain*, which for most native speakers will also have realizations with an unstressed vocoid nucleus, for example, [səˈsteɪn], the initial sibilant will have central resonance even without a separately discernible vocoid phase. Compare the different resonance in the initial sibilants in [sʲɪin] *seen* (front), [sə3v] *serve* (central) and [sˠɔ] *saw* (back). We can see the limitations of letter-shape transcriptions in this particular instance: if we write [səˈsteɪn], does it mean a long sibilant phase starting with central resonance or does it mean a very short vocoid phase between the two sibilants? In hand-written transcriptions (such as those in Kelly and Local [1989]) it is possible to avoid this ambiguity by writing the resonance symbols above the contoid symbols; this is more difficult in computer-generated typescript.

Another instance of the correlation between syllabicity and duration in unstressed syllables is furnished by English word pairs such as *lightning* and *lightening*. Whilst both may be pronounced [ˈlaɪtnɪŋ], the latter can also be pronounced [ˈlaɪtn̩ɪŋ], in which the alveolar nasal is longer than in the former word. In the case of laterals it may depend both on duration and resonance. A word like *saddling* may be [ˈsædlɪŋ] or [ˈsædɫ̩ɪŋ] in SBE; the back resonance in the second pronunciation indicates syllabicity.

Ladefoged ([2006], p. 238) also points out that stops can be syllabic in English. This would apply in cases like [wɪʃbˈbɪˈkɛfɫ] *we should be careful*, where the bilabial closure is held for longer than in cases like [wɪʃbɪˈtwiin] *wish between*. (The bilabial closure at the end of *should* is a case of assimilation, to be discussed in Chapter Seven.) However, Ladefoged's example of *today* is not quite the same. Since he indicates a release of the voiceless alveolar closure ([tʰˈdeɪ]), this would be better interpreted as a (brief) voiceless nucleus of the first syllable. This would be clearer, if we transcribed it as [tə̥ˈdeɪ]; consider also [pə̥ˈteɪtoʊ] *potato*. (Remember the voiceless vowels of Japanese in section 3.5.) Note that we could write the schwa symbol smaller and as a superscript, but do not forget that, as far as English is concerned at least, we cannot easily read duration into the letter symbols that we use.

The way stress is marked according to the conventions of the IPA poses a few questions that are difficult to answer, or at best they are not as straightforward as the convention suggests. The question as to where syllable boundaries fall is one that is not always easy to answer. In section 4.1.6 I gave the transcriptions [ɪkˈstɜmɪneɪt] *exterminate*, [ekˈsept] *except* and [ækˈsept] *accept*. with the boundary between the two syllables indicated by the stress mark according to the IPA conventions. In the case of the first example it is not necessarily in the right place. Why is it not [ɪksˈtɜmɪneɪt]? Since the rules of English onsets and codas (**phonotactics**) allow both [st] and [t] onsets and [s] and [ks] codas, it appears arbitrary to place the syllable before, or after, the [s]. There may be clues for either interpretation. If there is aspiration of the first [t] of *exterminate*, then it must be the sole onset consonant, because in the onsets [sp-], [st-] and [sk-] the voiceless stops are unaspirated. If there is no aspiration of the [t], then the onset of the second syllable must be [st-]. This does not give us a once-and-for-all answer, but indicates that the syllable boundary is variable depending on other aspects of articulation. However, even this categorical distinction does not reflect syllable boundaries consistently. If we take two contrasting combinations of words, *a tall* and *at all*, it is possible for speakers to distinguish between them in connected speech, as in (6.19).

(6.19) [əˈtʰɔɫ] *a tall*
 [ətˈɔɫ] *at all*
 [ətˈʔɔɫ] *at all*

In the first of the last two possibilities it appears fairly arbitrary to indicate the syllable boundary after the [t]. The only reason we do it is the phonological claim that [t] as sole onset consonant of a stressed syllable must be aspirated. But the argument is not really based on a detailed phonetic analysis of connected speech (whatever that might turn out to be); rather it is based on what happens when words are pronounced in isolation. One line of investigation might revolve around the relative durations of the closure phase of the alveolar stop. But whatever the outcome of our investigations, it is also the case that in some instances many speakers of Standard British English do not actually make the distinction. Another way of putting this would be that the realizations of the two lexically determined categories overlap. That is to say that both can be pronounced [əˈtʰɔɫ], though this is more likely in English English than in North America. The fact of the matter is that degrees of aspiration in intervocalic voiceless stops in English are variable. In continuous speech there are even more problematical cases. Ladefoged ([2006], p. 199) gives the spectrogram of an utterance of the sentence *I should have thought spectrograms were unreadable*. He points out that the whole phrase *should have* has no vocoid articulations and is completely voiceless. The first stress falls on *thought*, so Ladefoged transcribes the first part of the sentence up to and including the first stressed syllable: [aɪʃtfˈθɔt]. The question to be asked is why is the syllable boundary assumed to be just before the [θ]? It seems to be a completely arbitrary decision. It would be difficult to decide on any grounds where the boundary comes, but [aɪʃtˈfθɔt], [aɪʃˈtfθɔt] both seem possible, though [aɪˈʃtfθɔt] seems very unlikely with four contoid articulations in one onset. Reliance on phonotactic criteria is of no help in forms of natural conversation such as this, because none of the possible divisions into coda + onset occur in the lexical storage forms of English.

In post-tonic, intervocalic position, as in *reaper, letter, pocket*, the variability of aspiration can lead to a different view of syllable boundaries, namely **ambisyllabicity**. This means that the sound in question belongs to two syllables at the same time. (Whether this should have a phonetic interpretation in terms of dividing the duration of the contoid phase into two or an abstract phonological interpretation of category overlap is not a question I wish to address here.) We can say that stops have variable aspiration in ambisyllabic position, unlike in onsets where they are always aspirated (even if the degree of aspiration varies) or after [s] where they are not aspirated. There are also phonological arguments that can be given to support such an analysis: in words where the first, stressed syllable is 'short', such as *pepper, better, kicker*, we need to have a consonantal coda for the first syllable, that is, [bet] is a good English syllable, *[be] is not. However, a syllabic division: [bet.ə], where the full stop indicates the boundary, is not defensible either, because English vowels without an onset can all begin with a glottal closure, even in unstressed syllables, yet no speaker of SBE would say *[betʔə]. So the answer is that all single intervocalic consonants are interpreted as ambisyllabic.

I have used the IPA convention for marking the main stress in this book, because this is the near-universal convention in phonetics books and dictionaries using the IPA (and even the APA) system of notation that I am aware of. However, in my own teaching, in order to avoid questions of syllable boundaries, I use an acute accent above the appropriate vowel symbol: for example, [fáðə], [əbáʊt], [fətɔ́ɡɹəfə]. Secondary stress can be marked by a similar mark under the appropriate vowel symbol, or a grave accent over the symbol: for example, [dèkləɹéɪʃn] *declaration*, [fòʊtəɡɹǽfɪkl] *photographical*. As long as the transcription is consistent, it does not really matter which system you use, though it is useful to recognize them both.

One final point to be made here about syllables is that no matter what the phonetics may tell us, native speakers can usually perceive what constitutes a syllable and what does not. Of course, literate people may be influenced unduly by the spelling system of their language, but it is quite instructive to ask people to syllabify other people's languages. This gives us an insight into their own language without any encumbrance from writing conventions.

I will take just a few examples of variation in syllable structure and its perception: from English, Spanish, Arabic, Japanese and Scots Gaelic. If you say English monosyllabic words beginning with [s] + C, a native speaker of Spanish or Arabic will tell you you have spoken two syllables. This reflects the fact that in Spanish and Arabic such onsets are not permitted. [s] + C have to belong to two different syllables. Speakers of these languages have an [ɛ] or an [ɪ] in front of the [s] to ensure this syllabic division. This applies to native and loan vocabulary alike. So this is how Spanish and Arabic speakers hear English monosyllables such as *spike, stain, skin*.

In Japanese the syllable structure is very limited: mostly CV ± $C_{[nasal]}$. There is a complication in the case of Japanese in that many linguists consider Japanese to be a **moraic** language rather than one based on syllables (e.g., Tsujimura [1996]). The **mora** is a timing unit which can be made up of consonants and/or vowels. However, for the purposes of this simple demonstration, we do not need to engage with this particular issue, but I will return to it in section 6.5; all we need to know for the moment is that Japanese does not allow consonant clusters of the kind we find in English and many other languages. So when a Japanese speaker hears the Czech word [pr̩st], s/he hears it as four syllables. If asked to say the word, the likely outcome is [pirisɯto], which conforms to the requirements of Japanese syllable structure. (The late Professor Willi Haas, a native speaker of Czech, told me that he had himself tried this with a speaker of Japanese.)

The final example is from Scots Gaelic. There are quite a number of words which seem to the non-native speaker to be disyllabic, but are in fact monosyllabic. For instance, [marəv] *mairbh* 'dead' behaves as a monosyllable; for example, it cannot have an epenthetic glottal stop after the first vocoid, *[maʔrəv], which would be expected if the [a] was considered to be in a stressed open syllable, as in /u/ 'egg' = [uʔ]; and it is monosyllabic in Gaelic metrics. It is not a matter of duration, which can be highly variable and longer than a lexical schwa. Indeed, in many Scots Gaelic words the post-consonantal vocoid articulation is longer than the pre-consonantal one, for example, [faɫaːv] *falbh* 'going', and compare this with the lexical unstressed schwa in [ˈfaɫəv] *falamh* 'empty'. But nevertheless *falbh* is monosyllabic. Such words have idiosyncratic tonal patterns and are the only words that have the duration pattern given for *falbh*. The medial consonants involved are always [l m n r], which seem to be some kind of sonorant contoid 'interlude' overlaid onto the vocoid articulation.

So, the syllable is problematical from the phonetic point of view, but is nevertheless useful as a way of talking about stress and rhythm. We will continue to use the term when we need it, bearing in mind its less than firm basis.

6.5 Rhythm

If we look at a combination of the effects of stress, duration, differences in vocoid qualities and phonotactic constraints on syllable structure, we can describe the rhythmic patterns of a language, often quite distinct from one another. Let us start by looking at two languages which have very different rhythms, English and French. Originally the difference was referred to as a difference between stress-timed and syllable-timed rhythms. This was an oversimplification, based on stress patterns and syllable types. Even though the facts are more complicated, it is possible to see the basic differences by considering two sentences, one from each language, with the same meaning. These are given in phonetic transcription and orthographic form in (6.20) and (6.21).

(6.20) [hɪ ˈwent tə ðə juˈnaɪtɪd ˈsteɪts]
He went to the United States.

(6.21) [iletaleozetazyˈni]
Il est allé aux États-Unis.

In (6.21) I have not tried to separate the words in the phonetic transcription; syllable structure and word-boundaries are often anisomorphic in French because of the consonantal linking device known as **liaison**. In (6.20) there are three main stresses, an unstressed full vowel and four unstressed syllables with reduced vowels. Unless a speaker changes tempo in mid-utterance, the stresses come at regular intervals in English and it does not matter how many syllables there are in between. From the beginning of the utterance there is one syllable before the first stress, three before the second and one before the last stress, yet the intervals will be more or less of the same duration; hence the term stress-timed. In (6.21), on the other hand, there is only one main stress, but the preceding syllables each take up the same amount of time. This is what is meant by syllable-timed. Whereas in English there is an alternation between different vocoid qualities and different durations, in French the vocoid articulations are evenly timed and all have full vowel quality. It is possible to break up French sentences into smaller tone groups and put breaks in various places depending on the speaker's intentions and assumptions, as we saw for English in section 6.1. The important point to note here, though, is the difference in the time taken to utter each syllable: relatively constant in French, variable in English. Quite an extreme, but perfectly natural example of English rhythm with five reduced unstressed syllables between the two stresses is given by Gimson ([1962], p. 278), which I reproduce in a slightly adapted form in (6.22).

(6.22) ['haʊmnɪəvəsɬə'bɪi]
How many of us will there be?

(The [l] in *there* is another example of assimilation to be discussed in Chapter Seven.) Note that one word is monosyllabic, which in other circumstances would have two syllables: *many*. Even in short utterances monosyllabic words can occur without syllabicity between two vowels, for example, [aɪʔk̚'nɑsk] *I can ask*; the word *can* has no vowel in this instance and its consonants are distributed over two syllables. We can see that the word-initial [k] is, in fact, in coda position because it is glottally reinforced and unreleased. So, just as in French, word boundaries can be ignored in connected spoken English.

A further unit of rhythm is sometimes used, particularly for English but for other languages, too, the **foot**. The term refers to the stretch of syllables from one main stress up to, but not including, the next, so feet differ in their make-up depending on the number and type of syllables involved. In English, feet are often stress-initial, but do not have to be. Example (6.23) has three feet, each one starting with a stressed syllable; the boundary is marked by a vertical line. (6.24) has two feet, the first with an unstressed syllable preceding the tonic stress. (6.25) has a stress-final foot with three unstressed pretonic syllables.

(6.23) |Jóhn was the |bést of the |búnch.

(6.24) |He sént |móney.

(6.25) |He was a fán.

I do not intend to go into the details in this book, but for introductory discussions, see Abercrombie (1965, 1967), Clark and Yallop (1995), Davenport and Hannahs (2005). Above the level of the foot is the tone group, that we introduced in section 6.1. Various numbers of feet make up an intonational unit. In the examples (6.20)–(6.22) there is only one tone group in each: (6.20) contains three feet, (6.21) one, and (6.22) two. A single sentence may have more than one tone group, if the speaker wishes to have more than one focus of information, as we saw in many of the examples in (6.4).

Some languages have a mixture of both types of rhythm. German, like English, is said to have a heavy stress, which typically falls on the first syllable of the root morpheme in words of Germanic origin, and may have accompanying unstressed syllables, for example, *fáhren* 'to travel', *Fáhrer* 'driver', *fáhrend* 'itinerant', *Fáhrerei* 'driving around', *erfáhren* 'to experience', *Erfáhrung* 'experience', *Fáhrkarte* 'ticket'. However, modern German also has a large number of loanwords from Latin and Ancient Greek (not all learnèd words with a restricted distribution in the population), and their importation has brought with them a different stress and rhythmic pattern. Most of these words are stressed on the final syllable of the stem, and some have a penultimate stress + schwa; the pre-tonic syllables have full vowels in them, as we saw in some of the examples in section 4.4. In that sense these words are rhythmically more like French words. See Table 4.5 for a number of examples in addition to the following: [filozoˈfi] *Philosophie* 'philosophy', [bɪblɪoˈtek] *Bibliothek* 'library', [hypoˈtek] *Hypothek* 'mortgage', [økonoˈmi] *Ökonomie* 'economics', [filoˈloɡə] *Philologe* 'philologist', [hypoˈtezə] *Hypothese* 'hypothesis'. Even those loanwords that have a stress earlier in the word than this, even on the initial syllable, have full vowels in post-tonic positions, for example, [kɔˈleɡɪʊm] *Kollegium* 'group', [ˈtʏmpanɔn] *Tympanon* 'tympanum', and there are some Germanic words with this pattern, too, for example, [ˈaʌbaɪt] *Arbeit* 'work', [ˈhaɪmɑt] *Heimat* 'home(land)', [ˈbɪʃof] *Bischof* 'bishop'. (The last two may be pronounced with short vowels in the final syllable: [ˈhaɪmat], [ˈbɪʃɔf].) So, German has quite a variety of syllable patterning for different subsets of its vocabulary.

Another factor in rhythmic patterns is whether or not the language has a schwa-type vowel restricted to unstressed syllables, like English and German. Some languages do not, for example, Italian, Modern Greek and Japanese. Italian and Modern Greek have syllable-timed rhythm; note that there is a difference between schwa-less syllable-timed languages and those that have schwa as well, such as French. We have already said that Japanese is usually described as a moraic language. Basically this means that the timing unit is of relatively constant duration, just like the syllable in syllable-timed languages, but the constituents in Japanese are CV, V or C not followed by a V. In (6.26) I give examples of words with two, three and four moras; each mora is separated by a full stop.

(6.26) [to.ʃi]   year
       [a.ki]   autumn
       [ka.t.ta]   won
       [to.do.ke] deliver
       [ni.p.po.ŋ] Japan
       [ta.ke.za.o] bamboo pole

There is an interesting correlation between rhythmic patterns of spoken language and poetic and musical forms. This is a large area of investigation and I can only give two brief pointers to the kinds of issue that are involved. If you consider the rhythmic patterns of spoken English, it becomes clear that it fits well with the syncopated rhythms of rock music, as it has developed after World War II. Take the lyrics and music of the Beatles' song 'Sergeant Pepper's Lonely Hearts Club Band'. For copyright reasons I cannot reproduce even one line of a published song, but the main beats in the first two lines fall on *Sérgeant, Lónely, Héarts* and *Bánd; hópe, enjóy* and *shów*. This may not be quite the same rhythm as a spoken version of the same sentence; for example, in speech it would be normal to say [jʊɫ] *you'll*, rather than [jʊ wɨɫ], but it does not seem to be at odds with the rhythm of spoken English. If, on the other hand, we look at 'Within You Without You' (from the LP *Sergeant Pepper's Lonely Hearts Club Band*, Parlophone PCS 7027, side two, track one), which is set to a tune in an Indian style, the words do not fit neatly with the rhythm. Nearly all the syllables are lengthened, whether stressed or not in the spoken version, so most of the words are unnaturally drawn out. So *we, were, the, a* are all elongated and disyllabic words such as *between* and *people* are given syllabic durations of roughly equal length. I make no attempt to distinguish between the different durations of each syllable, just give an indication of where lengthening occurs. Listen to the song and consider the different rhythmic pattern from that of spoken English; try saying some of the sentences in normal conversational style for contrast. Of course, since music is based on sets of conventions, which do not necessarily have to be followed, there is no requirement for lyrics to fit the music according to the norms of colloquial English, but it is instructive to see how often they do. Look at a number of recent popular songs and see what stress patterns you find and how they relate to spoken English.

6.6 Practice

Practice marking stresses on written sentences of English. This can be done both on the orthographic form and as part of a phonetic transcription of them. Try the following and find other examples of your own to practise on.

> The whole world looked as though it had just stepped out of its bath.
> Something has got to be done about this business before too long.
> Are there a lot of them in Paris?
> She'll get very cross, if you don't hurry up.
> The captain was very particular about having all his buttons polished.

Continuous Speech

Chapter outline

7.1 Parametric interplay in disyllabic words	135
7.2 Connected speech phenomena	145
7.3 Transcription and practice	158

What we have discussed so far rarely goes beyond the level of the individual word, except for the discussion of rhythm at the end of Chapter Six. Many phonologists use the word as a basis for discussions of phonological patterns, so they give special status to the pronunciation of the word in isolation. This is referred to as the **citation** form or the **lexical entry** form, the one that is claimed to be stored by native speakers in their mental lexicon. But now it is time to look beyond the word to connected speech and this will shed further light on the issue of segmentation. To start with, however, I want to remain at a fairly modest level in order to present the details of interaction between the articulators in two syllables only. This will enable us to consider a way of representing parametric interplay in a written description. For this exercise I will restrict myself to English, but this is not to suggest that English is any different from any other language in this respect.

7.1 Parametric interplay in disyllabic words

In Chapter Five I pointed out that letter-shape transcriptions give the impression that connected speech is made up of discrete entities in a chain (**concatenation** is a technical term often used for this stringing together of linguistic units at any level). We now need to investigate the reality behind this impression a little more closely. Instead of considering the articulatory positions for one 'phone' followed by those of another in a way that suggests some kind of steady state for each individual 'phone' linked together by some rapid transitions, we should be looking at speech as a continuous interplay of moving articulators, which rarely take up a fixed position for anything more than a few milliseconds.

We can begin by considering the articulatory movements involved in the pronunciation of the English words *corned beef*. In the first instance I shall take a rather careful (and probably rather unnatural) pronunciation: [kʰɔndˑbɹiːf]. Notice that for this exercise we need a fairly narrow transcription, but I am not going to consider stress. It is best to take as a starting point the position of rest (Figure 7.1), that is, the one we use for normal breathing.

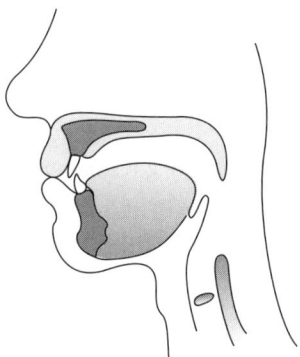

Figure 7.1 The position of rest.

Note that the lips are closed and the velum lowered, to allow for normal breathing through the nose. So our descriptions should start with a statement of the position of rest, as in (7.1).

(7.1) Starting from the position of rest, with the lips closed and neutral, the velum lowered and the tongue at rest,. . . .

This requires us to consider the movements any of these articulators will have to make to start an utterance. The next statement to make has to refer to the airstream, as in (7.2).

(7.2) Starting from the position of rest, with the lips closed and neutral, the velum lowered and the tongue at rest, after an intake of air, a chest pulse initiates an egressive pulmonic airstream.

While describing the required articulatory movements, it is important to keep in mind the different contributions of each of the main articulators: the vocal cords, the velum, the body of the tongue and the lips. If we are to describe a word beginning with [m], for example, the lips and the velum need to stay in their position of rest. The tongue, on the other hand, will move to the position required for whatever the following vowel will be during the bilabial closure; similarly, the lips will move to a rounded position, if the following vowel is rounded, or spread (or stay neutral), if it is not rounded. The vocal cords will have to vibrate from the beginning of the utterance.

In our case we need to change the tongue position to a velar contact, close the velum, and open and round the lips; at the same time the vocal cords will be held apart. It is very important to get the temporal connectives right in describing the sequence and overlap of movements, so we need to be precise about whether movement *x* is carried out *before*, *after* or *simultaneously with* another movement *y* or a hold phase. So we need to continue our description with the movements for the initial stop articulation, as in (7.3).

> (7.3) Starting from the position of rest, with the lips closed and neutral, the velum lowered and the tongue at rest, after an intake of air, a chest pulse initiates an egressive pulmonic airstream. The back of the tongue rises to make complete contact with the velum, as the velum itself is raised closing off the nasal cavities. At the same time the lips part and round slightly, and the vocal cords are held apart.

Note that 'at the same time' indicates (approximate) simultaneity.

We now have to indicate the movement from the consonant to the vowel, as in (7.4).

> (7.4) There is a brief hold phase, during which the lips continue to become rounder. Then the back of the tongue is moved away from the velum to the position of a back, open-mid vocoid in the region of CV6. The vocal cords then start to vibrate.

The hold phase is represented in Figure 7.2. Figure 7.3 is a vowel diagram for the vocoid articulation [ɔ]. In vocoid articulations the tip of the tongue is (usually) behind the bottom teeth, so it is unnecessary to say this each time we describe one. Note that there is a delay between the release of the velar closure and the onset of vibration of the vocal cords; this is the aspiration indicated in the transcription.

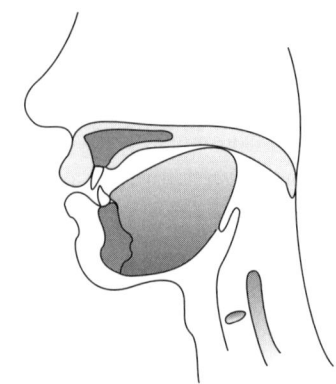

Figure 7.2 Position for [k].

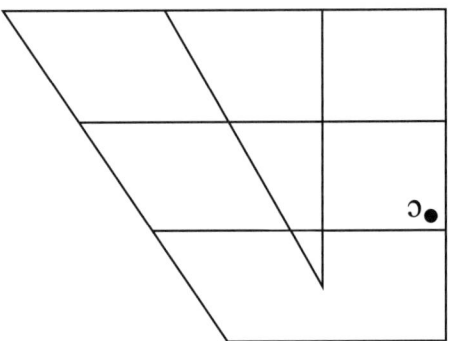

Figure 7.3 Vowel diagram for [ɔ].

The next phase is nasal, so we have to refer to the lowering of the velum and the movement to the next point of contact for the tongue, as in (7.5), with the position represented in Figure 7.4.

> (7.5) The tip of the tongue rises to form an alveolar closure, and the sides of the tongue come into contact with the upper molars. At the same time the velum is lowered, allowing air to escape through the nose. The vocal cords continue to vibrate and the lips are rounded.

It is very important to refer to the side contact of the tongue, since this produces a central rather than a lateral articulation. Although I have said 'at the same time' for the lowering of the velum, speakers typically lower the velum before the end of the vocoid articulation giving nasality to its final phase: [ɔ̃n].

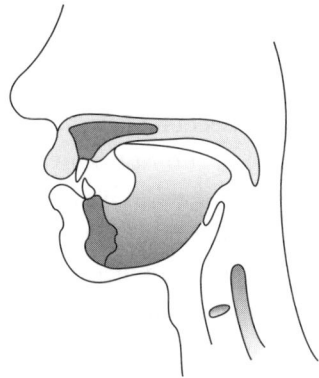

Figure 7.4 Position for [n].

The final sentence referring to the continuing vocal cord vibration and lip-rounding is not necessary, if we stick to the convention that an articulation continues until it is specifically referred to as ceasing, but it is quite helpful when doing this kind of exercise to remind oneself of the position of all the major articulators.

Next is the velic closure to stop the airflow escaping through the nose at the end of the first syllable. (7.6) is (7.5) with the extra statement added.

> (7.6) The tip of the tongue rises to form an alveolar closure, and the sides of the tongue come into contact with the upper molars. At the same time the velum is lowered, allowing air to escape through the nose. The vocal cords continue to vibrate. There is a hold phase during which the velum is closed, shutting off the nasal cavities, and the lips move to a neutral position.

Note that what we, as linguists, interpret as two consonants is produced by the closing of the velum part way through an alveolar stop hold phase. It is this movement of only one articulator that signals the change from one consonant to another, but movement of the articulators in itself is not a sufficient criterion for segmental status, if we insist on a segmental approach. Articulators move throughout vocoid articulations, whether they are monophthongs or diphthongs, the vocal cords start vibration part way into a vocoid articulation, and plosives have three phases produced by (at least) two movements, closure and release, yet none of these is usually interpreted as a change from one segment to another. From a purely articulatory point of view it is very difficult to pinpoint segment boundaries, and indeed steady states. The easiest steady state to discern is probably the hold phase of a stop, but even in this case there are changes in muscular tension as the closure movement prepares to alter to the release movement. (See, however, Pike [1943] for his peak and trough definition of a segment, referred to in section 5.1.)

The second oral stop phase of *corned* is unreleased, as is normal in connected English, which means it is held in place until the bilabial closure has been made. It is then released, and hence inaudible. The different possibilities of overlap of gestures and loss of some of them will be considered below. What is being described at the moment is a fairly careful, formal pronunciation (which is not necessarily the one people use in everyday conversation). (Note that when I use the word 'careful', there is no implication that such a pronunciation is, therefore, 'better' than any other. Linguists and phoneticians generally do not subscribe to the view that value judgments about what is and what is not 'correct' in linguistic usage are entailed in their investigations and descriptions.) (7.7) takes us into the beginning of the second syllable, and Figure 7.5 shows the overlap of the two stop positions.

(7.7) The tip of the tongue rises to form an alveolar closure, and the sides of the tongue come into contact with the upper molars. At the same time the velum is lowered, allowing air to escape through the nose. The vocal cords continue to vibrate. There is a hold phase during which the velum is closed, shutting off the nasal cavities, and the lips move to a neutral position. Towards the end of the hold phase the lips come together in a complete closure.

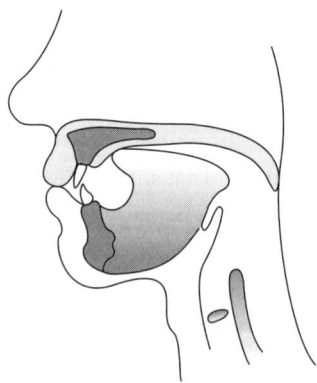

Figure 7.5 Overlap of [d] and [b].

The removal of the alveolar closure and side contact with the upper molars means that the body of the tongue can move into the position needed for the start of the next vocoid articulation [ɪi]. (7.8) takes us into this next phase.

> (7.8) Towards the end of the hold phase the lips come together in a complete closure. The alveolar and side contact is released and the main body of the tongue moves to the position of a front close-mid vocoid, considerably retracted from CV2. The bilabial closure is then released, as a new chest pulse initiates a new syllable, the lips spread and the tongue moves slightly forwards and upwards in the direction of CV1.

The amount of lip-spreading, and rounding, for that matter, is very variable in native speakers of English. The division into front and central with spread lips on the one hand, and back with rounded lips on the other (e.g., Gimson [1962]) is rather artificial and misleading. We may note that from a phonological point of view in English lip-rounding does not have a discriminating function of the kind we saw in French and German in Chapter Four.

Finally, we need to specify the articulation of [f], as in (7.9).

> (7.9) As the tongue is finishing its trajectory in a front-closing direction, the bottom lip is moved up towards the top teeth, which make light contact with the inside surface of the lip. At the same time the vocal cords cease vibrating. The air escapes with local audible friction. The articulators then return to the position of rest.

The inclusion of the final sentence is a reminder that articulation has finished. It is important to remember that in the case of utterance-final unreleased

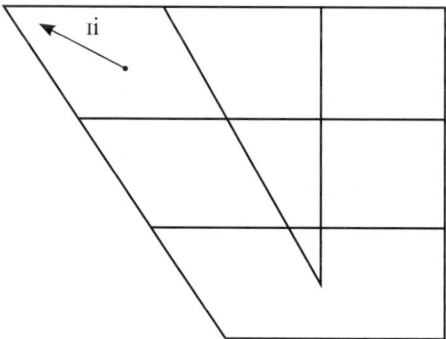

Figure 7.6 Vowel diagram of [ɪi].

stops, for example, the main articulators will return to the position of rest after all the others have been relaxed at the end of the utterance. If we wish, we can include a statement about the relative duraton of the vocoid phases of each syllable; in this case the first vocoid is relatively longer than the second, because the former has voicing in the following coda, whereas the latter does not. Note that the fact that the second syllable takes the primary stress, that is, *còrned béef*, does not change the relative durations.

(7.10) is a complete description, combining all statements we made above. The section in between the asterisks is the section to be replaced in the alternative pronunciations described in (7.11)–(7.13).

(7.10) Starting from the position of rest, with the lips closed and neutral, the velum lowered and the tongue at rest, after an intake of air, a chest pulse initiates an egressive pulmonic airstream. The back of the tongue rises to make complete contact with the velum, as the velum itself is raised, closing off the nasal cavities. At the same time the lips part and round slightly, and the vocal cords are held apart. There is a brief hold phase, during which the lips continue to become rounder. Then the back of the tongue is moved away from the velum to the position of a back, open-mid vocoid in the region of CV6. The vocal cords then start to vibrate. **The tip of the tongue rises to form an alveolar closure, and the sides of the tongue come into contact with the upper molars. At the same time the velum is lowered, allowing air to escape through the nose. The vocal cords continue to vibrate. There is a hold phase during which the velum is closed, shutting off the nasal cavities, and the lips move to a neutral position. Towards the end of the hold phase the lips come together in a complete closure. The alveolar and side contact is released and the main body of the tongue moves to the position of a front close-mid vocoid, considerably retracted from CV2. The bilabial closure is then released, as a new chest pulse initiates a new syllable, the lips spread and the tongue moves slightly forwards and upwards in the direction of CV1.** As the tongue is finishing its trajectory in a front-closing direction, the bottom lip is moved up towards the top teeth, which make light contact with the inside surface of the lip. At the same time the vocal cords cease vibrating. The air escapes with local audible friction. The articulators then return to the position of rest.

We can now consider alternative, more usual pronunciations of this sequence, with a particular focus on the coda+onset sequence: [ndˀb]. The following are all possible alternatives: [kʰɔmbˀbɪif], [kʰɔmmbɪif], [kʰɔmbɪif], and there will be varying degrees of nasality on the first vocoid. (I am not concerned with which is/are the most common, and I am not sure anyone actually knows.) The two phenomena displayed by these alternatives are usually referred to as assimilation and deletion, both of which we shall consider further in the next section. For now just note the differences in the descriptions, which I give as (7.11), (7.12) and (7.13), respectively. These only refer to the medial contoid phases; the rest of the description remains the same as in (7.10) in each case.

> (7.11) The lips come together in a complete closure. At the same time the velum is lowered, allowing air to escape through the nose. The vocal cords continue to vibrate. There is a hold phase during which the velum is closed, shutting off the nasal cavities, and the lips move to a neutral position. The bilabial closure is maintained, as a new chest pulse initiates a new syllable. During the bilabial closure the tongue moves from the back position to the position of a front close-mid vocoid, considerably retracted from CV2. The bilabial closure is then released, the lips spread and the tongue moves slightly forwards and upwards in the direction of CV1.

> (7.12) The lips come together in a complete closure. At the same time the velum is lowered, allowing air to escape through the nose. The vocal cords continue to vibrate. The bilabial closure is maintained, during which the velum continues to allow air to pass through the nose, and the lips move to a neutral position. The bilabial hold phase continues during which the velum is closed, shutting off the nasal cavities, as a new chest pulse initiates a new syllable. During the bilabial closure the tongue moves from the back position to the position of a front close-mid vocoid, considerably retracted from CV2. The bilabial closure is then released, the lips spread and the tongue moves slightly forwards and upwards in the direction of CV1.

> (7.13) The lips come together in a complete closure. At the same time the velum is lowered, allowing air to escape through the nose. The vocal cords continue to vibrate. The bilabial closure is maintained, during which the velum is closed, shutting off the nasal cavities, and the lips move to a neutral position as a new chest pulse initiates a new syllable. During the bilabial closure the tongue moves from the back position to the position of a front close-mid vocoid, considerably retracted from CV2. The bilabial closure is then released, the lips spread and the tongue moves slightly forwards and upwards in the direction of CV1.

The first two have more or less the same duration for the bilablial closure and the tongue movement from back to front. In the last version both the hold phase and the tongue movement are shorter. Figure 7.7 gives the movement of the tongue body during the bilabial hold phase in these cases.

This has been a deliberately extended consideration of articulatory movements and their interrelationships, in order to emphasize the complexity of

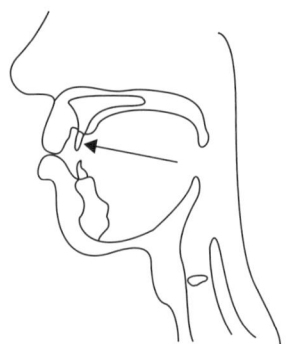

Figure 7.7 Tongue movement for [ɔ] to [ɪi].

what our letter-shape and diacritic transcriptions represent. I now want to consider one or two further examples of spoken English, covering phenomena that did not occur in *corned beef*, before going on to consider in more detail features of connected speech such as assimilation, that we have come across once or twice so far.

To exemplify the remaining articulatory details I shall take three simple monosyllables: [n̥ɒˀt̚] *hot*, [ˌgɑd̥] *guard* (with a released final stop) and [ˌgɜɫz̥] *girls*. In each case I will omit the details of the starting position, which is the same as in (7.10).

(7.14) [n̥ɒˀt̚]

The velum is closed, the lips part and become rounded, and, as the jaw lowers, the tongue takes up the position of a back, low vocoid, raised and considerably advanced from CV5. The vocal cords are held apart, as the egressive pulmonic air is expelled. The vocal cords then begin to vibrate, but after a brief vocoid phase are shut tightly together. At the same time as the glottal closure (or very slightly after it) the tip of the tongue rises to make a complete closure at the alveolar ridge, with the sides making contact with the upper molars. The articulators then return to the position of rest.

(7.15) [ˌgɑd̥]

The velum is closed and the back of the tongue is raised to make a complete contact with it. The vocal cords start vibrating just before the release of the velar stop. Then the tongue moves down to the position of a back, low vocoid, raised and considerably advanced from CV5, as the jaw lowers. The lips remain neutral or spread. The tip of the tongue then moves up to form a complete closure at the alveolar ridge, with the sides making contact with the upper molars. The vocal cords cease to vibrate and then the alveolar stop is released. The articulators then return to the position of rest.

(7.16) [ˌgɜɬzˌ]
The velum is closed and the back of the tongue is raised to make a complete contact with it. The vocal cords start vibrating just before the release of the velar stop. Then the tongue moves down to the position of a mid, central vocoid, as the jaw lowers slightly. The tip of the tongue moves up to make a complete contact on the median line of the oral cavity with no side contact with the upper teeth, allowing the air to escape laterally. At the same time the back of the tongue is raised in the direction of the velum, hollowing out the centre of the tongue and giving back resonance to the lateral. Then the sides of the tongue move up to make side contact with the upper molar, as the tip is lowered slightly to form a narrow groove through which the air escapes with local audible friction. During the friction the vocal cords cease to vibrate, and then the articulators return to the position of rest.

7.2 Connected speech phenomena

The phenomena to be discussed in the following sections are usually described in terms of some kind of process or change. (See, e.g., the definition of assimilation in Ladefoged [2006], p. 291.) In purely phonetic terms this is at best a metaphor for certain kinds of phonological relationships, at worst it presents a misleading picture. In any utterance a speaker uses a particular sequence of movements of his or her articulators, but in no sense changes one articulation into another during speech. The examples of assimilation of place of articulation in (7.11)–(7.13) are mutually exclusive alternatives to one another, and that is how I will present the phenomena we find in connected speech – as alternative pronunciations of the same lexical items.

7.2.1 Assimilation

It is possible to find alternations in any of the parametric features, but perhaps the most common is variation in the place of articulation. For instance, the final nasal of the English word *ten* typically shares its place of articulation with that of any obstruent in the onset of the following word, as in (7.17). (I have separated the words in the transcription to highlight the variation.)

(7.17) [tem men]   ten men
[tem fɹendz]   ten friends
[ten̪ θɪŋz]   ten things
[ten tents]   ten tents
[ten̪ tʃez]   ten chairs
[teŋ gɜɫz]   ten girls

The minus sign under [n] indicates a palatoalveolar contact. If the following word starts with a vowel, or is utterance-final, then the nasal is alveolar, for example, [ten egz] *ten eggs*, [ðə wə ten] *there were ten*. Note that some people, on occasion, especially as an indication of not wishing to continue with a particular topic of conversation, will use utterance-final bilabiality, as in (7.18).

(7.18) A: How many have you got?
B: [tem]

(Cf. also [noʊʔp̚] *nope* for *no*, and [jeʔp̚] for *yes*.)

The alternations in (7.17) are not random, they are rule-governed. Firstly, it is always the place of articulation of the onset consonant that is shared by the coda nasal. Secondly, it is not just any nasal that is subject to assimilatory variation. Thus, the coda [m] in *same girls* does not assimilate: *[seɪŋ gɜɫz], and nor does coda [ŋ]: *[sæm boʊθ] in *she sang both songs*. A further point to note is that assimilation in English is not obligatory; it is optional, but very common. There is also variation restricted to alternations between bilabial and labiodental points of contact, as in [fɜm mʌsɫz] *firm muscles*, [fɜm kɒntɹækt] *firm contract* but [fɜɱ fɹendz] *firm friends*. This is quite common amongst SBE speakers. (There are some English accents in which lexical [m] in a limited number of words, especially *some*, does actually assimilate to other places of articulation, e.g., [sʌŋ gɜɫz] *some girls*, but most [m]-final words do not. I use the term 'lexical' of a sound to refer to the sound of the lexical entry form spoken in isolation.)

It is not just the lexical alveolar nasal that is subject to assimilatory variation in this way; the oral alveolar stops are, too. In (7.19) and (7.20) I give a range of examples for each one. It is important to note that the coda stops must be unreleased, if they are assimilated; *[gʊb bɔɪ] for *good boy* with a release phase between the two bilabial closures is not possible.

(7.19) [hɒʔp̚ paɪz]   hot pies
[hɒʔp̚ fʊud]   hot food

[hɒʔt̚ θɪŋz]	hot things
[hɒʔt̚ deɪz]	hot days
[hɒʔt̚ tʃiiz]	hot cheese
[hɒʔk̚ keɪks]	hot cakes

(7.20)	[gʊb̚ paɪz]	good pies
	[gʊb̚ fuud]	good food
	[gʊd̚ θɪŋz]	good things
	[gʊd̚ deɪz]	good days
	[gʊd̚ tʃiiz]	good cheese
	[gʊg̚ keɪks]	good cakes

Assimilation of this type where a sound shares a feature or features with the following one is referred to as **regressive** or **anticipatory** assimilation. (It is also called **right-to-left** assimilation in segmental concatenation approaches.) It can work the other way, however, as in the examples of syllabic nasals in (7.21). This is called **progressive** or **perseverative** assimilation (**left-to-right**) and is less common in English than the regressive type.

(7.21)	[hæʔpm]	happen
	[kɒʔtn]	cotton
	[θɪʔknz]	thickens

If the preceding stop is released into a vocoid (schwa), then no assimilation takes place, for example, [hæpən], [θɪkən].

Another kind of place assimilation occurs in English when one of [t d s z] is followed by [j] or [ʃ]. Phonologists often refer to this as 'palatalization', but in fact the alternation is between alveolars and palatoalveolars. (No doubt the term 'palatoalveolarization' is rather off-putting.) In (7.22) I give examples with [j].

(7.22)	[mɪs jʊ] [mɪʃ jʊ]	miss you
	[wəz jʌŋ] [wəʒ jʌŋ]	was young
	[hɪt jʊ] [hɪtʃ jʊ]	hit you
	[wʊd jʊ] [wʊdʒ jʊ]	would you

The extent to which there is a palatal approximant phase varies along with the duration of the friction, so we find [mɪʃ ʃʊ], [mɪʃʊ], [wʊdʒʊ], for instance. Again, this kind of assimilation is usually optional, though in my own speech [hæʒ ʃɪ] *has she*, for instance, is obligatory. With more than two consonants the extent of the assimilation is variable, too; consider the different possibilities in (7.23) and try to decide which you do.

(7.23) [stjuudnt]   student
[stʃjuudnt]
[ʃtʃjuudnt]
[lɑst jɪə]   last year
[lɑs̪t ʃɪə]
[lɑʃt ʃɪə]

Although I have transcribed the assimilated sounds as [ʃ] and [ʒ], they are not always the same as lexical [ʃ] and [ʒ] in *sheep* and *massage*, respectively. Tongue contact is not necessarily exactly the same, and lip-rounding may be absent from the assimilated ones. Local (1992) investigated a number of instances of assimilated and lexical palatoalveolars, as in sentences like *This shop is a fish shop*, and showed that there were indeed differences between the two types. Nolan, Holst and Kühnert (1996) have also investigated the range of possible articulations for a [sʃ] sequence. This brings us once again to the issue of letter-shape transcriptions. Since letters are discrete from one another, any kind of blending of one articulation into another, such as a slow shift from alveolar to palatoalveolar contact, is impossible to transcribe. Provided we recognize the disparity between what actually occurs in instances of place assimilation and how we represent it in our transcriptions, then our over-simplified letter-representations will suffice. The same applies to the cases of assimilation in (7.17), (7.19) and (7.20); it is not a question of assimilated or not assimilated, but rather one of degrees of assimilation.

Yet another kind of place assimilation affects English [θ] and [ð], though the alternations are different in each case. Both assimilate to an adjacent (preceding or following) [s] or [z] in terms of place of articulation. Again there is an oversimplification in the transcription of the alternants as alveolar, as there are a number of slightly different points of contact. Consider the examples in (7.24).

(7.24) [lɪz sɪŋks]   Liz thinks
[boʊs saɪdz]   both sides
[ðɪs sɪŋ]   this thing
[boʊs zuuz]   both zoos
[loʊz zuuz]   loathe zoos
[loʊz sʌn]   loathe sun
[mɪs zæt]   miss that
[wɔz zæt]   was that

In the case of [ð] there are other circumstances in which assimilation takes place, but both place and manner of articulation are involved. When a lateral or a nasal precede lexical [ð], it is very common to find assimilation to a (dental) lateral approximant or a (dental) nasal stop, as in (7.25).

(7.25) [ɔɫ l̪ə]   all the
       [fɹəm n̪ə] from the
       [ɪn̪ n̪ə]   in the
       [bɹɪŋ n̪ə] bring the

Notice that in the case of the lateral the first one is velarized but the second one is not. In the case of *in the* we see different features in different assimilatory relationships, that is, [nasal] and [stop] are progressive, while [dental] is regressive. It is also interesting to note that there is a distinction of duration of the nasal between *in the* and *in a*, which native speakers use as a cue to which is being said. The duration of either one is very short, especially in unstressed syllables, and the difference itself is very small, but it is of phonological signifance to native speakers of English, and so is usually 'obvious' to them. Try saying [ɪn̪ n̪ə] and [ɪn ə] any number of times in any order and see if others can tell which you are saying. (Whether in the first example the nasal is dental or alveolar, which it is for some speakers, does not matter for the purposes of testing duration differences.)

As we have already said, in English the assimilation discussed above is optional, but very common, and indeed normal for many speakers, but now we can consider a language where assimilation is obligatory. It also involves both progressive and regressive assimilation of different features at the same time. Modern Greek has a number of unstressed forms that end in [n̪] when spoken in isolation or before vowels, for example, some of the forms of the definite article and the negative particle, [ðen̪]. So we find alternations between the nominative (subject) form and the accusative (object) form of nouns beginning with a voiceless stop in isolation, and similar alternations in verbs with and without a preceding negative particle, as exemplified in (7.26) and (7.27), respectively.

(7.26) [i porṭa]   the door (nom)
       [ṭim borṭa]   the door (acc)
       [i ṭrapeza]   the bank (nom)
       [ṭin̪ d̪rapeza] the bank (acc)
       [i kori]   the girl (nom)
       [ṭiŋ gori]   the girl (acc)

(7.27) [pirazi]   it matters
       [ðem birazi] it doesn't matter

[ʈraɣuðo]	I sing
[ðen̪ d̪raɣuðo]	I don't sing
[klin̪is]	you close
[ðeŋ glin̪is]	you don't close

Voicing assimilation is progressive, and place assimilation is regressive.

We have now moved on to other features that assimilate. Phonation characteristics can also be shared by sounds in contact. The voicing in the examples of Modern Greek above furnishes examples of this. It also occurs in French, especially in cases of common collocations, for example, [kɔgdø] *coque d'œuf* 'egg-shell', whereas *coque* in other environments is [kɔk], and [ʃmɛ̃tfɛʁ] *chemin de fer* 'railway'. In French both voice and voicelessness can be shared by two adjacent obstruents; the lexical phonation of the second consonant is the one that is shared.

Nasality may also be shared by English consonants in some environments. In section 7.1 one of the alternatives for *corned beef* was [kʰɔmmbɹif]. As well as regressive place assimilation there is progressive nasal assimilation of the final stop of *corned*. There are also limited examples of regressive nasal assimilation in English, for example, [wʊnnt] *wouldn't*, though *hidden* would not be *[hɪnn]. German has similar nasal assimilation in cases where a preposition ending in a nasal immediately precedes the definite article, for example, [ɪn nen], *in den*, [ɪn ni] *in die* 'into the' (the former masculine, the latter feminine).

In the examples in (7.25) manner assimilation is also involved. In some varieties of English, stops, especially those that are lexically alveolar, can alternate with fricatives and approximants, depending on the manner of the following consonant; the place of articulation also varies according to the following consonant. So, in Stockport, for instance, the forms in (7.28) are common (see Lodge [1984]). (The vocoid articulations are different from those of standard British English (SBE), hence the different symbols; see Chapter Eight.)

(7.28)	[dɛʋ ʋof]	dead (= very) rough
	[dɛj joŋg]	dead young
	[tɛw̃ wemen]	ten women
	[tɛl̃ ladz]	ten lads

Notice that in the last example the final lateral of *ten* is not velarized, any more than a final [m] or [n] would be in this word. We will return to variation in manner of articulation in section 7.2.2 on lenition.

All these examples have dealt with adjacent sounds in one way or another. However, some phonetic features seem to work over a greater distance. We have already noted resonance in English laterals and *r*-variants (see section 3.6 and the introduction to Chapter Six) as such a feature, and in a word in utterance-final position velarization affects the whole of the final coda; for example, [sɔlᵞtᵞ] *salt*, [fiilᵞdᵞ] *field* are narrow representations of these words. But there are vocoid features which also have this characteristic in some languages. Languages which use this system of vocoid assimilation in lexical and morphological discrimination are usually referred to as **harmony** languages. There is a large literature on these languages, many of which are found in Africa, but since a phonological description of the workings of the systems is complex, I do not intend to go into details here. What we need to note, however, is that vocoid articulations in particular over a number of syllables share one or more features. There are a number of commonly cited examples (not from Africa), for example, Finnish, Hungarian and Turkish. I will look briefly at Turkish.

In native Turkish words the vowels in each syllable have to agree with each other in terms of frontness or backness. As in many languages, the low, central vowel [a] patterns with the back vowels. (7.29) contains a number of examples showing this harmony pattern. (In Turkish orthography the high, back, spread vowel is written with an undotted *i*.)

(7.29) [tʃodʒuk]   *çocuk* (boy)
      [tytyn]   *tütün* (tobacco)
      [kibrit]   *kibrit* (match)
      [oda]   *oda* (room)
      [kutu]   *kutu* (box)
      [kɯbrɯs]   *Kıbrıs* (Cyprus)

There is a further limitation on the possible sequence of vowels: spread vowels go with spread vowels, but rounded ones can be followed by low, spread, as in *oda* in (7.29), or high, rounded ones, as in *çocuk*. Note that I am using the features [high] and [low] relatively, that is, phonologically, as Turkish only distinguishes two tongue heights. In phonetic terms there is considerable variation within each of these categories, for example, what I transcribe broadly as [e] may be anything between [e] and [æ] in terms of lowness.

The resultant sequences of vowels in Turkish are summed up in Table 7.1. One consequence of these limitations is that [o] and [ø] can only occur in the first syllable of a native Turkish word. There are a lot of loanwords

Table 7.1 Turkish vowel harmony

[i] or [e] are followed by [i] or [e]
[ɯ] or [a] are followed by [ɯ] or [a]
[y] or [ø] are followed by [y] or [e]
[u] or [o] are followed by [u] or [a]

in Turkish, which do not fit the pattern, for example, [otobys] *otobüs* 'bus' (from French); [dʒami] *cami* 'mosque' (from Arabic). However, Turkish is a language that uses a lot of suffixation to produce sets of related vocabulary, and the vowels of the suffixes all have to harmonize with the final stem vowel, whether the word is native or a loanword, as exemplified in (7.30).

(7.30)
[tʃodʒuklar]	çocuklar	(boys)
[kibritler]	kibritler	(matches)
[hatɯrlamak]	hatırlamak	(to remember)
[øksyrmek]	öksürmek	(to cough)
[tytyndʒy]	tütüncü	(tobacconist)
[tytyndʒyde]	tütüncüde	(at the tobacconist's)
[kɯbrɯsta]	Kıbrısta	(in Cyprus)
[odada]	odada	(in the room)
[odalar]	odalar	(rooms)
[hukukdʒu]	hukukcu	(lawyer)
[otobyste]	otobüste	(in the bus)
[otelde]	otelde	(in the hotel)

Try to work out each of the separate stems and suffixes, and check that they follow the harmony pattern. There are consonantal alternations in some of the suffixes; can you explain them from a phonetic point of view?

This presentation of the Turkish harmony system has been simplified. From what we have said about resonance features it is very unlikely that the consonants are not involved as well. For a more detailed discussion of the harmony system, which discusses the consonants as well, see Waterson (1956). There are even more complicated harmony systems such as that found in the group of related dialects referred to as Kalenjin, a southern Nilotic language spoken in Kenya, in which the phonetic relationships in the vowels and the consonants are not so straightforward. A discussion of such systems would lead us into a discussion of the relationship between phonetics and phonology, which would go beyond the scope of this book. (See, however, Local and Lodge [2004], Lodge, Local and Harlow [in prep.], Lodge [to appear].)

Some languages display what we might call purely phonetic harmony, that is, there is no associated grammatical meaning with the alternations of the kind we saw in Turkish. Lass ([1984], p. 303) gives an example from East Fife (Scotland), where the final unstressed vocoid articulation of the ending usually written -*y* varies according to the tongue-height of the preceding stressed vocoid in disyllabic words, as in (7.31).

(7.31) [pysë]   *pussy*
      [këʔë]   *kitty*

Some French speakers also use harmony in the pre-tonic unstressed mid vowels, as in (7.32). In this case the tongue-height of the final (stressed) vowel determines whether the preceding stem-vowel is high-mid or low-mid. (See Dell [1980], p. 189.)

(7.32) [sede]   *céder*   (to surrender)
      [sɛdʁa] *cédera*   ((he/she) will surrender)

Interestingly, some French speakers spell *cédera* with a grave accent: *cèdera*, no doubt partly under the influence of the [ɛ] in the stem and the related verb form *cède* 'he/she surrenders' with the same vocoid [ɛ].

7.2.2 Lenition and fortition

These are traditional terms, which are not phonetic terms. They mean 'weakening' and 'strengthening', respectively, and are used most often with reference to historical developments in various languages. They do have a phonetic basis, though. Lenition relates to the degree of obstruction in the oral cavity between the articulators. Stops, that is, those with the greatest degree of obstruction, are seen as the 'strongest' articulations and the low vocoids as the 'weakest'. In many instances of historical development a sound can be lost completely, and so loss is the 'weakest' stage of all. For instance, the bilabial stop in Vulgar Latin (i.e., the spoken language, as opposed to the written, Classical variety) *parabolare* 'to speak' (along with two syllables in this case) has been lost in French *parler* and Italian *parlare*, both of which languages are descendants of Latin. So we can establish a gradual development through slightly different degrees of stricture, as in Figure 7.8. (Compare this with the schema in Lass [1984], p. 178, in which he incorporates another dimension, that of voicing, that need not concern us here.) So lenition, and fortition, which is a change in the opposite direction, i.e. right to left in Figure 7.8, is related to the

[stop] → [affricate] → [fricative] → [approximant] → [vocoid] → ∅

Figure 7.8 Lenition schema.

manner of articulation. As an example from historical linguistic development I will take one instance of the so-called High German sound shift, which affected the voiceless stops. It is assumed to have taken place between AD 400 and 700, and was one of the distinguishing characteristics which marked High German, and subsequently modern standard German, from the other Germanic dialects at the time, the modern descendants of which include Dutch and English. If we compare some words of modern English with their equivalents in modern German, we can see a pattern of stops, affricates and fricatives that we can relate to part of the lenition schema in Figure 7.8. I will take the alveolars by way of exemplification in (7.33); the first row exemplifies word-initial position, the second row intervocalic and the third word-final.

(7.33) [tɛn] *ten* [tsen] *zehn*
      [wɔtə] *water* [vasʌ] *Wasser*
      [ðæt] *that* [das] *das*

Although lenition is seen as an essentially historical process, there are examples in phonological alternations, too. The High German sound shift has a very close parallel in the English spoken in Liverpool. Here most speakers have affricates rather than stops in word-initial position and fricatives in intervocalic and final position, so we find: [tsɛn], [wɔsə] and [das] for the English words in (7.33). There is variation in the exact type and place of contact, as well as phonation variability, but the pattern is remarkably like that of High German. (See also the discussion in section 5.3.) Even in SBE in continuous speech speakers may use fricatives rather than stops in intervocalic position, for example, [bɪɣə] *bigger*, [læzə] *ladder*. In Spanish, another descendant of Latin, there are alternations between stops and approximants that reflect the historical development, for example, [baŋka] *banca* 'bank', but [la βaŋka] *la banca* 'the bank'; the latter is intervocalic, as in [aβer] *haber* 'to have'.

Fortition seems to be less common than lenition, but can be exemplified in the historical development of Vulgar Latin [majore] 'bigger' into French [maʒœʁ] with a fricative rather than an approximant, and Italian [maddʒiore] with an affricate.

7.2.3 Dearticulation

We have seen a number of cases where the articulation involves features additional to a single oral obstruction, such as two points of contact, glottal reinforcement, velarization. These are often referred to as 'secondary' articulations, but it is not at all clear why some aspects of articulation should be singled out as 'primary' and others 'secondary', other than by an arbitrary convention. And are there 'tertiary' articulations? It is possible in some of these cases to remove one or more of the articulatory gestures and retain a different, but similar sound. For instance, if we consider a velarized lateral [ɫ], it has tongue contact at the alveolar ridge and a raised back of the tongue. If the alveolar contact is taken away, we have a vocoid articulation [o] or [ɤ], depending on lip-position, and this is both a historical development that we find in, for example, earlier forms of French and Portuguese, and an alternation in many varieties of English, for example, London [fɪo] *fill*, but [fɪlɪn] *filling*, where the velarized lateral of other accents has been dearticulated, but still alternates with the non-velarized lateral. It is clear from this development that the so-called secondary feature of velarization is the important clue for syllable-final /l/ in many varieties of English. Dearticulation removes the 'primary' articulation and leaves behind the 'secondary' one. It is often difficult to tell whether an alveolar contact has been made when listening to colloquial speech, but this makes no difference to comprehension. (For further comment on this, see Carter [2003], p. 238.)

Another example is furnished by the alternations and developments involving glottally reinforced stops. In English glottally reinforced [ʔt], in particular, but also to a lesser extent [ʔp] and [ʔk], can loose the oral contact, leaving a simple glottal stop [ʔ]. English is not the only language where this development has taken place. Burmese has reduced the earlier contrasts in the final stops to just [ʔ]; and in Malay there are obligatory alternations between [ʔk] and [ʔ], for example, [galaʔ] : [galaʔkan] 'encouragement'. In some Malay dialects, for example, Kelantan and Trengganu, the only coda stop allowed is [ʔ].

In a similar way voiceless obstruents alternate with [h]. If the oral articulation is taken away, the position of the vocal cords remains the same and a vocoid posture of some kind is taken up in the mouth. In Malay [s] and [h] alternate, for example, [kipas] or [kipah] (= [kipa̤]) *fan*. In Liverpool, too, we find examples such as [wɒh] *what*, and [sʊmhən] *something*.

Some phonologists refer to this as another kind of lenition, for example, Harris (1994), but it is clearly not allied to the degree of obstruction schema that we established in Figure 7.8 from a phonetic point of view. The interpretation here is more in line with that offered by Lass ([1984], pp. 177–181), which he presents as a different kind of lenition from the one based on manner of articulation.

7.2.4 Timing variation, 'deletion' and 'insertion'

The phenomena I want to discuss in this section are usually handled as deletion or insertion, or sometimes alternations with zero, but I have already sounded a warning about this over-simplified interpretation in section 5.2. What we find is variation in the relative timing of articulatory movements. Nevertheless, there are cases where it is helpful from a phonological point of view to see some of the alternant forms as alternants with zero in comparison with other possibilities. So, in English we can hear both [lɑst wiɪk] and [lɑs wiɪk] for *last week*. In the latter example we are indicating that there is no stop phase, and that the consonantal phase [-stw-] is shorter than [-sw-]. From a phonological perspective, like many of the phenomena we have considered in this chapter, in English this alternation with zero is optional, but rule-governed. There are only certain circumstances under which it can take place. The three consonants of the longer variant have to be distributed as follows: CC+C, where + indicates a morpheme boundary, and the second one must be a stop. (7.34) has a range of possibilities, some of which involve assimilation of place as well.

(7.34) [lɑs tɹeɪn]   *last train*
       [lɑʃ jɪə]   *last year*
       [poʊsmən]   *postman*
       [lɪfs]   *lifts*
       [ɑst]   *asked*
       [sen ten]   *send ten*
       [wɪmmɪl]   *windmill*
       [fɹenz]   *friends*
       [hæŋ kɑt]   *hand-cart*

On the other hand, there are a number of other examples, which seem to fit the environment for the alternation, but, in fact, are not subject to loss of the stop articulation, as in (7.35).

(7.35) [mɪlkmən]   *milkman*
       [sɔlt maɪn]   *salt mine*
       [sent mɔ]   *sent more*
       [semp mɔ]   *sent more*

Work out what is different between the examples in (7.34) and those in (7.35). Your answer will involve at least one of the phonetic features you have learnt about. Can you also find any examples that fit the environment template, which will be more precise once you have found the answer to the above problem, but which are not able to alternate with a stopless variant? If you find any, can you think of any reason why they do not participate in such alternations? So, we have an optional phonological rule of English with a partly phonetic explanation of the circumstances in which it operates. ('Partly', because the morpheme boundary stipulation is not a phonetic one.)

Examples of insertion would be instances of liaison in French and English. In French, certain consonants alternate with zero depending on whether the following sound is a vowel or a consonant. This occurs in the same circumstances that we discussed in section 2.9.3 in the phonological definition of consonants and vowels in French; in the case of liaison a consonant, such as the [z] of the plural definite article, occurs when a vowel follows, but not when a consonant does, as in the examples in (7.36).

(7.36) [lezɔm]   les hommes   (the men)
      [lezwazo]   les oiseaux   (the birds)
      [lefam]   les femmes   (the women)
      [lewiski]   les whiskeys   (the whiskies)

The [z] is a link between the two vowels.

In English a similar phenomenon occurs with [ɹ], which is used as a link between two non-high vowels, as in (7.37).

(7.37) [fɑ saɪd]   far side
      [fɑɹ ɒf]   far off
      [fɔ ʃedz]   four sheds
      [fɔɹ egz]   four eggs
      [bɪgə bɔɪ]   bigger boy
      [bɪgəɹ aɪz]   bigger eyes
      [lɔ suut]   law suit
      [lɔɹ əv]   law of
      [tʃaɪnə tıi]   China tea
      [tʃaɪnəɹ ən]   China and

Notice that it is not restricted to cases where there is orthographic (and, therefore, historical) *r*.

Both these phenomena can be viewed as alternations with zero, so why are some cases called 'deletion' and others 'insertion'. The answer relates to what the isolated, lexical form of the word is, its citation form. So, as [lɑst] is the citation form of *last*, [lɑs] is seen as losing its final stop, hence it is a case of deletion; on the other hand, since the citation forms of French *les* and British English *far* are [le] and [fɑ], the link is seen as being inserted. Whether or not this view of the mechanisms of phonology is justified is not something we can discuss here, but we can see that the names of these phenomena are not phonetic in nature, but bring with them a whole theoretical package. Similarly, the other phenomena discussed in section 7.2 are often treated as though they were processes, as we noted at the beginning. In order to be able to assess the validity of such an approach to phonology, we need to have a thorough understanding of the phonetic basis (or otherwise) of the phenomena we are dealing with. (For an extended discussion of this issue, see Lodge [to appear].)

7.3 Transcription and practice

There are two books that deal with connected English speech: G. Brown (1977) *Listening to spoken English*, which deals with RP speakers from radio and television broadcasts, and L. Shockey (2003) *Sound patterns of spoken English*, which deals with colloquial styles of pronunciation in a variety of accents including American ones.

Besides transcribing from tape/CD it is quite useful to practise transcribing written texts and to indicate various possible pronunciations of the same words, taking into account the connected speech phenomena we have discussed in section 7.2. For example, always indicate where linking *r* could occur. When transcribing sentences or longer texts, it is convenient to leave gaps between words. This makes the transcription easier to read, but remember it is a convention taken over from standard orthography. For reduced forms, for example, *I'm, you'd, he's, she'll*, it is more convenient not to break them up, as in the spelling forms, but do not put in apostrophes. As a general rule regarding punctuation, do not use it: no capital letters, no commas, question marks, colons, etc.

> **Sample text 1**
> Transcribe and indicate in particular places where assimilation is likely to occur.
>
> What about coming to our sale of work? It's being held in the village hall next Saturday morning. It doesn't open 'til eleven but you'd better be there a bit beforehand so as you can have a look round. The jumble stall always fascinates me and we seem to have collected a rather superior lot this time. I've got my eye on a dear little brass candlestick. At present it's as black as the ace of spades, but when I've given it a good cleaning up, it'll look just right on top of the sideboard in the

dining room. I hope no one else gets it first, while I'm on the ticket desk. Perhaps you'll get it for me; now you'll simply have to come!

Sample text 2

Transcribe and indicate in particular the most likely instances of zero realizations.

Ernest could hardly be blamed for what happened next. The postman tripped over the handbag and bumped his head on the wardrobe. A loud yell came from the poor man, as Mrs Lamb rushed down the hall-way. 'Get out of the way, you useless boy!' she shouted at Ernest. 'Wait 'til your father gets home.' 'It's hardly my fault; I didn't leave the bag down there', he protested. 'Nonsense, it *is* your fault. You left the thing in the way. You could've moved it.' 'How you can come to that conclusion is quite beyond my comprehension', said Ernest and banged the door in their faces.

Sample text 3

Transcribe and indicate in particular the most likely instances of lenition.

At what time are you going to the exhibition? I thought I heard you tell your brother this morning that you expected to meet him there at about two. Would you like to join us? We've got to leave early to catch the four o'clock train, because we don't live here now. We live in a bigger house out in the country and I want to get home before it's dark, even though I won't be driving. But you could stay later, especially if you've got plans for the evening with your brother. Anyway, think about it and let me know what you decide.

As regards articulatory descriptions, follow the examples above and describe any two (or more) syllable sequences from a language you know, for example, *Prince Charles, green peas, chemin de fer, guten Morgen*. To practise parametric representations try to represent the word boundary contoid sequences in *corned beef* as described above; follow the model of those in section 3.8, but add a parameter for velic activity.

Map of England, Scotland and Wales.

Varieties of English 8

Chapter outline

8.1 [ʊ] versus [ʌ]	162
8.2 Rhoticity	164
8.3 Variation in vowel systems	166
8.4 Consonants	176
8.5 Practice	182

We have only looked at standard British English (SBE) and General American (GA) in any detail, when discussing English examples, but I have pointed out that it is very likely that neither of these is your own accent or the accent of people you know at home. Language varies from speaker to speaker and from place to place; this is the object of study for sociolinguistics. So it is quite likely in any group of people that no two of them speak alike. This is not just a matter of voice quality, but of detailed phonetic differences, some of which are shared with other speakers, some of which are not. To take a simple example: a person from Manchester will pronounce the word *cat* [kʰaʔ], a person from Liverpool [kˣah], a person from London [kʰæʔ]. The Mancunian and the Liverpudlian share the same vowel quality; the Mancunian and the Londoner share the same onset and coda consonant articulations.

In this chapter I want to consider some of the phonetic details of accent variation in the hope that at least some readers will be able to pinpoint similar details in their own type of speech. I will divide the features up into similar types and indicate areas where they can be found. However, it is important to remember that individual speakers, even from the same geographical area, may have finely graded differences in the phonetic details of their speech. The notion of a uniform, homogenous 'Yorkshire accent', an 'Edinburgh accent' or 'a London accent' is difficult to maintain. Speakers vary within these areas, though they may have some characteristics in common, so to claim that X has a Yorkshire accent makes sense, provided we recognize that 'a Yorkshire accent' does not equate with 'the' Yorkshire accent; in other words, it is interpreted as one of many similar accents found in Yorkshire. Whereas at one time the idea of stable rural dialects may have had some basis in reality in that people did not necessarily move about much or have contact with speakers from other areas, in the 21st century mobility and interaction with speakers from elsewhere is now the norm. Just consider the number of clearly different accents you hear in one day; this number will be greatly increased, if you watch television for part of the time. Changes in lifestyle during the 20th century have meant that people of all kinds interact with one another quite frequently in everyday life.

Two further points need to be made. There are, in fact, no clear-cut boundaries between dialect areas, except where, in former times, some impenetrable geographical obstacle intervened. Since the development of improved modes of transport, such obstacles have diminished in significance. For instance, the Pennines down the centre of Northern England were once difficult to travel through, but the trans-Pennine railways of the 19th century and more recently the M62 motorway have changed that. The other point is that dialects and accents do not follow the administrative local government boundaries of towns, cities and counties. For example, the main features of a Norfolk accent (or should we say accents?) are not found in the extreme west of the county near the borders with Cambridgeshire in the Fens, but are found in the northeast of Suffolk from Lowestoft down to Halesworth, Southwold and beyond.

So, let us first of all consider just two major distinguishing features of accents of English, one restricted to England, the other applying much further afield. It is important to note that I do not use the proposed broad transcription that I introduced in Chapter Four for SBE, in particular the vowel symbols. If we are comparing phonetic details, then we need to indicate differences in the symbols we choose. This means that each accent I represent has its own set of symbols, sometimes fairly narrow, other times more broad.

8.1 [ʊ] versus [ʌ]

In section 4.1.1 we looked at the six so-called short vowels in SBE: [ɪ e æ ɒ ʌ ʊ]. However, in many accents of English (in England), usually described as 'Northern', there are only five: [ɪ ɛ a ɒ ʊ]. Note that I have used two different

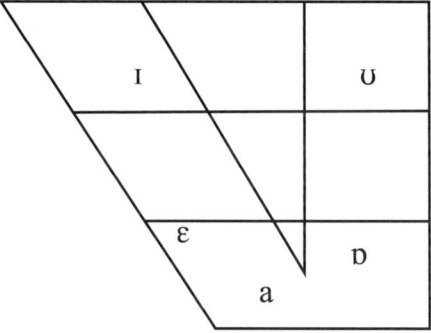

Figure 8.1 Northern English vowels.

symbols [ɛ] and [a]; this is to indicate the different qualities of these vowels in northern accents. (Given the warning above, note that [ɛ] is the vowel in *bed* in northern accents; the vowel in *fair* would be given a length mark: [fɛː] to differentiate it, and to indicate that the rhythmic patterns are not the same as for SBE.) Figure 8.1 gives the articulations on a vowel diagram.

Words which contain [ʌ] in SBE have [ʊ] in areas of England from the Scottish border down to Shropshire, North Oxfordshire and the Wash. Since there are no sharp boundaries, there are areas of fluctuation where both may be heard, for example, the West Norfolk and Cambridgeshire Fens. So in this northern area most speakers use [ʊ] as the stressed vowel in the examples with [ʌ] in Table 4.1, as in (8.1).

(8.1) [kʊd] *cud*   [θʊndə] *thunder*   [pɹədʊkʃn] *production*

This produces a number of homophones, for example, *could/cud, put/putt, book/buck*. In the West Midlands, around and in Birmingham, most speakers have an unrounded articulation in these words: [ɤ], but still no contrast.

There are also speakers who try to make the distinction, though not in a consistent way, nor in line with the SBE lexical distribution of the sounds. Such mixed, and to some extent artificial accents are referred to by sociolinguists as **hypercorrect** (see, for instance, Trudgill [1986, 2000]), that is, such speakers misunderstand the details of the phonological system of the accent they are trying to adopt and so produce forms that neither their own original accent nor the one they are trying to adopt would use. In relation to the case under discussion some speakers attempt to produce the [ʌ] vowel, often producing an articulation in the area of [æ] or [ə]. But typically they fluctuate between this and [ʊ], and they will use it in words which have [ʊ] in SBE, for example, [pət] *put*, [bətʃə] *butcher*, [bək] *book*.

8.2 Rhoticity

The other example is rhoticity, that is, the occurrence of coda /r/, which we discussed in Chapter Four in relation to differences between SBE and GA. (Note that I use slant lines and an ordinary *r*-symbol to indicate a phonological entity which has a variety of phonetic realizations.) Within the British Isles rhoticity occurs, though it is on the decrease in some areas. For instance, in the South-East of England, in the 1970s, when I was recording speakers for my book on accent variation (Lodge [1984]), only speakers over about forty years of age still used rhoticity. Today it is very difficult to find a local rhotic speaker in Sussex, for example. On the other hand, there are areas, even in England, where it is still quite widespread, for example, the West Country (including urban Bristol) and parts of urban Lancashire (e.g., Bury). In addition, it is the norm in Scotland and in both Northern Ireland and the Republic. The commonest articulations for /r/ in rhotic accents are an alveolar approximant [ɹ] or a retroflex approximant [ɻ]. Retroflex articulation affects more than just the approximant in the coda. All coda consonants involved in what we might call an *r*-coda, that is, one containing an /r/, are retroflex, and in many cases the articulation of the preceding nuclear vowel is affected, too. This is not surprising since the tip of the tongue is either curled back or retracted for the retroflexion, so this tongue posture is retained for the whole of the rhyme. Even in speakers who omit the approximant posture, the retroflexion remains, so we find realizations such as those in (8.2).

(8.2) [kɑɻɖ] [kɑd] *card*
[bɜɻn̺ḛ] [bɜn̺ḛ] *Burnley (a town in Lancashire)*

Some speakers in the rhotic areas of Lancashire do not have a coda approximant, that is, are non-rhotic, but the preceding vocoid articulation is short before another consonant. (The received wisdom is that historical loss of rhoticity from the 18th century onwards resulted in compensatory lengthening of the preceding vowel phase, i.e., the lengthening of the vowel phase compensates for the loss of coda *r*; see, e.g., Beal [1999], p. 105–118.) So we find forms such as [wɜk] *work*, [tʃɜtʃ] *church*, [sɜv] *serve*, with a vocoid duration no longer than for [sɛt] *set* or [man] *man*. I should point out here that vocoid duration in this accent is not the same as for SBE; there is a distinction between short and long articulations which is consistent across different stressed environments.

In the United States, where rhoticity is standard, by no means all speakers use it. Many speakers from the Southern states and Eastern New England have no rhoticity at all, e.g. [fɑm] *farm*, [fɑðə] *father*, [fɔə] *four* (New York), [fouə] *four* (Southern States) and some have no intervocalic [ɹ] either, for example, [kæi] (disyllabic) *carry*, [vei] *very*, [bɛːɪŋ] *bearing* (see Harris [1994], p. 234). Most African American speakers were non-rhotic, though this is changing to some extent. At one time black Americans not just from the South had no rhoticity, though some used [ɝ] in the appropriate words. Also a broad New York accent has no rhoticity, but diphthongs occur in words which have rhoticity in other accents, for example, [bɜɪd] *bird*. Watch a number of American films or TV programmes and see if you can find differences in the occurrence of rhoticity.

As was pointed out in section 4.2, rhotic accents vary in the number of vocoid articulations that they allow before coda /r/. Harris ([1994], pp. 230–265) deals with variation in the occurrence of /r/ in a wide range of accents, mainly from a phonological perspective, but a number of points can be made drawing on his material. Only in a few rhotic accents, namely relatively broad Scottish ones do we find a full set of vocoid articulations preceding coda /r/, giving examples such as those in (8.3); I have given a trill for the articulation of /r/, which it often is in such accents, and it may be voiceless before voiceless sounds or utterance-finally. I discuss the vowel system of many Scottish accents further in section 8.3.1.

(8.3) [fir] *fear*   [pʉr] *poor*   [wʌɪr] *wire*   [flʌʏr] *flour*
      [per] *pear*   [por] *pour*   [hɛr] *her*   [fɔr] *for*
      [far] *far*   [pʌr] *purr*   [fɪr] *fir*

In other rhotic accents centering diphthongs often occur before /r/ but not elsewhere, as in [faɪəɹ] *fire*, and [puəɹ] *poor*. This is the origin of the centring diphthongs in non-rhotic accents in such words, for example, *fire, poor, there, hour*. In yet other accents /r/ occurs in the syllable nucleus as a rhotacized vocoid, as we noted in some American accents in section 4.2, Table 4.2, for example, [bɝd] *bird*, [kɝl] *curl*, [fɝrl] *fertile*. So, in most rhotic accents the range of vocoid qualities is (i) different from before other contoid articulations, and (ii) more limited.

8.3 Variation in vowel systems

As we saw in section 8.1, northern English accents have one fewer vowel in the short set. There are other systems, however, that have more or fewer distinctions overall in comparison with SBE or GA. For instance, Californians and Canadians usually have the same unrounded vocoid in both *cot* and *caught*, [kẍt], the lips being spread or neutral. I have used a narrow transcription to indicate that it is not quite the same quality as either GA [ɑ] or [ɔ] with spread or neutral lips. In fact, it is really the vowel systems that vary in particular accents, though we will also consider some of the consonantal variation, too, below.

I will take further examples of vocoid variation separately.

8.3.1 Scotland

In most accents from Lowland Scotland the vocoid articulations are rather different from those of other varieties. First, the articulations are more peripheral; second, their duration does not vary much, except under certain specific conditions. (We need not be concerned about the details of this phenomenon, usually referred to as the Scottish Vowel Length Rule (SVLR), but see, e.g., Lass [1984], pp. 32–34.) Third, there are far fewer diphthongal articulations than in many varieties of English (see our description of SBE above in Chapter Four). In Table 8.1 I give transcriptions of the monophthongal vocoids of an Edinburgh accent, and Figure 8.2 gives them on a vowel diagram.

Notice that there are fewer distinctions than in SBE or GA: *food* and *put* have the same vowel, so *fool* and *full* will be homophonous; *fat* and *calm* have the same vowel, so *cam* will be pronounced the same as the latter example; *pot* and *thought* have the same vowel, so *cot* and *caught* are homophonous. The [ʉ] articulation may be even further forward, that is, [ʏ] or even [y]. Some speakers have different lexical distributions, so [ʉ] may occur in what would be termed broad Scottish accents in words like *house*, *mouse* and *trousers* as well. Note, too, that unlike the North of England, most Scottish accents have [ʌ].

Table 8.1 Scottish monophthongs

[fit] *feet*	[fʉd] *food*	[fɪt] *fit*	[pʉt] *put*
[fet] *fate*	[bot] *boat*	[mɛt] *met*	[pɔt] *pot*
[fat] *fat*	[kam] *calm*	[kʌt] *cut*	[θɔt] *thought*

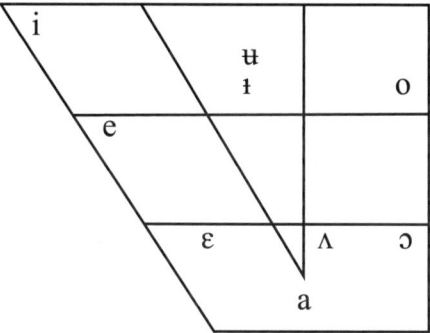

Figure 8.2 Scottish monophthongs.

The diphthongs are [ɔɪ] in *boy*, [ʌɪ] in *fine* and [ʌʏ] in *town*. The last two vary according to the SVLR, at least in some speakers (see, however, Lodge [1984] and Agutter [1986]), with [aɪ] and [aʉ], respectively. For the unstressed vowels, see section 8.3.6.

8.3.2 East Anglia

In East Anglia, especially in rural areas, there are more distinct vocoid articulations than in many other English accents. This is because some of the distinctions made in Middle English, which have disappeared in most varieties, have been maintained by East Anglian speakers. On the other hand, distinctions made elsewhere have been merged. In Table 8.2 I give the main vocoid articulations found in Norwich; Figure 8.3 is a vowel diagram for the monophthongs.

Table 8.2 Norwich vowels

[fiit] *feet*	[fuːd] *food*	[fɪt] *fit*	[pʊt] *put*
[fæɪt] *fate*	[mʊun] *moan*	[mɛt] *met*	[pɑt] *pot*
[fæt] *fat*	[kaːm] *calm*	[kʌt] *cut*	[θɔt] *thought*
[fɛː] *fear*	[fɛː] *fair*	[mʌʊn] *mown*	[pɔt] *port*
[fɜː] *fur*	[pɜː] *pure*	[faɪt] *fight*	[tæʏn] *town*
[bɔɪ] *boy*			

In the speech of very old Norwich inhabitants and still in the rural areas of Norfolk a further distinction is made between the vowel in *rain* [ɹæɪn] and

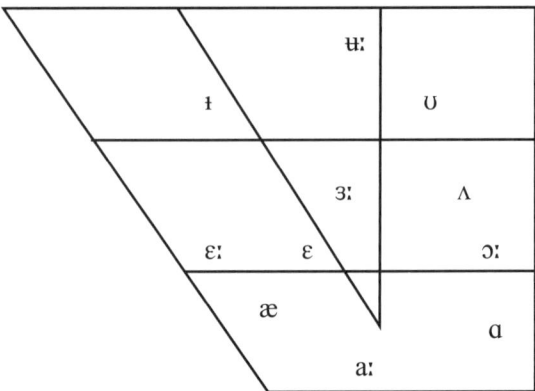

Figure 8.3 Norwich monophthongs.

day [dæɪ] on the one hand, and [mɛːk] *make* and [teːk] *take* on the other. (This distinction is reflected in the spelling: *ai/ay* and *aCe*, where C = any consonant letter, respectively.) So *gait* and *gate* are not homophonous, as they are in SBE. There are also variations in the lexical incidence of some of the vowels, but the details need not concern us here. Note that there is no distinction between *fear* and *fair*, and that *pure* and *purr* are homophonous. [j] does not occur before any vowel after another consonant, for example, [fʉː] *few*, [hʉːdʒ] *huge*, [ʃɜː] *sure* and [kʉːt] *cute*, which is usually homophonous with *coot*.

Two particular characteristics of the Norwich vowel system are worth mentioning. Vowels, especially the low vowels [æ] and [ɑ], are often lengthened. Interestingly, this even occurs before glottal stops and glottally reinforced oral stops, which is considered an environment where short duration of vocoids occurs in most accents of English. For example, we find [kæːʔ] *cat* and [ʃɑːʔp] *shop*. (The latter form to a speaker from elsewhere in the South-East sounds like *sharp*.) However, this lengthening does not make them phonological long vowels; they still have to have a following consonant. The other phenomenon is found both within morphologically complex words and in connected speech; it is often referred to as **smoothing**, which is really a non-phonetic term (like lenition, for instance), to describe monophthongization. When a phonologically long vowel, including the diphthongs, combines with a schwa, the articulation is a long monophthong, usually of a different quality from the long vowel in isolation. The commonest combinations are *V+ing* and *V+it*; both these morphemes in Norwich have an unstressed schwa, [-ən], [əʔ], respectively; and *V+and*. In (8.4) I give a few examples.

(8.4) [dɯː] *do*   [dɜːn] *doing*   [dɜː?] *do it*
      [sæɪ] *say*   [sæːn] *saying*   [sæː?] *say it*
      [gʊu] *go*   [gɔːn] *going*   [gɔːn] *go and*

8.3.3 Jamaican Creole

In varieties of English that have developed in places where English was an imposed, colonial language, we find very different vowel systems, with either five or ten distinctions only. In the case of ten distinctions there are five short and five long vocoids. Jamaican Creole (see, for instance, Wells [1967, 1973]) has such a system, plus two diphthongs. Clearly, with fewer vowel distinctions the lexical incidence is very different from British and American English. In Table 8.3 I give the stressed vowel distinctions; Figure 8.4 is a vowel diagram for the monophthongs, both long and short.

The mid vowels vary from [e] to [ɛ] and [o] to [ɔ]. In some cases there is no consistent pattern of correlation in the lexical incidence of the vowels. Some words which have [ʌ] in SBE have [a], whereas others have [o]. Of course, it must be remembered that the origins of this creole come from a variety of Englishes anyway, reflecting the different origins of the native English

Table 8.3 Jamaican stressed vowels

[fiːt] *feet*	[fuːd] *food*	[fit] *fit*	[put] *put*
[feːt] *fate*	[boːt] *boat*	[met] *met*	[pat] *pot*
[fat] *fat*	[kaːm] *calm*	[kat] *cut*	[taːt] *thought*
[faɪt] *fight*	[toʊn] *town*	[taɪ] *toy*	[son] *son*

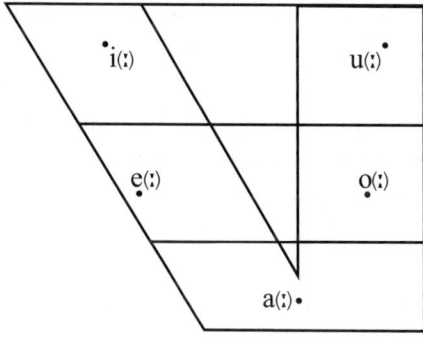

Figure 8.4 Jamaican long and short monophthongs.

speakers who came into contact with the black speakers. Rhoticity is variable, especially in unstressed syllables, for example, [ʃaːp] *sharp*, [gorl] *girl*, [sistor] or [sista] *sister*. As can be seen from these examples, full vowels occur in unstressed syllables; there is no schwa. This gives a distinctive rhythm to the language.

The main descendant of Jamaican Creole is London Jamaican, which has retained most of the original features, but is not rhotic. (For a detailed account of London Jamaican, see Sebba [1993]; note that some young white Londoners have some features of this accent today.)

8.3.4 Kenyan English

Another reduced vowel system, in this case with only five vowels, three diphthongs and no schwa, is that spoken in Kenya. In fact, many of the African Englishes have simple vowel systems of this kind. It is also the case that in the ex-colonial countries there is typically a continuum from what might be termed a pidginized variety for minimal interactions at markets and shops to a fully fledged standard variety for official purposes, for example, higher education and international interaction. The accent associated with this standard variety is not SBE or even some older form of RP (as it, no doubt, was for a few speakers, in the colonial period), but has its own regional characteristics. This is true of black Africa, India and parts of South-East Asia. Note that, for the most part, these local varieties are no-one's native language, though a major exception to this are the many native speakers of Indian English. Along this continuum all the varieties have features of the local languages, too. This is how the regional standard accents of many countries in Africa have developed. In certain circumstances, especially in instances of code-switching, when English is used, it is often virtually incomprehensible to a native speaker from Britain or the United States. For instance, in small townships in Kenya, when interaction is undertaken in a mixture of English, Swahili and the local language(s), English may take on features of a local language, for example, syllabic features of Kalenjin, a language with so-called [ATR]-harmony. (For a detailed account of such interactions, see Muthwii [1994].)

Lexical incidence is even more constrained than in Jamaican Creole with its short and long pairs. In Table 8.4 I give some examples, with a vowel diagram in Figure 8.5.

This means that there are many more homophones than in native-speaker English, for example, *bad*, *bard*, *bird* and *bud* are all pronounced [bad]. Again there is variation in the mid vowels between [e] and [ɛ], and [o] and [ɔ],

Table 8.4 Kenyan vowels

[fit] *feet*	[fud] *food*	[fit] *fit*	[put] *put*
[fet] *fate*	[bot] *boat*	[met] *met*	[pot] *pot*
[fat] *fat*	[kam] *calm*	[kat] *cut*	[θot] *thought*
[faɪt] *fight*	[toʊn] *town*	[bɔɪ] *boy*	[san] *son*

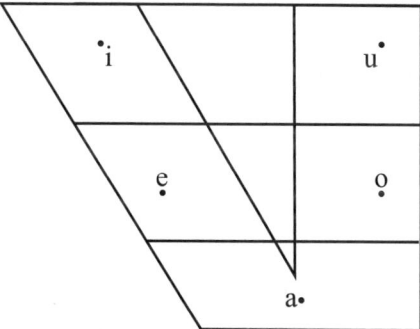

Figure 8.5 Kenyan monophthongs.

and the duration of vocoid articulations is variable. Some of the variation (in both vowels and consonants) can be accounted for by features from the local languages, for instance, a Kikuyu speaker sounds different from a Kalenjin speaker. Since this accent is based largely on non-rhotic British varieties, there is no rhoticity, and final schwa is usually [a], for example, [faða] *father*, [bɾaða] *brother*, [foti] *forty*, though in pre-tonic positions and in some unstressed words, other vowels can occur, sometimes, it would seem, influenced by the spelling, for example, [akˈsept] *accept*, [pɾeˈdikt] *predict*, [oˈbe] *obey*, [in ðe ˈde] *in the day*. Example (8.5) is an utterance from a Kikuyu speaker, adapted from Muthwii (1994).

(8.5) [imadʒin ju a futiŋ fɔti kirɔmitas tu tu θiri des . . . . ðeris miʃonari dispɛnsari ðea ðe a putiŋ prɛnti osɔ]
Imagine you are footing (= walking) forty kilometers two to three days . . . . there is missionary dispensary there they are putting plenty also.

8.3.5 The legacy of Middle English /x/

In Middle English it is assumed that there was a distinctive voiceless fricative [ç] or [x] in codas, depending on the preceding vocoid articulation, front or back, respectively (remember the German pattern in section 4.4), which had disappeared by the modern English period. It has left a trace in the spelling system: most cases of *gh* in words like *fight* and *enough* indicate where it once occurred. (Remember that I warned against using spelling as a guide for learning about phonetics. This warning relates to current written English; for earlier periods written records are the only evidence we have, but they have to be interpreted carefully.) However, it did not disappear at the same rate over the whole of England and in the North it persisted much longer. (In some broad Scottish accents it still persists, e.g., [reçt] *right*.) Consequently, there are a number of accents, in particular in Lancashire and Yorkshire, where there are different vowel distinctions from in the southern accents and the lexical incidence is different. This is not the place to go into the details of the historical developments that took place, but in Table 8.5 I give some examples of the vocoid articulations involved and the distinctions maintained.

Table 8.5 Relics of Middle English /x/

[ɹɪit] *right*	[taːm] *time*	[weɪt] *weight*	[weːt] *wait*
[θæɤt] *thought*	[pɔːt] *port*		

The diphthongal vocoid in *thought* is the one that is more usual in Lancashire; in Yorkshire it is more likely to be [θoʊt], and the vowel in *right* may be [ɛɪ]. In some accents the [oʊ] diphthong will occur in words like *saw* as well.

Although it is assumed that the voiceless fricative had all but disappeared by the middle of the 19th century, it is amazing to see how long it takes for earlier forms to completely disappear. In the Survey of English Dialects (Orton and Halliday [1962–3]) one of the Lancashire informants, a woman of 72 recorded in 1954, still used a relic velar fricative in combination with a labiodental one in words like *enough* and *laugh*, and she even had a diphthong for the ME [ax] sequence: [lëʊxf] (1962–3: 1000) for what today, and indeed for most people at that time, would be pronounced [laf].

8.3.6 Unstressed vowel variation

In section 4.1.6 I briefly referred to variation between unstressed final [ɪ] and [i] in SBE. Although we have characterized English as a language with a stress-timed rhythm and a lot of reduced syllables, there is variation in the vocoid qualities in unstressed syllables. In some Midland and southern accents of

England there is clear diphthongization in [ɪi] or [ɹi], e.g London [lɛvlɹi], Birmingham [l̃ʌvɫi] *lovely*. Indeed, in broader accents from these areas, the movement for the diphthong is even greater: [əɪ], and this changes the rhythmic pattern of such words in comparison with SBE. Further north, in Scotland too, the unstressed quality is monophthongal and centralized, and may be low-mid for some speakers: [ɫʊvɫë], [ɫʊvɫë]. (See also the Scottish examples of vowel harmony in (7.31).)

Speakers from the North of England have a tendency to use non-reduced, unstressed vocoid articulations more than their southern counterparts. We noted a few such variants that even SBE speakers may use in section 4.1.6: I give further examples with northern vocoid qualities in (8.6).

(8.6) [ɛˈlɛktɹɪk] *electric*   [kɒmˈpleːn] *complain*
      [akˈsɛpt] *accept*   [sʊsˈpɛkt] *suspect (verb)*

Note that it is not all words that have such vocoid qualities, for example, *attend* would not be *[aˈtɛnd], only [əˈtɛnd].

The quality of what we have called schwa and transcribed [ə] in our broad transcriptions is also quite variable, especially in word-final position. A centralized low quality is to be heard in final position in a number of accents: [paɪpɐ] (London), [peːʔpɐ] (Durham) *paper*, or, slightly higher, as in [ɛdnbÄɾÄ] *Edinburgh* (Edinburgh). Even in SBE there is a tendency for final schwa to be lower than pre-tonic schwa.

In Norwich and Norfolk there are unstressed forms of words with schwa which do not occur in most other accents, for example, *they*, *by*, and *to* does not alternate between [tə] + consonant and [tʊ] + vowel. Consequently, linking /r/ (see section 7.2.4) occurs in contexts where it would not in most other accents, as in the examples in (8.7).

(8.7) [bəɹaːʔ] *by heart*
      [təɹəpaːʔi] *to a party*
      [gʊʊʔɹəpaːʔi] *go to a party*

Note that in the last example the [ɹ] occurs without a preceding schwa.

8.3.7 Comparisons

It is quite instructive to compare pronunciations across accents by taking a number of lexical items and giving the forms in a table. In Table 8.6 I give a number of forms to show both rhotic and non-rhotic varieties of English; in some cases I give alternatives for the same variant.

Table 8.6

	SBE	Lancashire	Norfolk	GA	Edinburgh	Kenya
bird	[bɜd]	[bɜɹd]/[bɜd]	[bɐ:d]	[bɝd]	[bʌɹd]	[bad]
serve	[sɜv]	[sɜɹv]/[sɜv]	[sɐ:v]	[sɝv]	[sɛɹv]	[sav]
cart	[kɑt]	[kaɹt]/[ka:t]	[ka:t]	[kɑɹt]	[kaɹt]	[kat]
more	[mɔ]	[mɔɹ]/[mɔə]	[mɔ:]	[mɔɹ]	[moɹ]	[mo]
sort	[sɔt]	[sɔɹt]/[sɔət]	[sɔ:t]	[sɔɹt]	[sɔɹt]	[sot]
fair	[fɛ]	[fɜɹ]/[fɜ:]	[fɛ:]	[fɛɹ]	[fɛɹ]	[fea]

Table 8.7

	SBE	Lancashire	Norfolk	GA	Edinburgh	Kenya
last	[lɑst]	[last]	[la:st]	[læst]*	[last]	[last]
man	[mæn]	[man]	[mæn]	[mæn]*	[man]	[man]
book	[bʊk]	[byːk]/[bʊk]	[bʊk]	[bʊk]	[bʏk]	[buk]
come	[kʌm]	[kʊm]	[kʌm]	[kʌ̃m]	[kʌm]	[kam]/[kom]
boat	[bəʊt]	[bɔːt]	[bʊʊt]/[bʊt]	[boʊt]	[bot]	[bot]
thought	[θɔt]	[θaʊt]	[θɔ:t]	[θɔt]	[θɔt]	[θot]
take	[teɪk]	[teːk]/[tɛk]	[tæɪk]/[teːk]	[teɪk]	[tek]	[tek]

*The vocoid phases of these words are typically quite long.

In Table 8.7 I give a number of examples of vowel variation and differences of lexical incidence. Try constructing your own tables of variation in the accents you know.

8.3.8 Some recent developments

In many of the accents of young speakers from the South-East of England there are two noticeable tendencies, in particular in female speakers. One is the fronting with or without unrounding of SBE [uu] and [ʊ]. So, *good food* may be [gʉd fʉ:d] or [gɨd fɨ:d]. Unrounding of [ɒ] usually with a neutral lip-position rather than spread has been taking place over quite a long period, and is quite widespread now, for example, [gɑt] *got*. In the transcription of accents of this kind the vocoid articulation of *last* and *farm* will have to be transcribed [ɑ:]. See if you can work out what you do yourself in the pronunciation of these vowels. The difference between central [ʉ:] and back [uu] is clearly visible on spectrograms (see Chapter Nine).

The other feature is nasalization of vocoids, even when there is no nasal consonant in the word. This occurs mostly in non-high vocoids, so we find [wẽʔ wẽðə] for *wet weather*, and London forms such as [fɑːṽẽ] *father*, [plãĩə] *player*. Many American speakers have clearly nasalized vowels, but usually only in the vicinity of nasal consonants, for example, [mæ̃n] *man*, [pẽn] *pen*, [plẽr̃i] *plenty*.

Other more general variation in vocoid articulations includes the relative height of the three short front vowels, [ɪ e æ] in SBE. In many northern speakers each is lower and could be transcribed [e ɛ a] for some speakers (see Lodge [1984]). Equally [ʊ] can be as low as (centralized) [o]. On the other hand, Australian accents typically have much higher versions: [i ɪ ɛ], respectively. In fact, it is sometimes difficult for British hearers to tell which of *pin* or *pen* is being uttered, if it is spoken in isolation with an Australian accent, or if the context does not make it clear which is intended by the speaker.

The extent to which accents heard frequently in the media have an effect on the accents used in everyday life is not clear; they may well have a fashionable effect that lasts only for a short time. However, there are two features of young people's speech in Britain that possibly reflect Australian accents. The diphthong in *stone* (SBE [stoʊn]) can be articulated with a relatively longer and greater tongue movement: [ɑəɨ] or [ɑəʏ] with lip-rounding towards the end. I have used three symbols rather than the usual two for a diphthong to emphasize the duration of the movement as a whole and the relative durations of the position through which the tongue moves. It has a duration more like that of a triphthong, but the trajectory of the tongue body is in one direction rather than two. I give a vowel diagram of the vocoid in Figure 8.6. Some young speakers, mainly from the South-East of England, use this articulation nowadays.

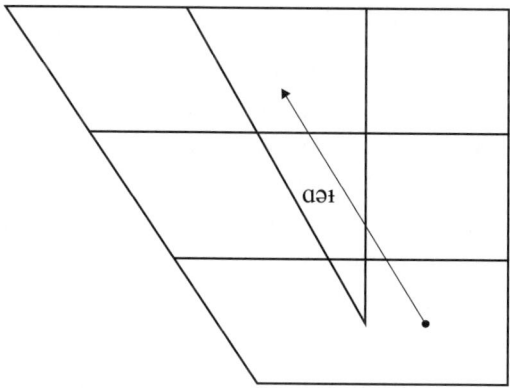

Figure 8.6 Vowel diagram for [ɑəɨ].

The other feature is intonational and we could call it Australian raising, although it also occurs in some speakers from Canada, America and New Zealand. Rather than letting the pitch fall at the end of a statement (see section 6.1), some English and a lot of Australian speakers use a rising tone. This can lead to communicative misunderstandings (not to mention irritation) on the part of the English speakers who are not used to this tone pattern.

8.4 Consonants

In terms of phonological contrasts the English consonant system varies much less than the vowels across different varieties. On the other hand, there are quite a number of interesting phonetic differences, some of which I will discuss in this section.

The phonological variation is restricted largely to whether or not an accent has /h/ and whether or not it has /ʍ/ as distinctive sounds. Many accents of English English have no words containing [h] at all. Of course, some speakers who are aware that the standard variety does have it may use it sporadically, if not hypercorrectly, for example, [ə heg] *an egg*. Lack of [h] is, in fact, a mark of English from England; native varieties in Scotland, Ireland, America, Australia, New Zealand and South Africa all have [h]. In Wales it is variable. In England the occurrence of [h] is restricted to the North-East, parts of the South-West and Norfolk (but not urban Norwich).

Earlier periods of English maintained a distinction between [w] in *wail* and [ʍ] in *whale*. By the late 18th century it was disappearing from large parts of England, but it is maintained in Scotland, Ireland, by many speakers in Canada and New Zealand, and by some in America.

In section 8.3.5 above we noted that a few broad, mostly rural Scottish accents have retained another consonant /x/ with the variants [ç] and [x] depending on the preceding vocoid articulation, for example, [hiç] *high*, [roxt] *wrought*. Most non-broad speakers retain it in words of Gaelic origin, for example, [drʌmʃʏç] *Drumsheuch* (name of a street in Edinburgh), [lɔx] *loch*.

The following variables are phonetic rather than phonological.

8.4.1 Glottal reinforcement

This is a widespread feature of many British accents; it is also on the increase in America. As we saw in section 2.2.1, SBE and most other regional British accents use glottal reinforcement in syllable-final position, usually without any release, for example, [kʌʔp̚] *cup*, [kʌʔt̚] *cut*, [kɪʔk̚] *kick*, [kʌʔp̚keɪʔk̚] *cup-cake*, [ʌˀt˺moʊst] *utmost*, [sɪˀk˺nəs] *sickness*. If there is a release, the glottal closure is released first, then the oral one. Otherwise the result would be an ejective. Indeed, ejectives are used by speakers in utterance-final position, though whether this is just a timing adjustment of the vocal cord activity with the oral closure, or there is some communicative meaning in their use in such circumstances, for example, an indication of finishing one's utterance, is not clear. So, a form like (8.8) is not unusual in a variety of accents (though this is a north-west Midlands variety).

(8.8) [av kʊm ɑm mɪ baːkˀ] *I've come on my bike.*

In the North-East and East Anglia speakers also use glottal reinforcement intervocalically, as in [peːˀpɐ] *paper*, [lɛˀtɐ] *letter*; [æːˀpi] *happy*, [pʊˀkə] *poker*. In this case the timing of the releases is slightly different in that either they are both released simultaneously, or the glottal closure may be released very slightly after the oral one. (Recall our discussion of the timing of vocal cord activity in section 5.3.)

8.4.2 Glottal stops

In terms of dearticulation that we discussed in section 7.2.3 a very likely development of glottally reinforced stops is a simple glottal stop without an oral gesture. (Note that we cannot predict future developments in language, but we can suggest what is likely and what is not. For instance, a change from glottally reinforced stops to homorganic nasals would be considered much less likely.) It may be that, at least for a time, speakers use an incomplete gesture in the direction of the point of contact, for example, the back of the tongue rises towards the velum during the glottal closure in a form such as [laɪʔ] *like*, but as the development continues the partial gesture is omitted, so that both *light* and *like* are articulated in the same way. In English accents, (non-initial) lexical [t] is the most likely to vary with a glottal stop, then [k] and least likely [p]. In some forms of London English (including what is usually referred to as Cockney) all three oral stops alternate with [ʔ], for example, [kɐʔ ə tˢɔɪ] *cup of tea*, [lɛʔɐ] *letter*, [kɪʔ də bɔo] *kick the ball*, and alternations with [p] are becoming more common generally in the South-East, especially before [ɫ], for example, [pɹiʔɫ] *people*, [kʌʔɫ] *couple*.

We also saw in section 2.2.1 that in many Lancashire and Yorkshire accents the glottal stop is used as the definite article. This means that glottal reinforcement can occur in word-initial position, too, and not just in the case of the voiceless stops. In (8.9) I give a selection of examples. Note again that the glottal closure is released before any other closure; in the case of word-initial voiceless stops in stressed syllables they are released with aspiration, just as they would be without a preceding glottal stop.

(8.9) [ˀpʰʊbz kɫoːzd] *the pub's closed*
[ɪmˀpʰʊb] *in the pub*
[ˀtʰaps bʊst] *the tap's bust*
[ɪnˀtʰæʊn] *in the town*
[ˀkɫaks stɒpt] *the clock's stopped*
[ɪŋˀkʰɪtʃɪn] *in the kitchen*
[ˀbʊs ɪz kʰʊmɪn] *the bus is coming*
[amˀbʊs] *on the bus*
[ˀdʊsbɪnz ɛmˀptɪ] *the dustbin's empty*
[ɪnˀdʊsbɪn] *in the dustbin*
[ˀɡeːmz fɪnɪʃt] *the game's finished*
[wɪ wʊŋˀɡeːm] *we won the game*
[ˀfɛns ɪz dʊn] *the fence is done*
[amˀfɛns] *on the fence*
[ˀsʊnz æʊʔ] *the sun's out*
[ɪnˀsʊn] *in the sun*
[ˀʃuuz ə njuu] *the shoes are new*
[ɪnˀʃuu] *in the shoe*
[ˀmɪɫz ʃʊt] *the mill's shut*
[əʔˀmɪɫ] *at the mill*
[ˀjaʔs ɡɑn] *the yacht's gone*
[anˀjaʔ] *on the yacht*

Note that in the case of *at the mill* the glottal closure is longer, as reflected in the transcription, than in, for example, [əʔ mantʃɛstə] *at Manchester*, where there is no definite article. In parts of Lancashire the form of the definite article before vowels is [ˀθ], as in (8.10).

(8.10) [ˀθeːɹɪəɫ] *the aerial*
[pʰʊʔ ˀθeːɹɪəɫ ʊp] *the aerial up*
[ˀθɒspɪɫ] *the hospital*
[əʔ ˀθɒspɪɫ] *at the hospital*

8.4.3 Alternatives to [l] and [ɹ]

The lateral and approximant articulations alternate with vocoids, and /r/ has a number of non-approximant variants. These are the class of sounds that most phonologists refer to as 'liquids'. Note that when talking about realizational variation of an equivalent sound in different accents, it is convenient to use the phonological representation between slant lines; remember this has no particular implications as to what the realization might be.

The distribution of [l] and [ɫ] is that the former occurs in onsets and intervocalically, and the latter in codas and as an unstressed syllable; thus: [lɪtɫ] *little*, [fɪɫ] *fill*, [fɪlɪŋ] *filling*. When a vowel-initial unstressed word follows the lateral, the non-velarized variety is used in SBE, for example, [fɪl ɪt] *fill it*, just like [fɪlɪt] *fillet*. (Note that this is the British pronunciation of this word; Americans say [fɪˈleɪ].) This example shows that quite often word boundaries are not relevant to phonetic realizations in connected speech, as in example (6.18) in section 6.4, where we saw that *at all* and *a tall* can be pronounced the same.

However, the representation of laterals by means of one of two symbols is, in fact, an oversimplification, in rather the same way as it is an oversimplication to divide the roof of the mouth into just two areas of contact, palatal and velar, as we saw in section 2.8.9. Basically the bunching of the free part of the tongue in dental or alveolar lateral articulations can occur anywhere along the front-back axis of the mouth, and it is often determined by the surrounding vocoid articulations. There is certainly a third distinguishable possibility, namely a central kind of resonance, which we can transcribe [lə]. So speakers will vary as to which resonance they use under which circumstances. A common variation in syllable-initial position is between front resonance before front vowels and central resonance before central and back vowels, giving the following: [lʲet] *let*, [ləʌv] *love*, [ləʊk] *look*; back resonance will occur in syllable-final position after any vowel: [fɪɫ] *fill*, [fʊɫ] *full*. Other speakers vary between central resonance in initial position and back resonance in final position, for example, [ləet] *let*, [ləʊk] *look*; [fɪɫ] *fill*, [fʊɫ] *full*. Amongst old speakers in rural Norfolk there is variation in syllable-final position: front resonance after front vowels and central or back resonance after back vowels, for example, [fɪlʲ] *fill*, [smɛlʲ] *smell*, [fʊlə] *full*, [fɔɫ] *fall*. Try to work out what kind of resonance you have for your lateral articulation in various contexts, for example, in *leave, luck, clear, clerk, fill, filling, salt, little,* and whether you have alveolar contact in syllable-final and syllabic positions (see section 7.2.3).

In 7.2.3 I discussed dearticulation of laterals in syllable-final position in English (and in the history of other languages). Most London speakers have no alveolar contact, so the tongue bunches in a back vocoid position, with or without lip-rounding; the quality is usually an advanced [o/ɤ]. (In the transcriptions I will use just [o] for simplicity, but don't forget the variability of the lip-position.) In some cases there is alternation in the same morpheme in different phonological environments. I give a number of examples in (8.11).

(8.11) [fɪo] *fill*   [fɪlɪn] *filling*   [tɛo] *tell*   [tɛlɪn] *telling*
       [pæo] *pal*   [pælii] *pally*   [fʊo] *full*   [dɒo] *doll*
       [fɔo] *fall*   [ʋo] *hull*   [fæɪo] *fail*   [fʊuo] *fool*
       [gʌuo] *goal*   [gʌulii] *goalie* [fɔo?] *fault* [fɪod] *filled*

The variability of /r/ has been referred to briefly in our discussion of General American in section 4.2 and in section 8.2 under rhoticity. The main variants are an alveolar approximant [ɹ] or a retroflex one [ɻ], even in non-rhotic accents. For example, speakers in Norwich, which is non-rhotic, vary from individual to individual between the two, for example, [nɑɹɪdʒ] or [nɑːɻɪdʒ] *Norwich*. (The lengthening of the vocoid seems to be more likely with the retroflex version.) We also noted in 2.9.6 that speakers in the West Midlands use a tap in intervocalic and post-consonantal positions, for example, [fɛɾii] *ferry*, [θɾii] *three*. Many Scottish speakers also use a tap in these environments. Incidentally, the apical trill [r], which is supposedly typically Scottish, is, in fact, rare in Scottish speakers today, the two main variants being the alveolar approximant [ɹ] and the tap [ɾ]. One variant that is disappearing is the uvular approximant [ʁ], which was quite widespread fifty years ago in the North-East of England. (Those readers who know the British comedy series *Last of the summer wine* should watch episodes from the 1980s in which Nora Batty's husband, Wally, appears. The actor, Joe Gladwin, uses a uvular approximant. He also did voice-overs for the Hovis adverts of the time, e.g., [ɪ wəʁ ə gʁeːʔ beːkə wəʁ aʊə dad] *He were a great baker, were our dad*.)

A recent development of /r/ in non-rhotic accents is the increase in the use of [ʋ]. Since the Second World War this form of articulation has been on the increase amongst adult speakers. It has long been recognized as a form used by young children during the early stages of acquisition; after the age of about seven or eight there is a replacement by [ɹ], the adult target. However, there are now far more adults using the labiodental approximant, so the transition to an alveolar posture does not occur. So, this is yet another feature of speech in modern Britain that you should listen out for and see whether, in fact, you use the labiodental variant yourself. It seems that rhotic speakers do not use the labiodental articulation, at least not before another consonant. Whether or not linking *r* (see section 7.2.4) matches the labiodental articulation in all individuals needs systematic investigation.

One possible explanation for the almost universal occurrence of [ʋ] in young English children is that many adults use either slight lip-rounding or a labiodental posture without any contact when articulating [ɹ]. Since young children use both their eyes and ears to observe their carers' speech production, they can see any different position of the lips, and can replicate it much more easily than try to work out the relatively difficult posture of the tongue near to the alveolar ridge. Since, too, it is assumed that children know more of the adult phonology than they can produce in the early stages, when motor control is far from perfect, it is also assumed that they try to produce differences that they are aware of, even if it is in a non-adult way. So, in the first attempts a child may produce [w] for adult [w] and [ɹ], and then change the articulation of the latter by mimicking the lip-position of the adult speakers, producing [ʋ]. How the later transition to [ɹ] occurs (or not, as the case may be) is more difficult to explain, as there is no obvious phonetic continuity between [ʋ] and [ɹ]. It seems that working out the alveolar approximant posture is difficult for some speakers at least. Since future developments cannot be predicted, it is impossible to say whether new generations of children with parents who use [ʋ] will also use [ʋ], or whether interaction with [ɹ]-users will maintain [ɹ]. Note, too, that metaphors of competition between forms are sometimes used, but there is no evidence that one single form is the norm or ideal to be aimed at; all the evidence suggests that variation is the norm, so alternatives co-exist, but not necessarily as competitors.

Kelly and Local (1986) show that in their informants' speech the following patterns of resonance, that is, frontness and backness, in /l/ and /r/, as exemplified in Table 8.8. Try to work out what kind of resonance you use in your version of /r/, and see if what you do for both /l/ and /r/ fits with the findings of Kelly and Local.

Table 8.8 Resonance features of /l/ and /r/

1. [l] front	[ʋ] back
2. [ɹ] front	[l] back
3. [l] front	[ɹ] back

8.4.4 Lenition

We discussed this in section 7.2.2 as a phenomenon found in many languages, both as a historical process of development and involved in alternating forms in some varieties of English. In English the commonest place for lenition to occur is intervocalically. This can occur even in SBE, for example, [peɪɸə] *paper*, [lesə] *letter*, [kɪçɪŋ] *kicking*, [ɹʌβə] *rubber*, [læzə] *ladder*, [wæɣɪŋ] *wagging*. The British accent that has quite striking instances of lenition in varying degrees is Liverpool. What are voiceless stops in other accents of English are affricated in initial position of a stressed syllable, for example, [tˢɛn] *ten*, [kˣʊm] *come*; in intervocalic or final position they may be fricatives, for example, [bɛɪçə] *baker*, [bʊx] *book*.

8.5 Practice

Listen to as many varieties of English as you can, and practise transcribing them. There are a number of recordings available, usually accompanying books, that are a good starting point, for example, Hughes, Trudgill and Watt (2005). For extra practice listening to less usual sounds being used in English, watch cartoon films such as Deputy Dawg, Looney Tunes or Walt Disney's Mickey Mouse. For instance, Deputy Dawg and Goofy use implosives rather than egressive stops. Sample transcriptions of various British and American English accents can be found in numerous studies, for example, Trudgill (1974), Wells (1982), Lodge (1984), Sebba (1993) and Shockey (2003).

Acoustic Phonetics 9

Chapter Outline

9.1	Sound waves	185
9.2	Periodic waves	187
9.3	Frequencies and formants	190
9.4	Contoid articulations	206
9.5	Approximants	216
9.6	Narrow-band spectrograms and harmonics	218
9.7	Practice and further reading	222

Having looked at articulation in some detail, it is now time to consider the acoustic analysis of speech. The imbalance in terms of chapters on each aspect of speech is not intended to reflect relative importance. Although there is a tendency these days to rely more on acoustic analysis than, say, impressionistic transcription, I would suggest that both are equally important, as is an understanding of the relationship between the two, articulation and acoustics. Every articulatory movement and posture has its own acoustic effects. However, in a book of this nature it is probably only necessary to understand the basics of acoustic analysis and leave the theoretical aspects to other publications. (It is rather like learning to drive a car: it is not necessary to understand the theory and workings of the internal combustion engine and the computational help it gets in order to drive successfully.) So, sufficient useful information about acoustic phonetics can be given in one chapter to provide a basis for analysis and for checking our articulatory descriptions. Remember that in section 2.9.4 I said that the articulatory descriptions of the cardinal vowels were somewhat dubious, especially as regards the back ones; acoustic analysis helps us to confirm (or otherwise) what we think we hear. Similarly, if we find it difficult to determine whether an articulation is a stop or a fricative, or a fricative or an approximant, then we can use acoustic clues to decide. It is not a question of one form of description of speech being better or more reliable than the other (despite the fact that one looks more 'scientific' because it is based on an understanding of acoustics), rather they can support one another and are often simply alternative ways of interpreting the facts of articulation. To take a simple example, let us consider Silverman's discussion of nasal sounds involved in nasal assimilation in languages like English and Dutch ([2006], pp. 61–69). He emphasizes the acoustic cues that hearers can use to determine the place of articulation of a nasal stop, which I list in Table 9.1. The technical terms, **formant** and **anti-formant**, will be explained below. Each of these cues has its articulatory correlate. I give these in Table 9.2. Silverman chooses to discuss the issue he is concerned with in acoustic terms because he is emphasizing the rôle of the hearer (who is also a speaker) in phonological patterning. But as phoneticians, don't forget we, too, are hearers – hearers with extra training. The acoustic cues in Table 9.1 help us to confirm (or otherwise) what we hear as linguists.

Table 9.1 Acoustic cues for place of nasals from Silverman ([2006], p. 62)

(1) the formant transitions out of the nasal;
(2) the formant transitions into the nasal consonant;
(3) the location of the nasal anti-formant during the oral closure;
(4) the duration of nasalization on the preceding vowel.

Table 9.2 Articulatory correlates of acoustic cues

(1) place of release of oral stop mechanism;
(2) place of closure for oral stop mechanism;
(3) lowered velum and place of contact of oral closure;
(4) time (from start of utterance) when the velum is lowered.

We must now turn to a consideration of the basics of acoustic phonetics. The following sections will present a description of the nature of sound waves, the acoustic correlates of the major sound types discussed in Chapters Two and Three, and an introduction to the interpretation of spectrograms. One particular point needs to be emphasized: no two utterances are ever exactly

Acoustic Phonetics

alike, even made by the same speaker. Human beings are not capable of producing carbon copies of anything they utter. Add to this, that all human beings are different from one another in physical terms, then you can begin to appreciate that the acoustic qualities of any linguistic sounds are going to vary, however slightly, from one speaker to the next, since acoustic qualities are determined by the physical characteristics of the person making the sound (or thing, if it is a non-linguistic sound). So, what linguists have to do is look for generalities across speakers, but these are relative characteristics, not absolute ones. For example, when we come to look at the acoustic qualities of vocoid articulations, it is the relative differences of each vocoid for each speaker that are important. Of course, we can also do the acoustic equivalent of measuring articulation against a set of ideal articulations, as we did with the Cardinal Vowels, and take the acoustic properties of the original recording as a baseline. For the most part, however, this is unnecessary, and we can simply plot the relative distances of the vocoid articulations of a speaker's vowel system from one another, and, if it is of relevance to the project in hand, average the measurements across speakers.

9.1 Sound waves

In Chapter One we noted that the molecules in the air are disturbed by sounds (of any kind). These disturbances are known as **pressure fluctuations**, which, when they reach the hearer, cause her/his eardrum to move. The molecules of the air move together and then apart in various ways, producing a **sound wave**. In order to investigate the nature of these fluctuations we need some form of wave-analyzer in the form of an acoustic analysis computer program. There are several available and some are downloadable from the Web (e.g., WaveSurfer or PRAAT). Different kinds of analysis are available from the program menus, some of which I shall discuss in this chapter.

There are three aspects of sounds that can be distinguished: pitch, loudness and quality. We have come across each of these in the previous chapters; pitch changes were discussed in relation to tone and intonation systems (section 6.1); loudness relates to energy variation as reflected in stress patterns (section 6.2); and quality of individual sounds was discussed in detail in Chapters Two and Three.

In order to demonstrate the variations in air pressure we can give a visual representation of the waveform in Figure 9.1 of the two syllables *shoe box*, pronounced with a SBE accent: [ʃuubɒks].

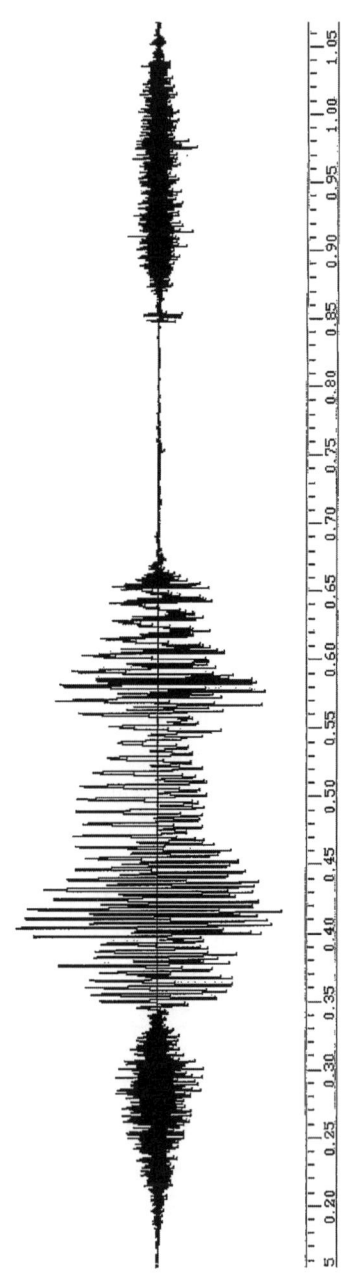

Figure 9.1 Waveform of *shoe box*.

Acoustic Phonetics   **187**

We have already noted that it is the rate of vibration of the vocal cords that determine these pitch changes. The movement of the vocal cords together and apart during vibration produces a series of fluctuations in air pressure with relatively regular peaks and troughs. If we measure the rate at which the peaks occur in terms of numbers of complete opening and closing movements (cycles) per second, this gives us an indication of the pitch. This is known as the **frequency** of the sound and is measured in Hertz (Hz). (The older way of expressing this measurement was 'cycles per second' (cps).) A sound with 200 cycles of pressure change per second is said to have a frequency of 200 Hz.

During the vocoid articulations, [ʊu] and [ɒ] in our example, the peaks and troughs are indicated by the (near-)vertical lines on either side of the baseline, which represents the ambient air pressure without any sound. The horizontal axis of the waveform represents time measured in milliseconds (thousandths of a second). The movement away from the baseline on the vertical axis indicates the **amplitude** of the sound, which relates to its loudness. In Figure 9.1 we can see that the sounds with the greatest amplitude are the vocoids; during the hold phase of a stop there is no airpressure disturbance, except for that registered by the vibrating vocal cords, if the stop is voiced. Compare [b] (voiced) with [k] (voiceless) in Figure 9.1. The fricatives have less amplitude than the vocoids, but, of course, more than the stops. Waveforms of the kind in Figure 9.1 are complex, and to appreciate fully just some of this complexity we need to focus on smaller time-frames than the 920 milliseconds of the complete utterance. For example, to determine the acoustic qualities of the vocoids we need finer visual detail than is available in Figure 9.1. We shall also need a different kind of visual representation, the spectrogram, to which we will return in section 9.3 below.

However, we can start by considering the structure of simple (non-linguistic) waves. Firstly, we need to distinguish between **periodic** and **aperiodic** waves. The former have regularly recurring patterns in their acoustic make-up, such as in vocoids in speech; the latter do not, they have a random or a non-repeating pattern, such as in the case of fricatives.

9.2 Periodic waves

Simple periodic waves are also called **sine** waves. They result from simple propagators of sound, such as tuning forks, or electronic tones. If we bang a tuning fork on a surface and then let it vibrate, the sound will fade over time,

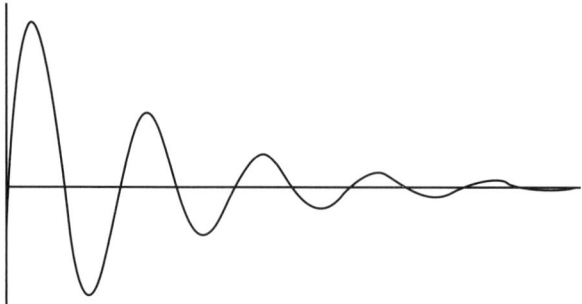

Figure 9.2 Fading sine wave.

as the movement of the prongs decreases. In Figure 9.2 I give a simple representation of a fading sine wave, where the amplitude decreases over time. On the other hand, if we produce an electronic tone, we can continue it for as long as we like, without fading. This is represented in Figure 9.3. Here we can see the three basic measurements we need: frequency (pitch), amplitude (loudness) and phase, the time at which the wave starts relative to other waves. In speech the timing of articulations is often made with reference to the start of utterance. In Figure 9.4 I have indicated where we take the measurements for frequency and amplitude.

A single cycle, which is marked by the horizontal arrow, is measured from the position of rest through each extreme point of displacement back to the

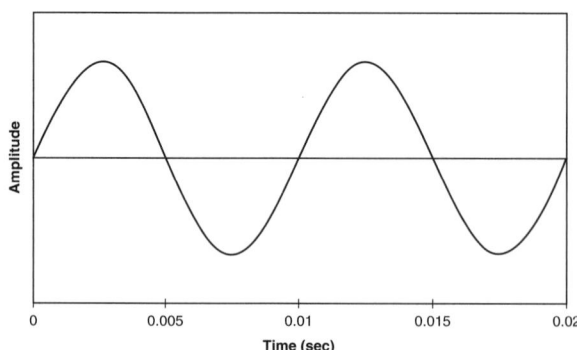

Figure 9.3 Constant sine wave.

Acoustic Phonetics

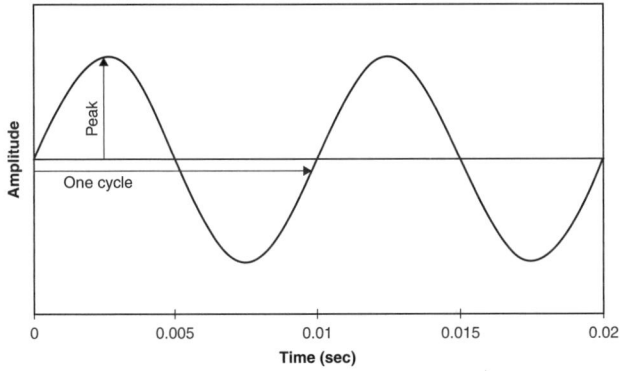

Figure 9.4 Constant sine wave [Figure 1.3 from Johnson [1997], p. 8]

position of rest. As we pointed out in section 6.1, the number of cycles per second of the wave is measured in Herz (Hz). Given the timescale along the horizontal axis given in milliseconds, what is the frequency in Hz of the wave in Figure 9.4? The amplitude is indicated by the vertical arrow, which gives the maximum deviation from the position of rest. It is usually measured in decibels (dB). This is a complex system of measurement and it is not necessary to go into the details here. (If you wish to pursue the details of measuring loudness, see Johnson [1997], pp. 51–54.)

Simple sine waves are really abstract constructs that rarely occur in actual sounds. A number of sine waves of different frequencies can be superimposed one on top of the other. Figure 9.5 gives examples of this. The closest sounds to these regular wave formations are those produced by means of simple physical structures, such as tubes. Brass instruments, such as the trumpet, or woodwind, such as the flute, are basically long tubes with a sound source, human lips blowing air, at one end and mechanisms for changing the size and shape of the tube, the valves of a trumpet and the slider of a trombone. Whereas a vibrating tuning fork is not surrounded by any container to modify its sound, a blown musical instrument has a tube which acts as a **resonator** to the sound source. A resonator makes the sound more complex and in the case of speech, we have seen that the sound source is the vocal cords vibrating in the glottis and the tube is made up of the throat and the oral cavity with or without the nasal cavities.

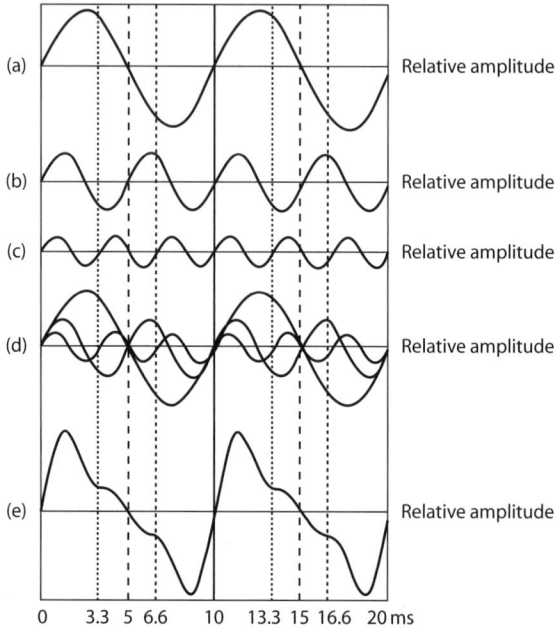

Figure 9.5 Complex sine waves.

9.3 Frequencies and formants

We saw in Chapter One, Figures 1.1 and 1.2, the plots of the changes in pitch of the fundamental frequency of two different English utterances. In Chapter Six, Figures 6.2–6.5 were spectrographic representations of further English utterances. In the case of the F0 plots, only a small amount of information relating to the frequencies involved is given, enough to demonstrate the intonation pattern that was used. But if we want fuller information about the other frequencies involved in the articulation, then we need the complete spectrogram. Spectrograms can be generated by a number of different software packages, such as those referred to above.

In the acoustic record of vowels we can see that there are patterns of horizontal dark bands for their duration. Some of these, in fact, change frequency during their articulation, but for the time being we will consider relatively steady-state articulations, in which the bands are horizontal. The dark bands represent the overtones of the fundamental frequency, also called **formants**. These overtones are a result of the complex nature of the vocal apparatus, and vary according to the positioning of the tongue in relation to the rest of the articulators in vocoid (and other) articulations. (The details of the relationship between the configuration of the articulators and the formant structures of linguistic sounds are complex and need not concern us here; for a proper treatment, see Ladefoged [1996] or Johnson [1997].) The differences in formant structure reflect the differences in quality of vocoid articulations.

If we take a simple monophthongal vocoid in the vicinity of CV1 [i] spoken in isolation, we will generate a spectrogram as in Figure 9.6. The horizontal axis represents time in milliseconds and the vertical axis the frequency (up to 7500 Hz). From this we can read the frequencies of the first, second and third formants (from the bottom of the representation upwards). In order to take a single measurement of the formant frequency we take roughly the median line of the dark band, as indicated by the arrows, so in Figure 9.6 the first formant (F1) is at 250 Hz, F2 at 2100 Hz and F3 at 3200 Hz.

As an initial comparison we can look at the formant structure of the position of rest, [ə], which is usually assumed to be: F1: 500; F2: 1500; F3: 2500 (see Ladefoged [2006], p. 182). Figure 9.7 is the spectrogram of an actual utterance of [ə]. This instance has a formant structure: F1: 550; F2: 1400; F3: 2750. For the moment, just notice two things: F1 of [i] is lower than for [ə], and F2 is higher.

In Figure 9.8 I give spectrograms of isolated [e], [ɛ] and [a]. Notice how F1 is progressively higher and F2 progressively lower. In Figure 9.9 we have [u], [o], [ɔ] and [ɑ]. Again, F1 is lower, the higher the tongue position is; on the other hand, F2 is relatively lower in the case of the back vowels compared to the front ones. Look at the distance between F2 and F3 in each case. Write out the formant structure for each of the vocoids in Figures 9.8 and 9.9.

The relationship between F1 and F2 determines the acoustic quality of the vocoid articulations. In an idealized schema, as in Figure 9.10, the F1 measurement correlates with the length of the pharyngeal cavity. The longer the cavity, the lower F1 will be; the shorter it is, the higher F1 will be. This correlates with tongue-height; the pharyngeal tube continues into the mouth and is narrowed in varying degrees by the movement up and down of the tongue. Similarly, F2 correlates with the length of the oral cavity in terms of frontness and backness of the tongue body. The longer the front cavity, the lower F2 will be (= back vowels); the shorter it is, the higher F2 will be (= front vowels). Schwa, as a central vowel has F1 and F2 values roughly in between the two extremes. For a more technical account of the acoustics of vocoids, see Johnson ([1997], pp. 91–109.)

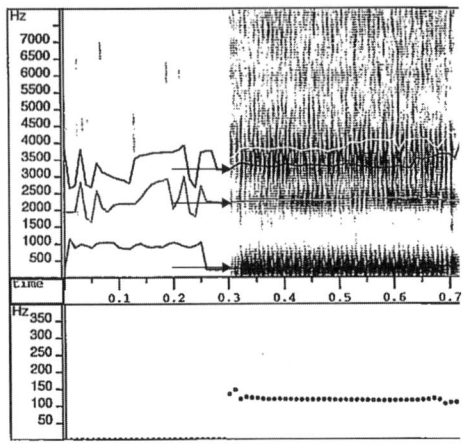

Figure 9.6 Spectrogram of [i].

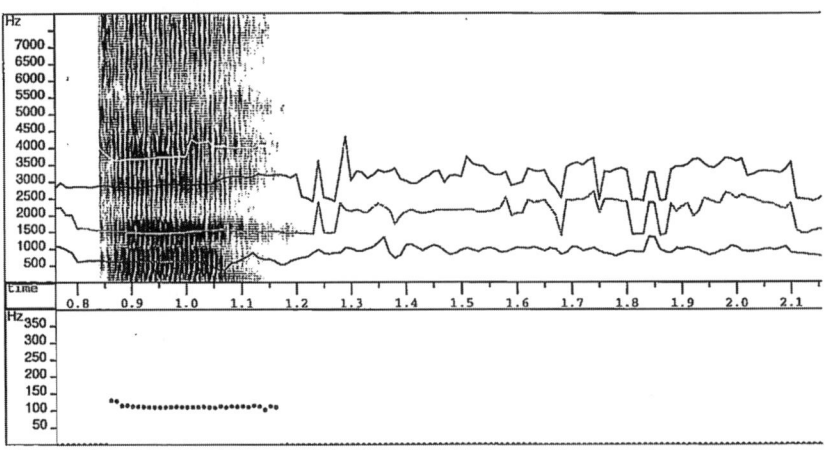

Figure 9.7 Spectrogram of [ə].

Acoustic Phonetics 193

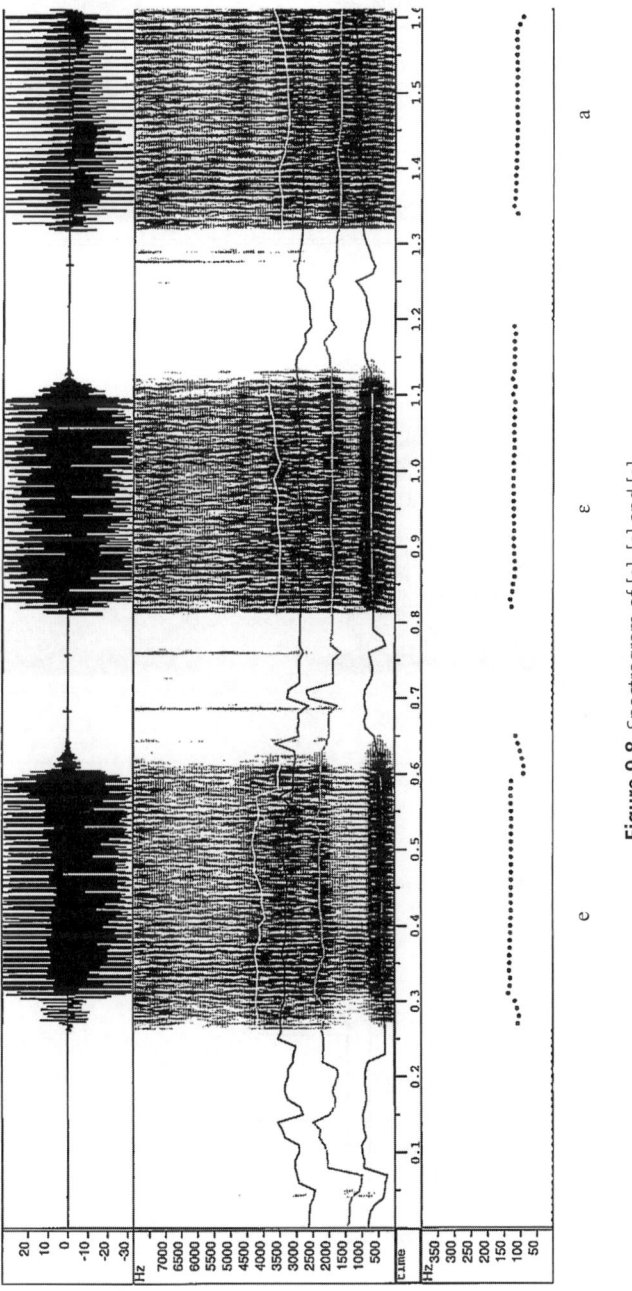

Figure 9.8 Spectrogram of [e], [ɛ] and [a].

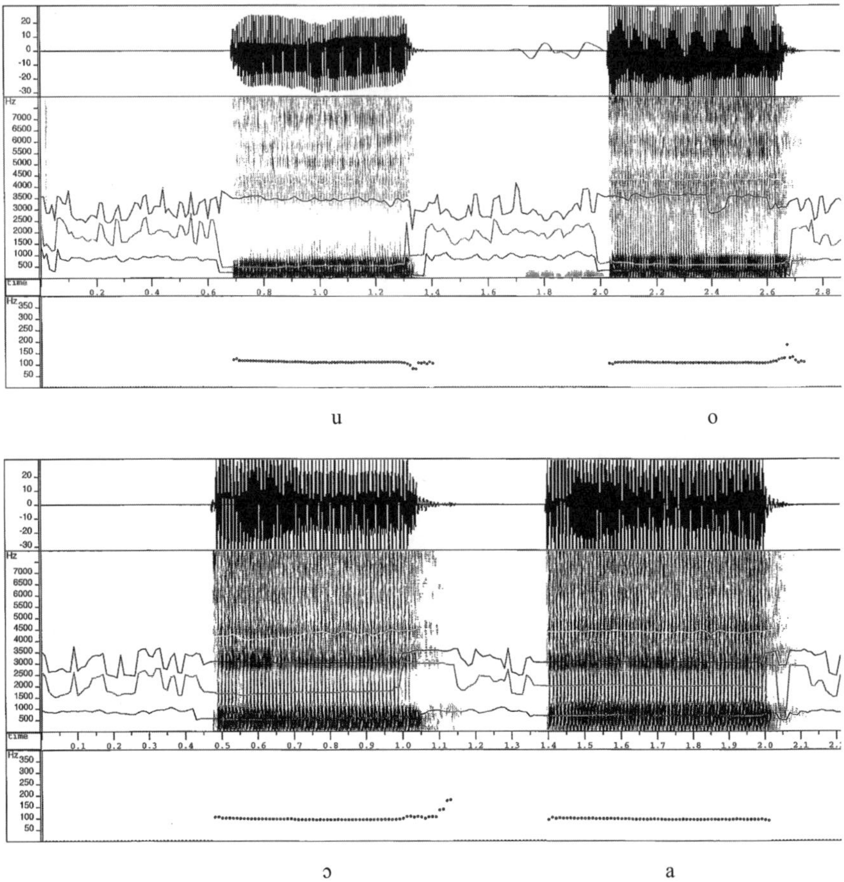

194 A Critical Introduction to Phonetics

u   o

ɔ   a

Figure 9.9 Spectrograms of [u], [o], [ɔ] and [ɑ].

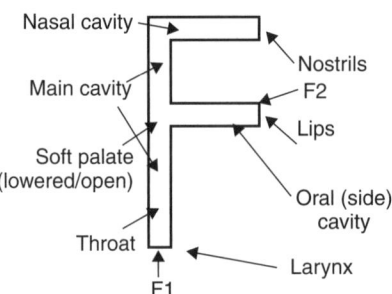

Figure 9.10 Stylized 'F' diagram of vocal tract marked with F1 & F2.

Acoustic Phonetics   195

The relationship between the formant structures and the articulatory descriptions can be seen if we plot F1 against F2 on what is known as a **formant chart**. The measurement of F1 in Hz is plotted against the vertical axis (also known as the **ordinate**); the measurement of F2 is plotted against the horizontal axis (also known as the **abscissa**). In order to allow a visual comparison between formant plots and the vowel diagrams we introduced in Chapter Two, the lowest frequencies on each axis are placed in the top right-hand corner of the chart. Figure 9.11 is a formant chart for the nine vocoid articulations of Figures 9.6–9.9. Figure 9.12 is a blank chart for you to photocopy and use, as required.

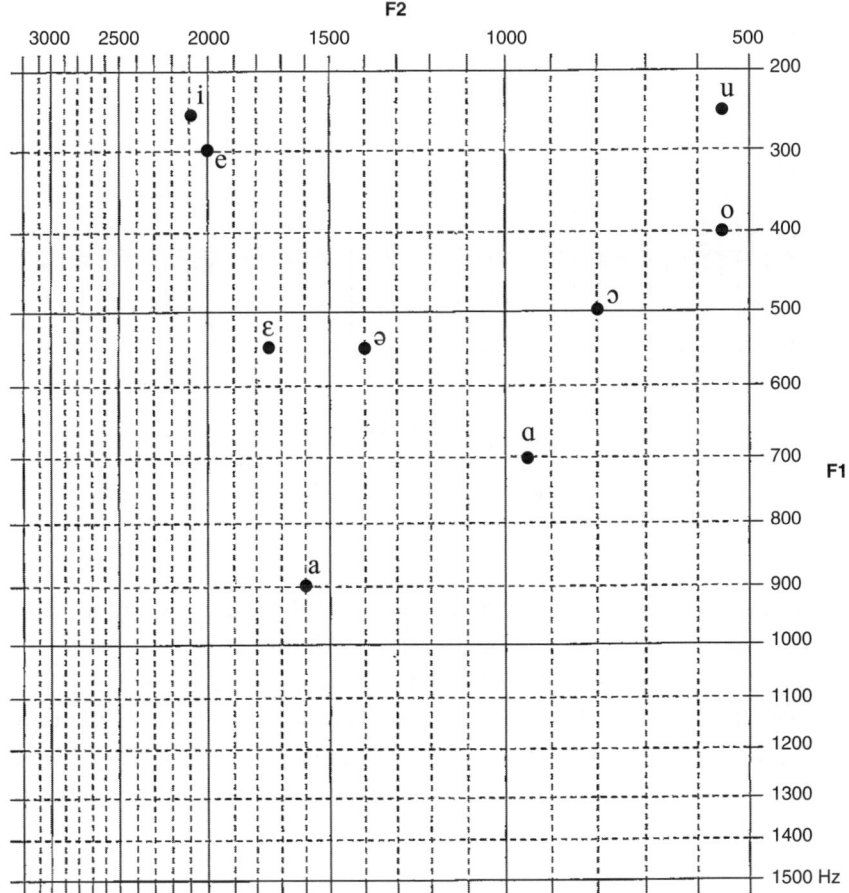

Figure 9.11 Formant chart for the vocoids in Figures 9.6–9.9.

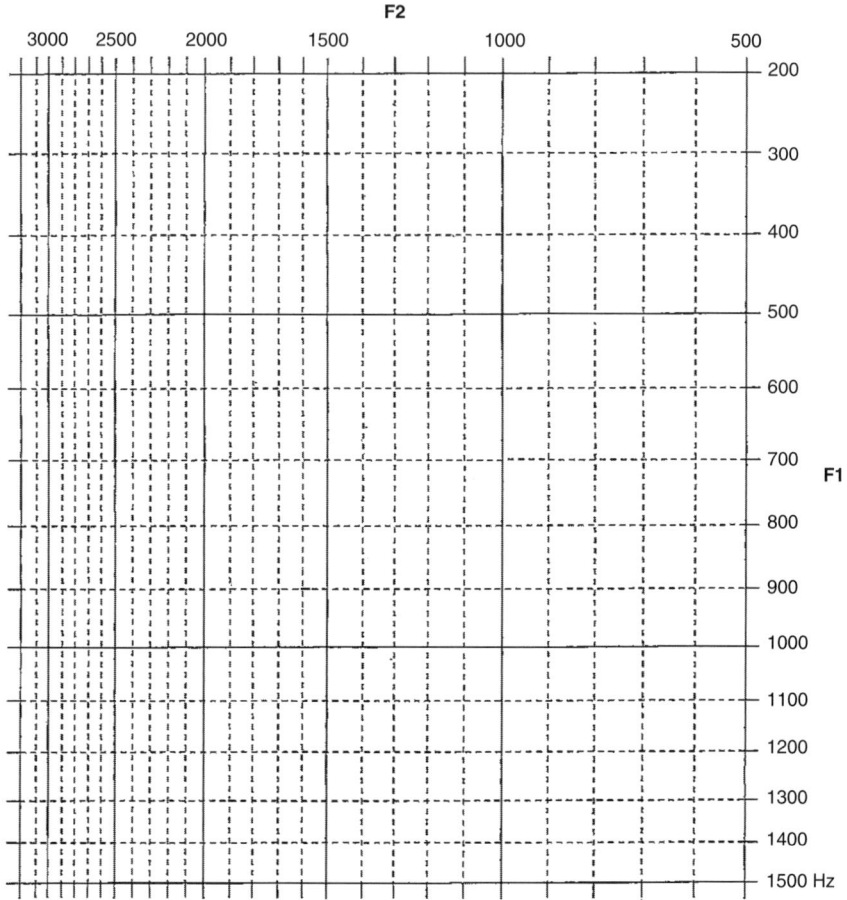

Figure 9.12 Blank formant chart.

The above, then, are samples of monophthongal vocoid articulations. But, we also saw that quite often the tongue is moved during vocoids, so I will demonstrate the effect on the spectrogram of articulating diphthongs. Figure 9.13 contains the spectrograms of [ai], [ao] and [iə], pronounced with relatively equal positions. Notice how the movement of the tongue is clearly captured by the movements of the formants. We can plot these, too, on a formant chart, as in Figure 9.14.

By using the formant structures of Figures 9.6–9.9, and by making your own spectrograms and using the readings from them, make formant charts for the following diphthongs: [ei], [ɑu], [ɔə], [oi]. Note that if you use the formant

Acoustic Phonetics

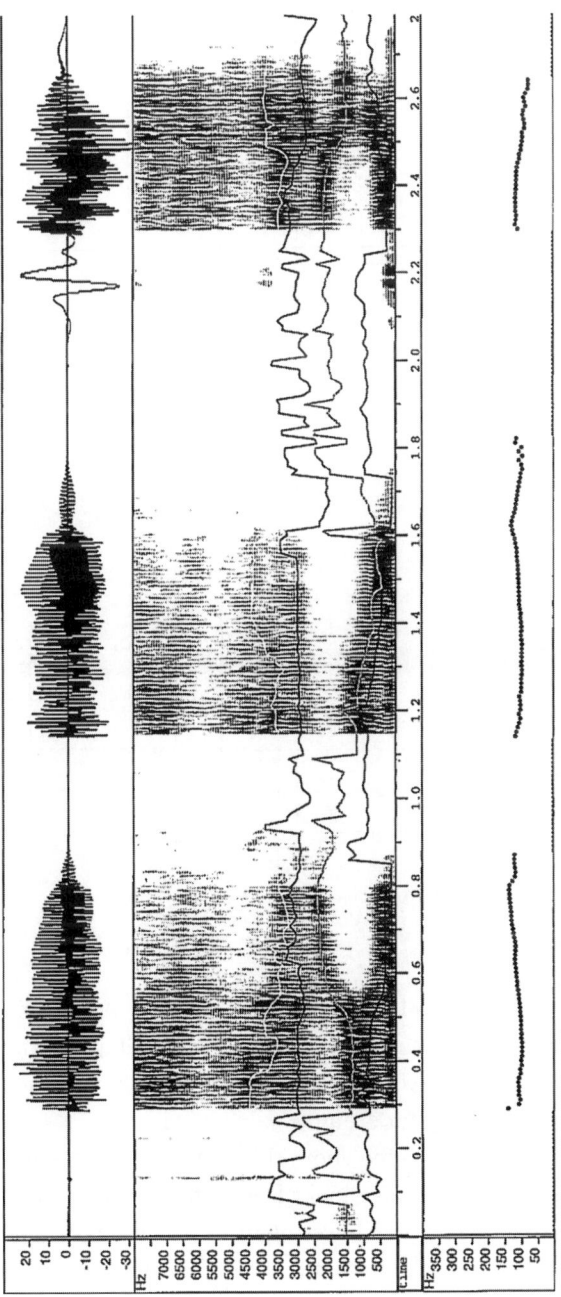

Figure 9.13 Spectrogram of [ai], [ao] and [iə].

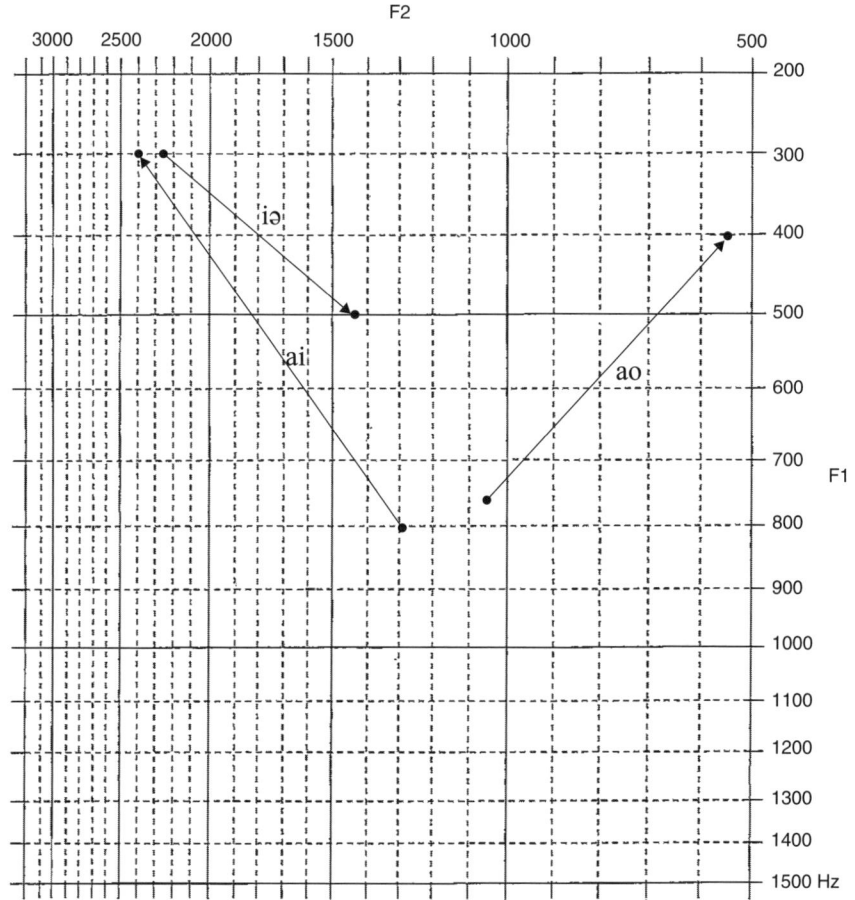

Figure 9.14 Formant chart of [ai], [ao] and [iə].

measurements in Figure 9.11, the results for the diphthongs will be conjectural; using your own recordings will give you real readings. Compare the two sets of measurements. Also compare the measurements of all the instances of what I have transcribed [a], for example.

We have not yet said anything about the acoustic effects of lip-position or nasality. Of the vocoids we have looked at so far, five are spread, three are rounded. Rounding involves the lowering of F2 and F3, as can be seen in the spectrograms of [iy] and [ɯu] in Figure 9.15. The effect on the formant plots can be seen in Figure 9.16. In [iy] F2 goes from 2250 Hz to 2050 Hz, and F3 from 3400 Hz to 2550 Hz.

Acoustic Phonetics

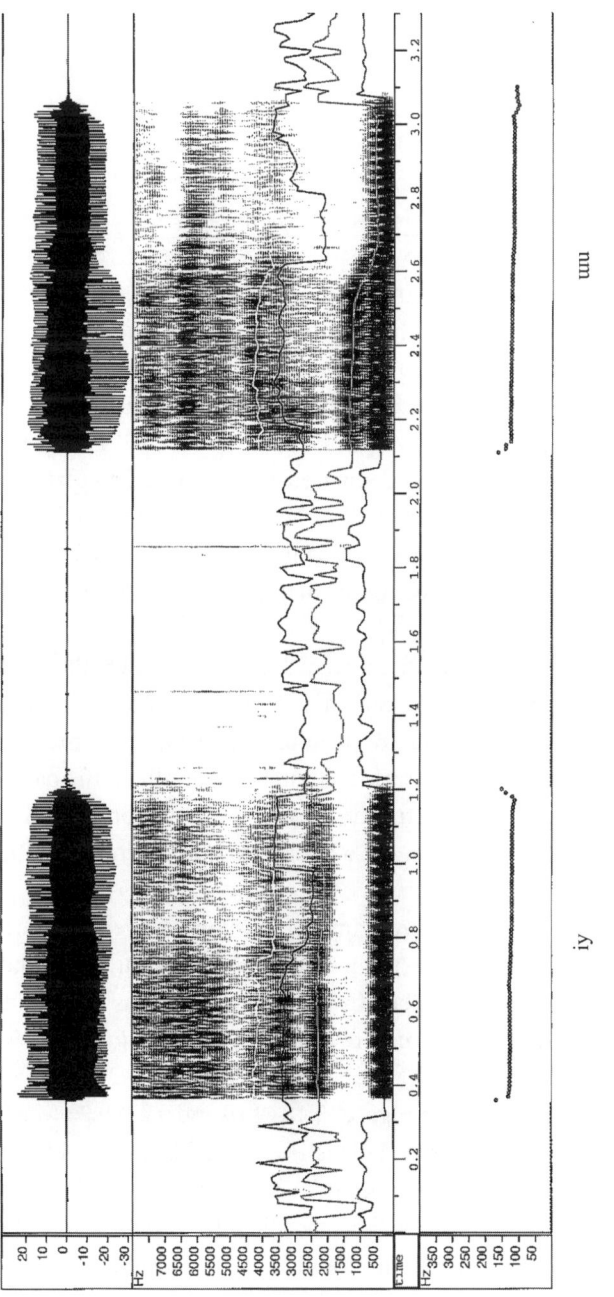

Figure 9.15 Spectrograms of [iy] and [ɯɯ].

With the addition of nasality, the pharyngeal tube is extended to the nostrils by lowering the velum. This gives particular nasal formants in both contoid and vocoid articulations. Since the tube is so long, the first formant is usually low at c.250–300 Hz, and the nasal formants appear quite faint on spectrograms because of the loss of acoustic energy in the sound as it travels over the surfaces of this long tube. Figure 9.16 gives the spectrogram of [ɛɛ̃] and Figure 9.17 that of [ɔɔ̃]. They both show the loss of energy in the fainter nasalized portions, though the nasal formants themselves are not evident.

We are now in a position to consider the acoustics of vocoid articulations of a particular speaker speaking his/her native language, for our purposes English. In Figure 9.18 I give the front vowels [ɪ], [e] and [æ]; in Figure 9.19 the central and back vowels [ʊ], [ʌ] and [ɒ]. Figure 9.20 is a formant chart for all six. If you compare these with the vocoid articulations in Figures 9.6–9.9, you can see the relative positions of F1 and F2. For instance, F1 is higher and F2 lower in [ɪ], as compared to [i], so in articulatory terms [ɪ] is lower and more retracted than [i]. Note that the (phonologically) back vowels have non-peripheral qualities, as indicated especially by F2; for example, [ɒ] is centralized compared to cardinal [ɑ] in Figure 9.9 and English [ɑ] in Figure 9.21.

A word of warning is necessary regarding the traces on the spectrograms that track the formants. These can vary during the vocoid articulation, so I have usually used the mid-point of the phase to take measurements. However, the software does not always track accurately, especially in the back vowels in which F1 and F2 are very close together, so there may be apparent discrepancies between the readings based on the actual formant positions and the position of the traces.

Figure 9.21 contains spectrograms of the long vowels [ɜ], [ɔ] and [ɑ]. Construct a formant chart for them. The diphthongs [aɪ], [aʊ] and [oʊ] are given in Figure 9.22. We can see from the spectrograms of [ɪi] and [ʊu] in Figure 9.23 their diphthongal nature as compared to [i] in Figure 9.6 and [u] in Figure 9.9.

The vocoid articulations in Figures 9.18–9.19 and 9.21–9.23 were all said in isolation rather than in words. This is because adding contoid articulations makes the spectrograms more complex even for the vocoid phases, and I shall discuss the details in section 9.4. Try recording the vowels of your own system in isolation and produce spectrograms of them and formant charts.

Acoustic Phonetics 201

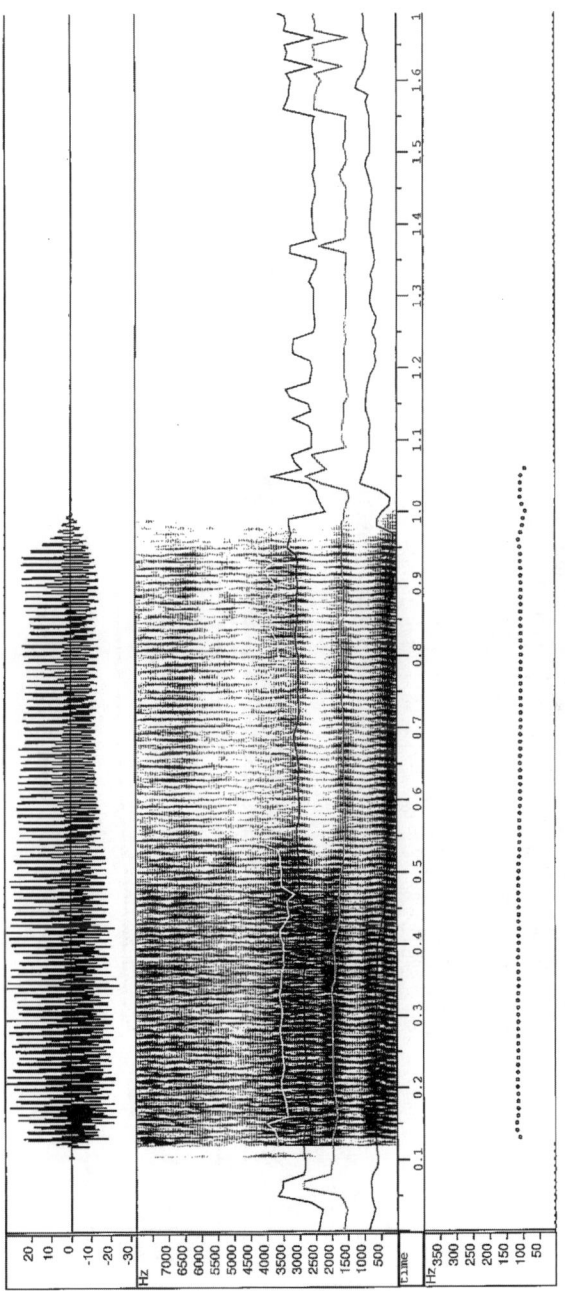

Figure 9.16 Spectrograms of [εɛ̃].

202 A Critical Introduction to Phonetics

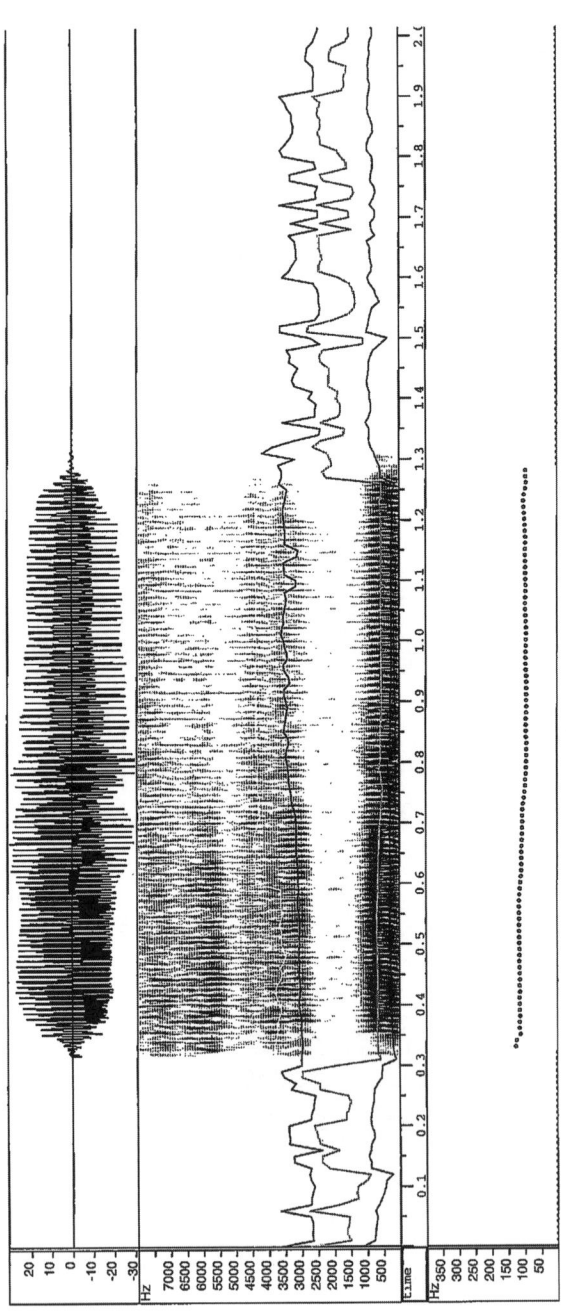

Figure 9.17 Spectrograms of [ɔ̃ʃ].

Acoustic Phonetics **203**

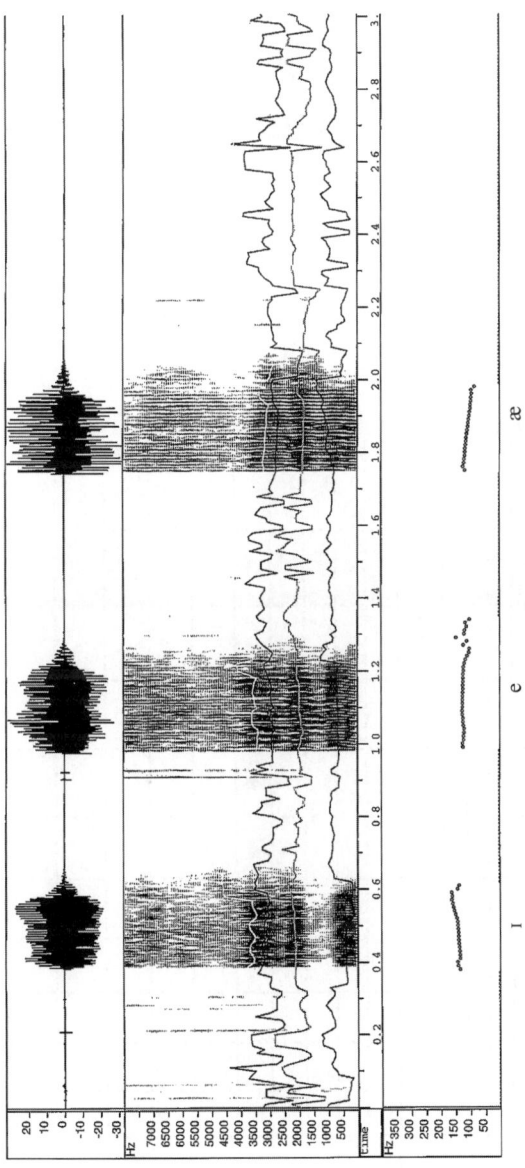

Figure 9.18 Spectrograms of [ɪ], [e] and [æ].

204 A Critical Introduction to Phonetics

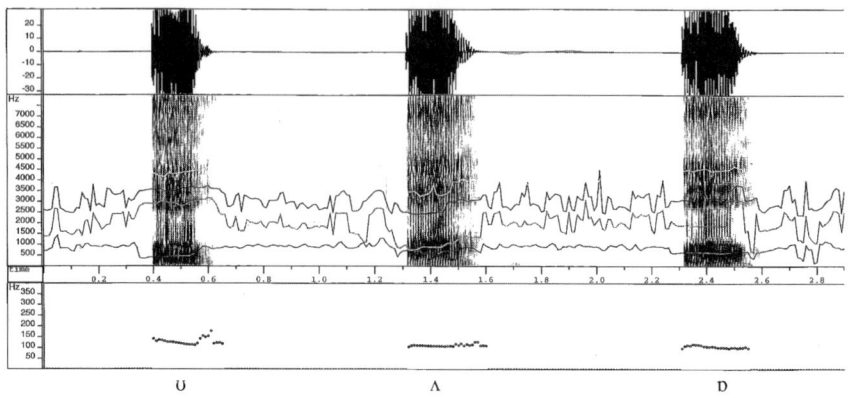

Figure 9.19 Spectrograms of [ʊ], [ʌ] and [ɒ].

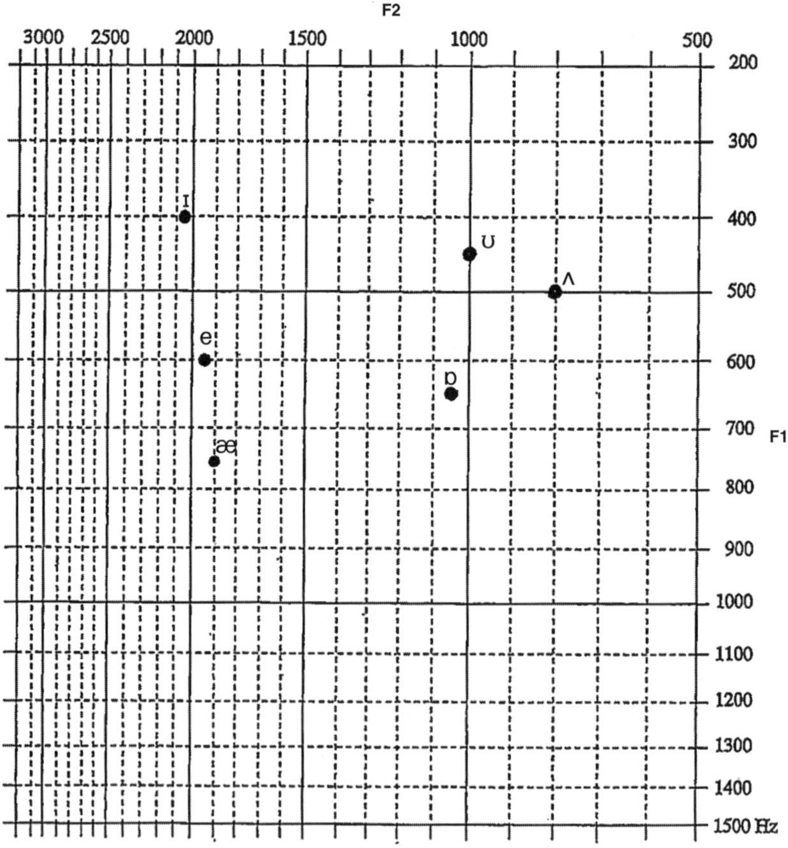

Figure 9.20 Formant chart of English short vowels.

Acoustic Phonetics 205

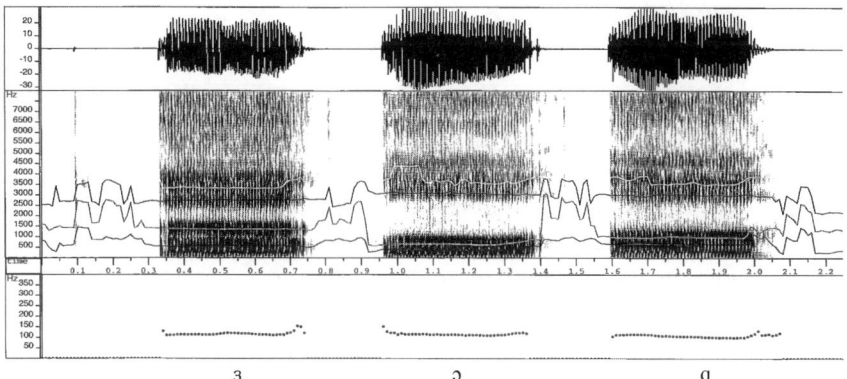

Figure 9.21 Spectrogram of [ɜ], [ɔ] and [ɑ].

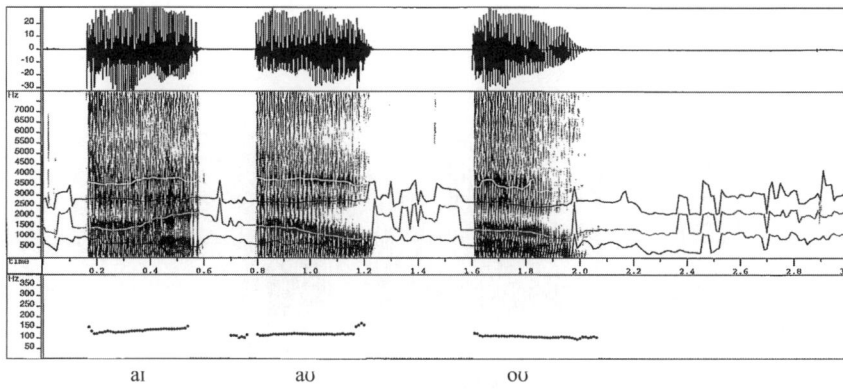

Figure 9.22 Spectrogram of [aɪ], [aʊ] and [oʊ].

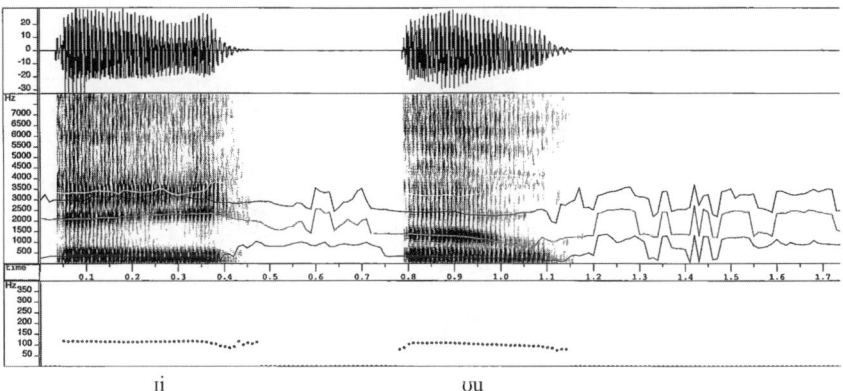

Figure 9.23 Spectrogram of [ɪi] and [ʊu].

9.4 Contoid articulations

If we add contoid articulations to the vocoids, as in Figure 9.24 [pʊt] *put*, we can see that the vocoid phase, which is still represented by the dark horizontal bands, is no longer a simple steady state (compare this with [ʊ] in Figure 9.19). Why is this? At the very beginning of this chapter I pointed out that every articulatory movement has its own acoustic effects. If you think of the details of articulation that are involved in producing [pʊt] (see Chapter Seven), then we have a bilabial hold and release at one end of the vocoid and an alveolar closure at the other. For the latter the tongue has to move from its relatively back position for [ʊ] to make apico-alveolar and lateral contacts. As the tongue moves forward, the formant structure changes accordingly, so F2 curves upwards and F3 downwards. If the vocoid is relatively low, as in [kɔt] *caught* in Figure 9.25, F1 will lower slightly, as the tongue body rises towards the alveolar ridge.

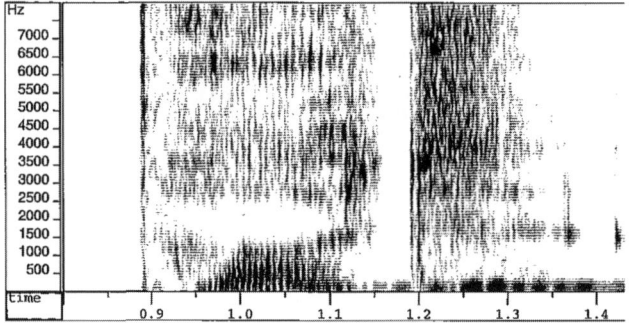

Figure 9.24 Spectrogram of [pʊt].

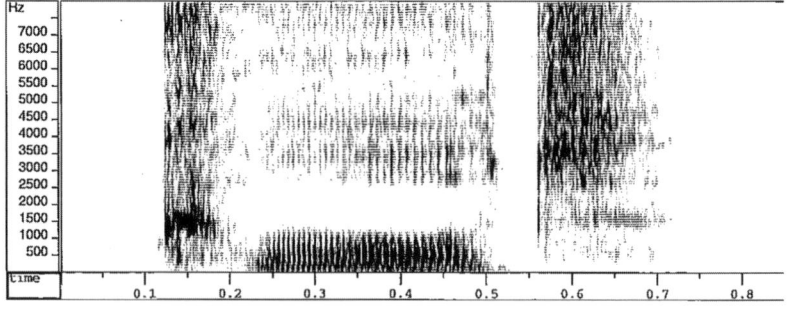

Figure 9.25 Spectrogram of [kɔt].

These changes in formant structure are usually referred to as **transitions** (e.g. Ladefoged [2006], pp. 192, 198). We should guard against seeing this term as indicating anything subsidiary; if we insist on segments as the focus of analysis, this term could suggest a subsidiary rôle for them, which is unjustified, given that they reflect the place of articulation. So, in using this term it is important to remember that they are just as significant in interpreting an acoustic record as the steady-state phases.

So, it is clear that we will find it much more difficult to fix on a steady state from the acoustic point of view when speech is continuous, even in just one CVC word. If you look at the spectrograms in Chapter Six, Figures 6.2–6.5, in which the utterances are quite long, it is even more difficult to find steady states. Of course, there are some, in particular, the hold phases of oral stops, since no air is escaping. We shall also see below that fricatives, too, usually have a stable phase. Nevertheless it is quite hard to determine exactly where the steady state for vocoid articulations is. Ladefoged ([2006], pp. 197–202) segments the spectrograms he presents, but this seems to be on a visual basis rather than an acoustic one. In order to demonstrate the difficulties involved in segmentation from an acoustic point of view, make a spectrogram of an English monosyllabic word with the structure: oral stop – vowel – oral stop, such as *put*, *caught* or *bed*. Most software enables you to excise chunks of the spectrogram by means of moving left and right cursors into appropriate positions and then play the excised part through the speaker(s). Try to isolate only the steady-state vocoid phase in your recording. Note that if you record, say, *bed*, and isolate the complete vocoid phase with the transitions included, you will still hear *bed*, with just parts of the stop phases removed. This is because the transitions are the cues you use in identifying place of articulation for the stops. When you have managed to isolate just the vocoid phase without the transitions, you will probably find that it sounds very unlike a section of human speech, largely because it is so short.

Whether or not we think it is appropriate at some level of linguistic analysis to segment acoustic records of speech, we need to be able to appreciate and interpret its non-vocoid aspects by considering their acoustic characteristics.

9.4.1 Stops

As we have already noted, there is no acoustic record for the hold phase of a stop. There is one exception to this statement, namely that the vibration of the vocal cords during the hold phase of voiced stops is evident as a series of striations along the baseline of the spectrogram, which, as in the case of the much longer striations in the vocoid spectrograms, represent each vibration of the vocal cords. The spectrogram in Figure 9.26 is the utterance [apabap] with a final release, which demonstrates the difference between voiceless and voiced bilabial stops.

The sharp spike that corresponds to the burst of noise at the release of a stop is clearly marked by arrows. Even in final position, where the release is weakest, there is a similar spike, albeit fainter. The voicing striations during [b] are absent during [p]. Recall the voice onset and cessation times presented in sections 3.3 and 5.3; we can measure in milliseconds the period before voicing begins in articulations that we transcribed [ˬb] and when it ceases in [bˬ]. If we take the spectrogram of the English word *bed* spoken in isolation in Figure 9.27, we can see that the initial stop is not voiced at all and the final stop is voiceless at the release.

9.4.2 Place of articulation

We can now return to the cues for place of articulation in stops. There are different patterns of formant structure immediately after the burst of release, and the particular pattern for a single place of articulation varies according to the accompanying vocoid articulation. Equally, there are different patterns at the closure phase of stops. In Figure 9.28 I give the spectrograms of the following nonsense monosyllables: [bib], [bub], [bab], [bɔb].

Note the different patterns of F1, F2 and F3 as they move into and out of the vocoid articulations. It is necessary to acknowledge that the different instances in Figure 9.28 are not all equally readable. This is typical of acoustic records and may reflect, in part, the amount of energy used in the individual articulation, the particular vocoid quality involved, as well as the individual speaker's voice quality. The example that is easiest to see is that of [bab]. F2 and F3 curve upwards slightly at the release of the first stop; F2 curves downwards before the closure of the second stop. Usually F3 also curves downwards at this point, but it is not obvious in this particular spectrogram. An upward curve of a formant indicates an increase in frequency, whereas a downward curve indicates a decrease.

In 9.29 I give the spectrograms for [did], [dud], [dad], [dɔd] and in 9.30 for [gig], [gug], [gag], [gɔg].

In the case of alveolar contact F2 and F3 start relatively higher than with bilabial contact at the point of release. F2 lowers in those cases where the

Acoustic Phonetics 209

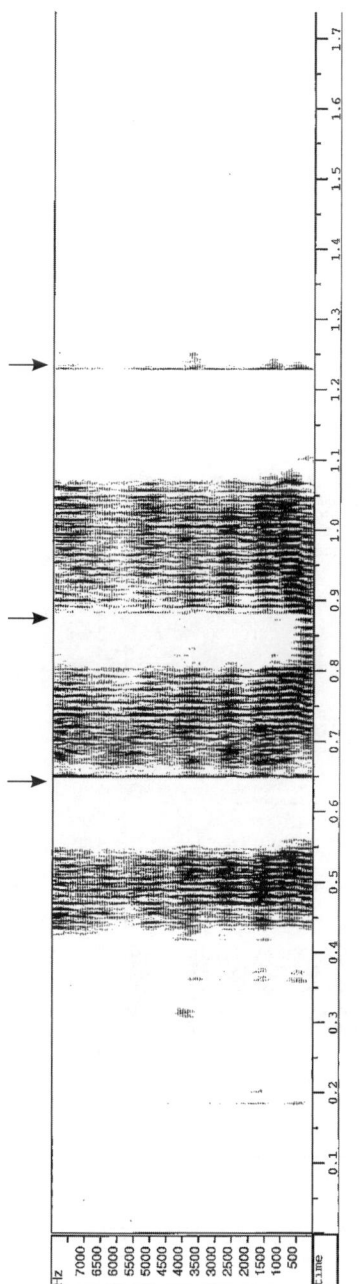

Figure 9.26 Spectrogram of [apabap].

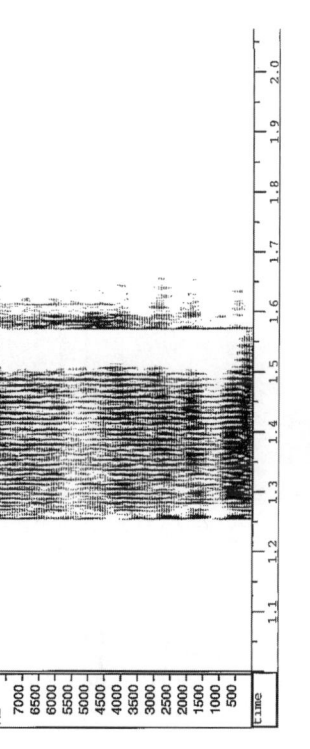

Figure 9.27 Spectrogram of [ˌbedˌ].

210 A Critical Introduction to Phonetics

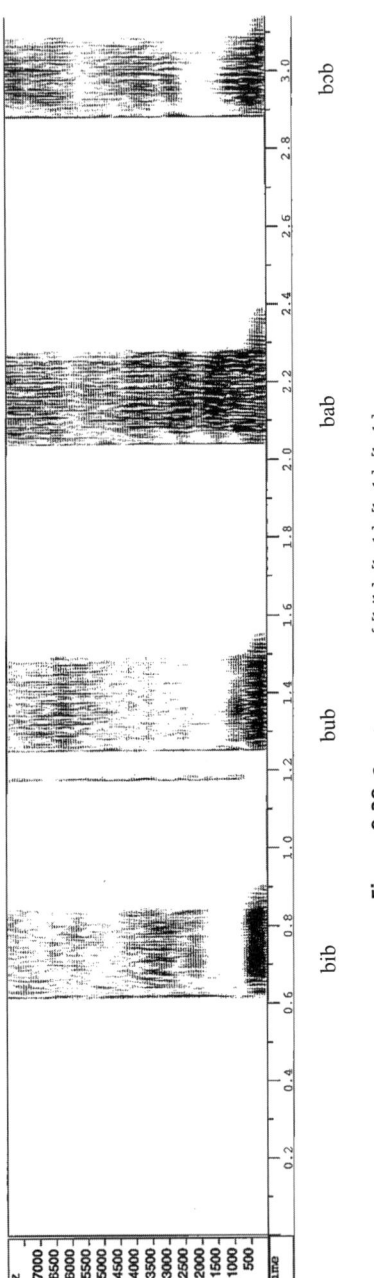

Figure 9.28 Spectrograms of [bɪb], [bʊb], [bab], [bɔb].

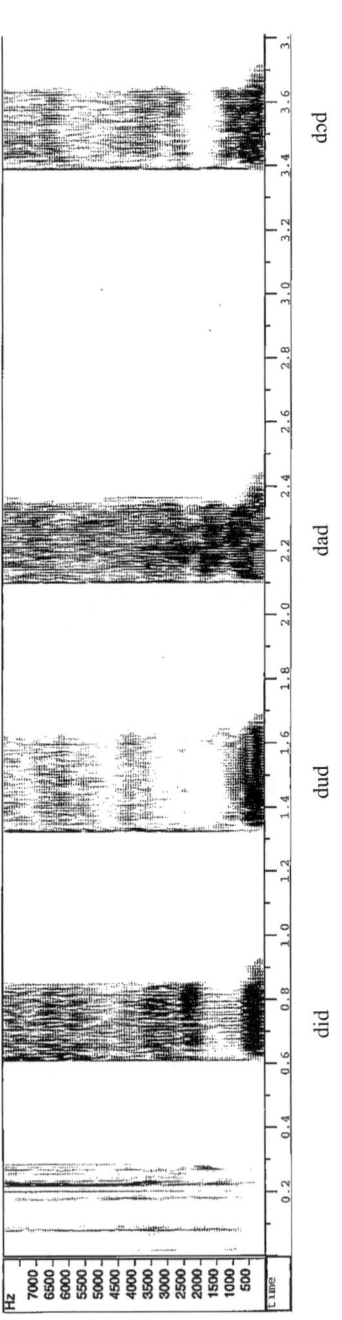

Figure 9.29 Spectrograms of [dɪd], [dʊd], [dad], [dɔd].

Acoustic Phonetics 211

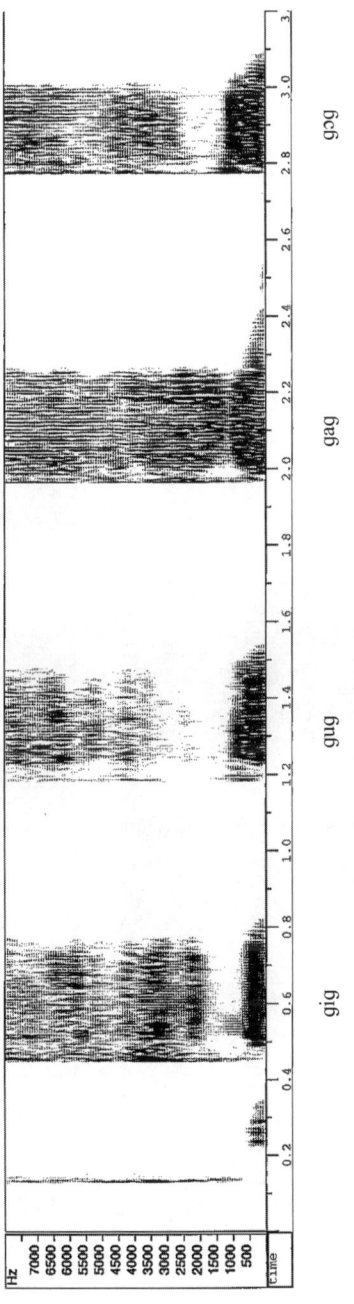

Figure 9.30 Spectrograms of [gig], [gug], [gag], [gɔg].

212 A Critical Introduction to Phonetics

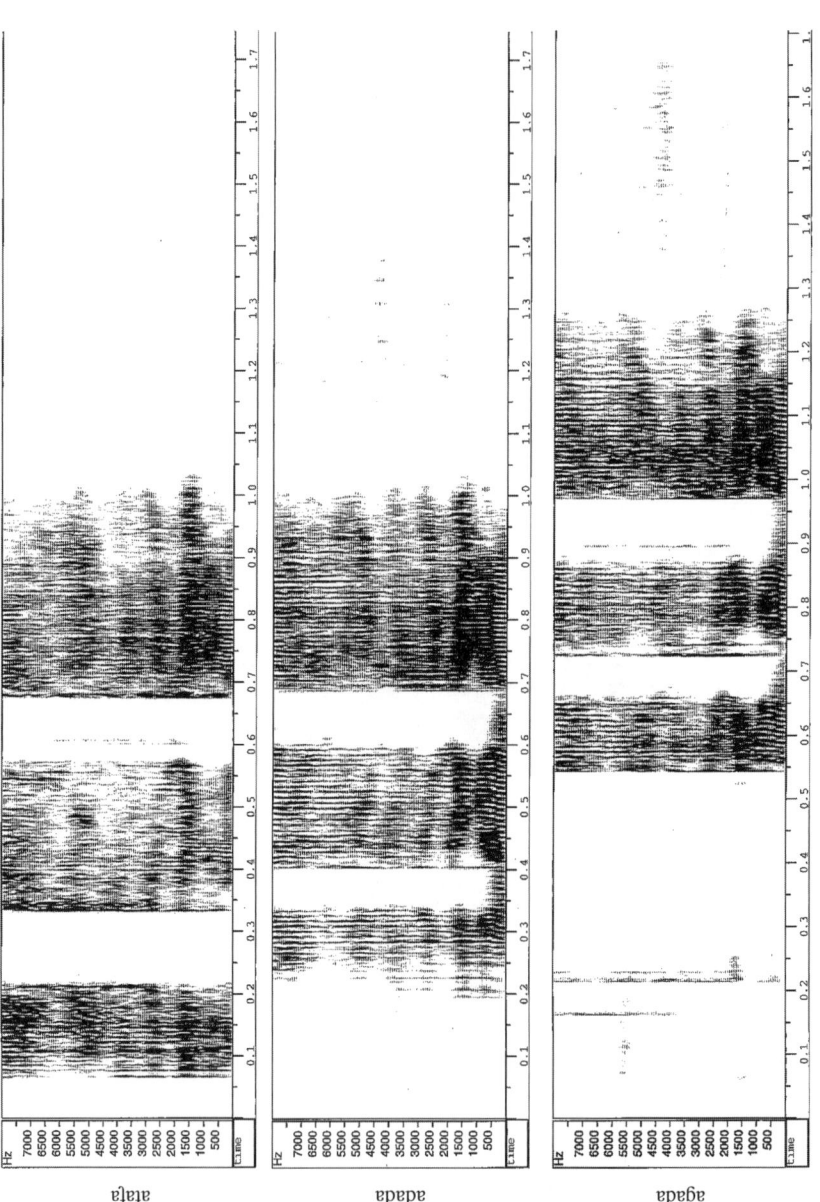

Figure 9.31 Spectrograms of [ataṭa], [adaḍa], [agaḓa].

vocoid phase requires a significant movement of the tongue, as in [dud], [dad], and [dɔd]. On the other hand, this is not the case with [did], where the vocoid is front and high and much closer to the alveolar ridge than the other instances in Figure 9.29. F2 then rises again before the closure of the second stop.

Velar contact shows a decrease in F2 and F3 at release and a pincer movement of those two formants at closure. The latter is most noticeable in [gig].

For a set of idealized representations of the release phases of [b], [d] and [g], see Johnson ([1997], p. 135).

Retroflexion usually lowers F3 and F4; compare the transitions in the alveolar and retroflex pairs and the velar-retroflex pair in Figure 9.31. The lowering of F3 is particularly noticeable before the closure of the second stop.

We will consider the acoustic effects of other places in the following sections.

9.4.3 Aperiodic sounds: fricatives

We have so far looked at periodic sound waves, and lack of acoustic energy. Aperiodic waves have random patterns, which are a characteristic of **noise**. This is what we find in the case of fricatives. The frequencies for fricatives are much higher than for the other sound types and we need to look at the frequency scale on spectrograms up to about 8000 Hz. In Figure 9.32 are the spectrograms of [fɪʃ], [θætʃ], [sauθ] and [ʃiif].

The sibilants [s] and [ʃ] have the most energy, with the greatest intensity between 4750 Hz and 5500 Hz for the former and lower for the latter at between 1750 Hz and 2500 Hz. The other two fricatives have much less intensity and are sometimes quite difficult to see on spectrograms. [f] and [θ] are also very similar to one another, even in the formant transitions, and are often difficult for hearers to differentiate, even native speakers of English, most of whom have a phonological contrast between them. This acoustic similarity is usually given as the reason why young native acquirers of English do not differentiate them until quite late, and some adults do not differentiate them at all. (I have a recording of a bilingual English-Cypriot Greek speaker from London who only uses [f] in English and even uses it in Greek, e.g., [falasa] for standard Greek [θalasa] 'sea'.)

Three further voiceless fricatives are represented in the spectrograms in Figure 9.33: [aça], [axa], [aχa]. Compare the different displays of the fricatives in Figures 9.32 and 9.33, and see if you can work out the details of the differences. Note that the second formants of the vocoid phases continue through

214 A Critical Introduction to Phonetics

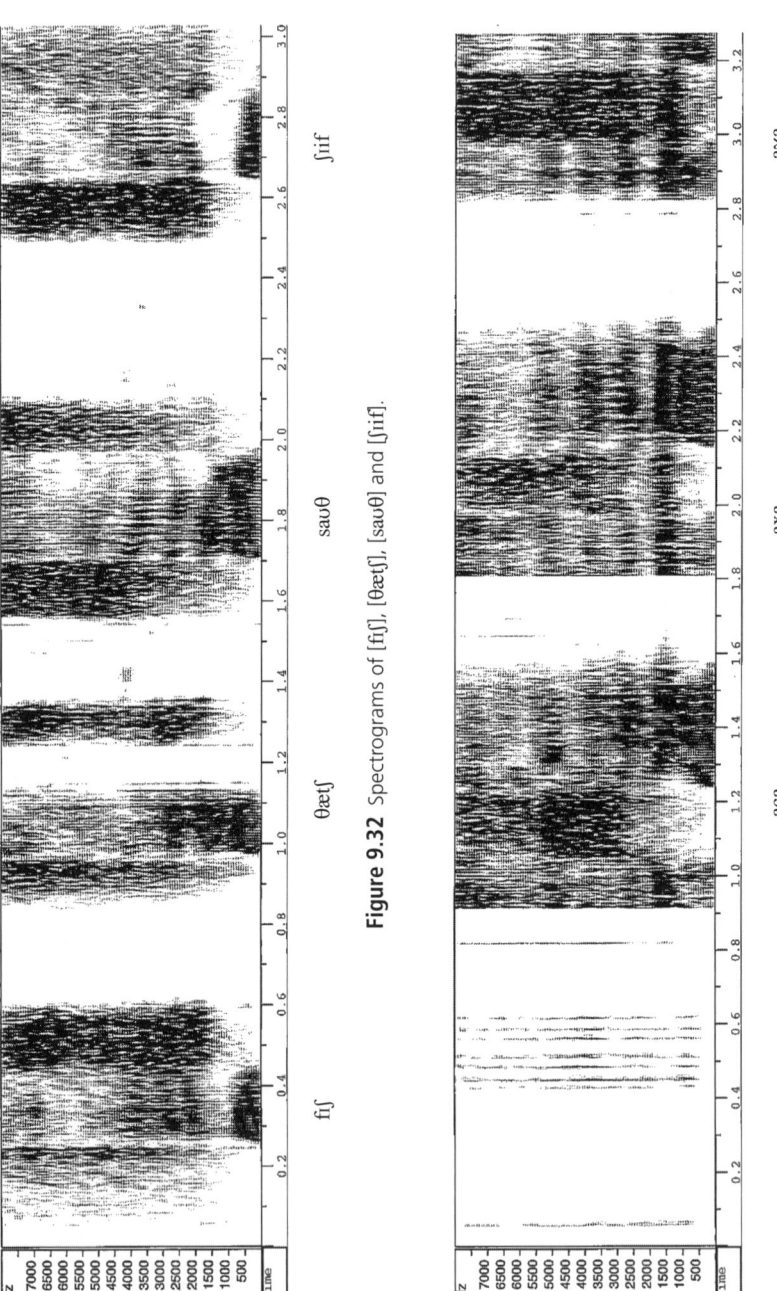

Figure 9.32 Spectrograms of [fɪʃ], [θæt͡ʃ], [saʊθ] and [ʃiif].

Figure 9.33 Spectrograms of [aça], [axa], [aχa].

Acoustic Phonetics **215**

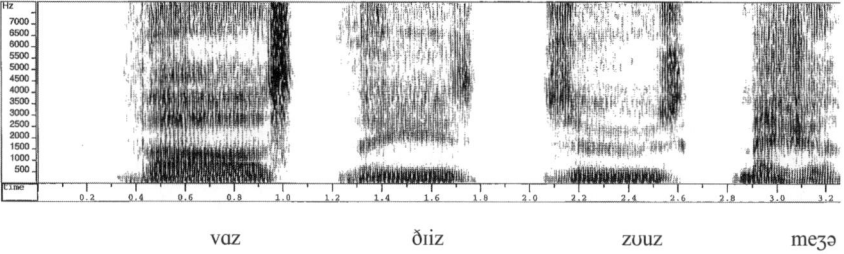

Figure 9.34 Spectrograms of [vɑz], [ðɹiz], [zʊuz], [mɛʒə].

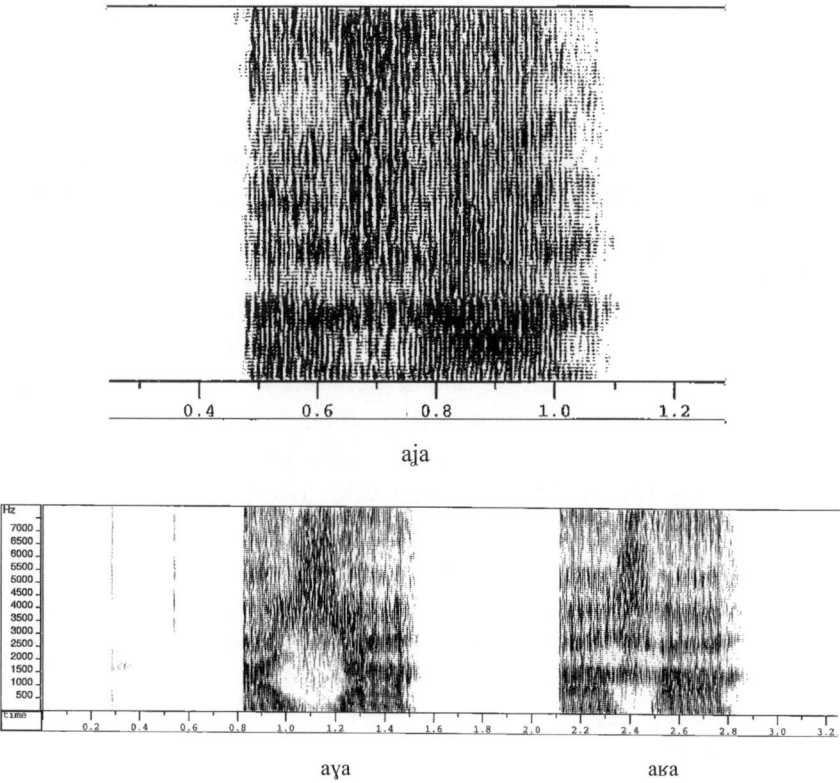

Figure 9.35 Spectrograms of [aja], [aɣa], [aʁa].

the friction giving an indication of the position of tongue contact on the front-back axis.

As with the stops, the voiced fricatives have the voicing striations at the baseline of the spectrogram, as in the examples in Figure 9.34: [vɑz], [ðɹiz], [zʊuz], [meʒə]. In Figure 9.35 are the spectrograms of [aja], [aɣa], [aʁa]. Compare the spectrograms of the voiced fricatives with those of their vocieless partners and see if they match, except for the voicing striations. The greatest intensity spread throughout the frequency range is associated with uvular contact.

9.4.4 Nasal contoids

As we noted above in connection with nasal vocoids, the nasal cavity adds specific nasal resonances to the spectra. These are usually at fixed locations of about 250–300 Hz, 2000 Hz and 3000 Hz. So even in nasal stops there is a formant structure on the spectrograms, because the air is escaping through the nasal cavities and the sound has the resonances appropriate to the location of the oral closure. Although there are distinctive formant transitions for the different places of articulation, they do not always show up well on spectrograms. Figure 9.36 has spectrograms of the sequences [abama], [adana], [agaŋa] to demonstrate the difference between oral and nasal voiced stops at the same place of articulation.

In Table 9.1 from Silverman (2006) we came across the term 'anti-formant'. This is of relevance to nasals, since it is the effect of the side chamber, the mouth, in relation to the energy peaks in the larynx-to-nostrils cavity. The air does not escape through the lips because of the oral closure, so the energy that is diverted into the mouth 'bounces back', as it were, into the energy in the main airstream. This produces an energy valley rather than an energy peak; this valley is what we refer to as an anti-formant. Its frequency level varies in accordance with the position of the oral stoppage; the longer the oral cavity (as with a bilabial closure), the lower the anti-formant, so velar and uvular nasal stops produce higher anti-formants than alveolar and bilabial ones.

9.5 Approximants

Since approximants have no close contact between articulators and some of them are, in fact, brief vocoids, as we noted in section 2.9.3, it should be no surprise to learn that they have formant structures similar to those we

Acoustic Phonetics 217

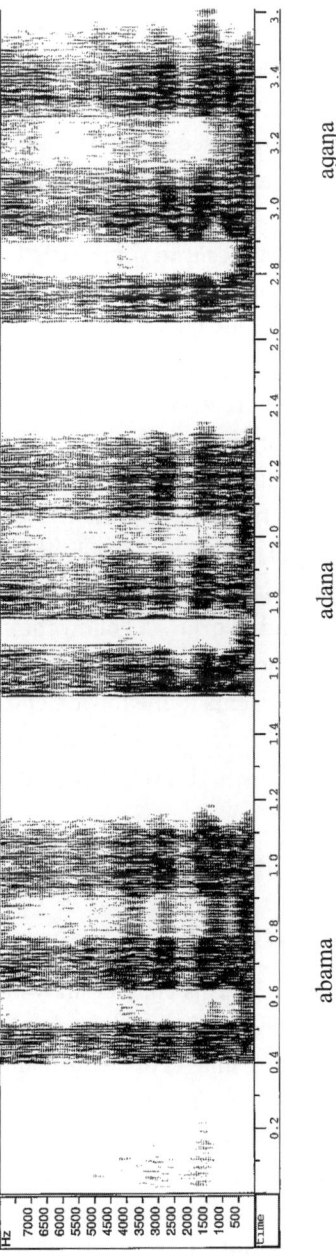

Figure 9.36 Spectrograms of [abama], [adana], [agaŋa].

discussed in section 9.3 above. In the case of the lateral approximant, this has a formant structure dependent on its resonance. An initial lateral in English typically has formants in the region of 250 Hz, 1200 Hz and 2400 Hz, but a velarized one has a different structure. Consider the examples in Figure 9.37: [let], [lʌɫ], [lɪtɫ]. Note that the higher formants often have lower intensity. In the initial laterals of these examples F2 is in the region of 1600 Hz, indicating relatively front resonance, as opposed to the relatively back resonance of the velarized examples with F2 at around 1000 Hz. Compare this F2 measurement with that of [ʊ] in Figure 9.20.

The other approximants that occur in some varieties of English, [j], [w], [ɹ] and [ɻ], all have formant structures similar to the vocoids they are related to. Figure 9.38 gives spectrograms for [aja], [awa], [aɹa] and [aɻa]. [j] has a similar structure to [i], [w] to [u] and both [ɹ] and [ɻ] have similarities with [ə]. Compare the shapes in Figure 9.38 with those in Figures 9.6, 9.7 and 9.9.

The other commonly occurring approximant in English is the labiodental [ʋ], which has a different structure, as in Figure 9.39. Here F1 and F3 dip slightly during the approximation and F2 remains steady.

To demonstrate the tongue movements involved in words that only contain vocoids and approximants, consider the examples in Figure 9.40: [jɔɹaɪ] *your eye*; [juuɫ] *Yule*; [eɹə] *error* and [weɫ] *well*. Follow the changes in the first three formants and relate them to the discussion of vocoids and approximants above. Try to relate the tongue movements to the movements of the formants.

For a comparison between fricatives and their related approximants, consider the spectrograms in Figure 9.41: [ajaja], [aɣaɰa] and [aɣawa].

9.6 Narrow-band spectrograms and harmonics

The spectrograms used so far in this chapter are what are called **wide-band** spectrograms. These are good for showing the general acoustic shape of an utterance, and produce smeared images of the formants. The software samples the utterance using short windows for analysis and gives accurate representations on the temporal dimension. For most linguistic purposes wide-band spectrograms are adequate. If, however, we wish to have more detail of the frequency structure of an utterance, the sampling can occur using long analysis windows, giving us **narrow-band** spectrograms. These can blur the edges of

Acoustic Phonetics 219

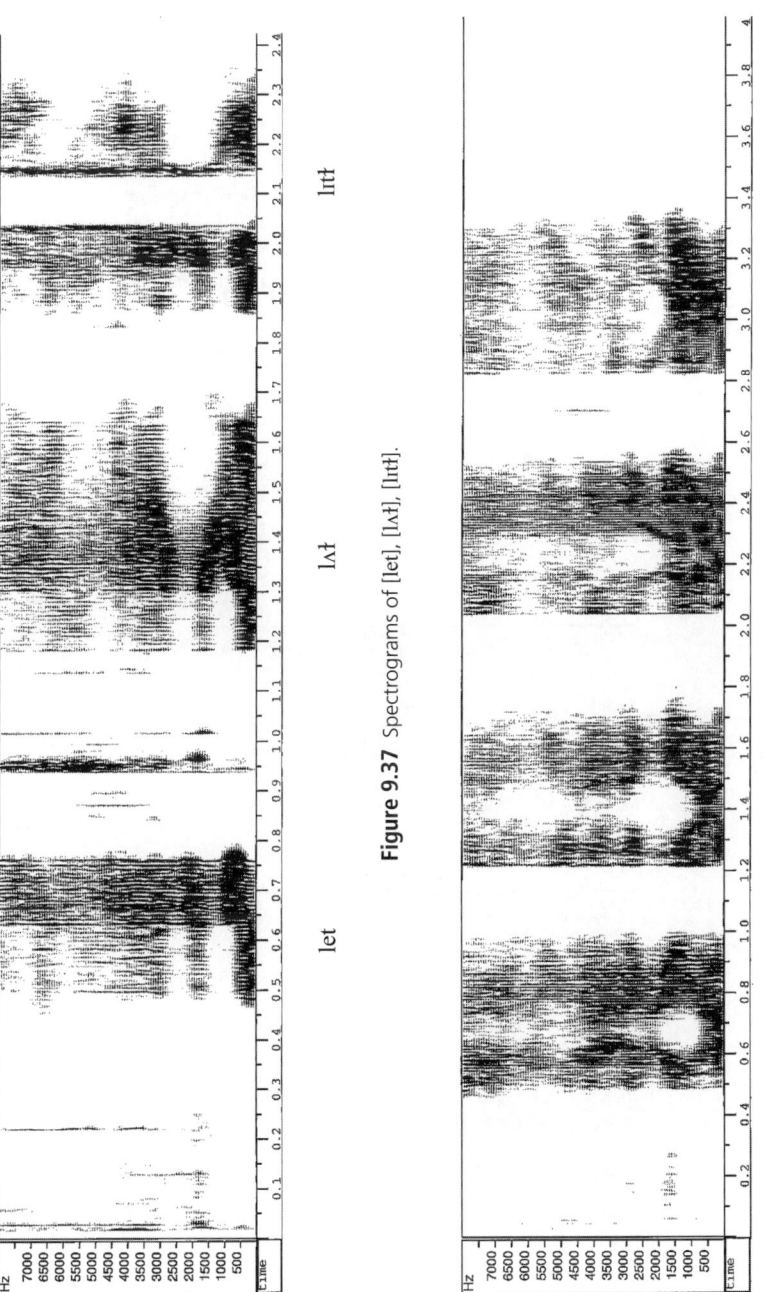

Figure 9.37 Spectrograms of [lɛt], [lʌɫ], [lɪtɫ].

Figure 9.38 Spectrograms of [aja], [awa], [aɹa] and [aɹa].

220 A Critical Introduction to Phonetics

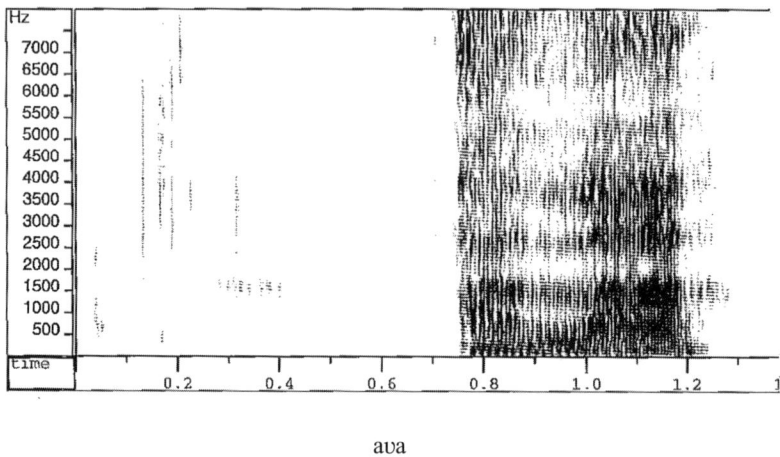

aʋa

Figure 9.39 Spectrogram of [aʋa].

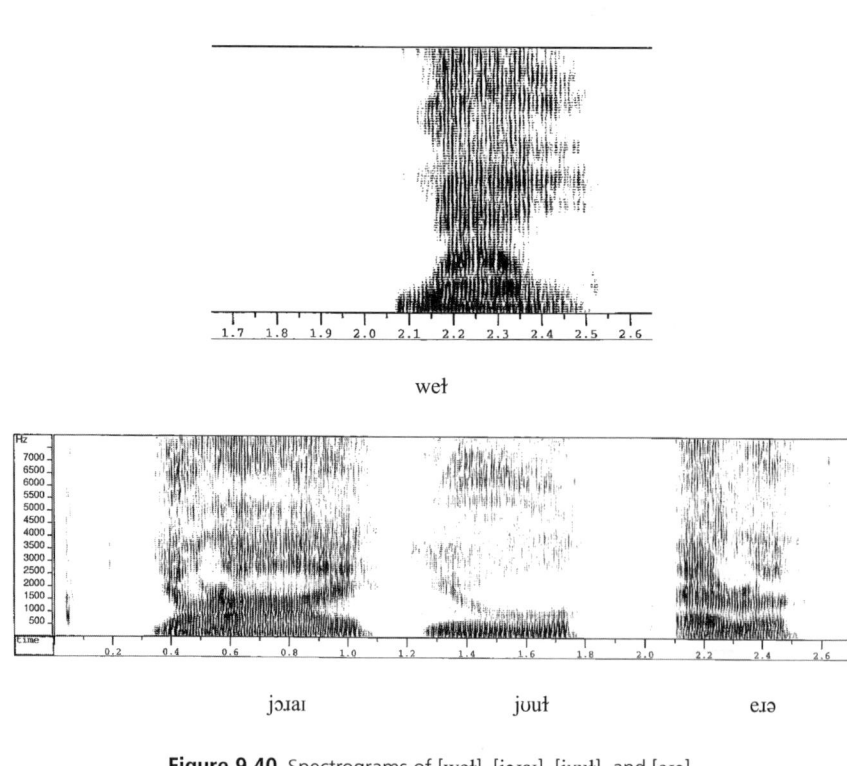

weɫ

jɔɹaɪ   juʊɫ   eɹə

Figure 9.40 Spectrograms of [weɫ], [jɔɹaɪ], [juʊɫ], and [eɹə].

Acoustic Phonetics 221

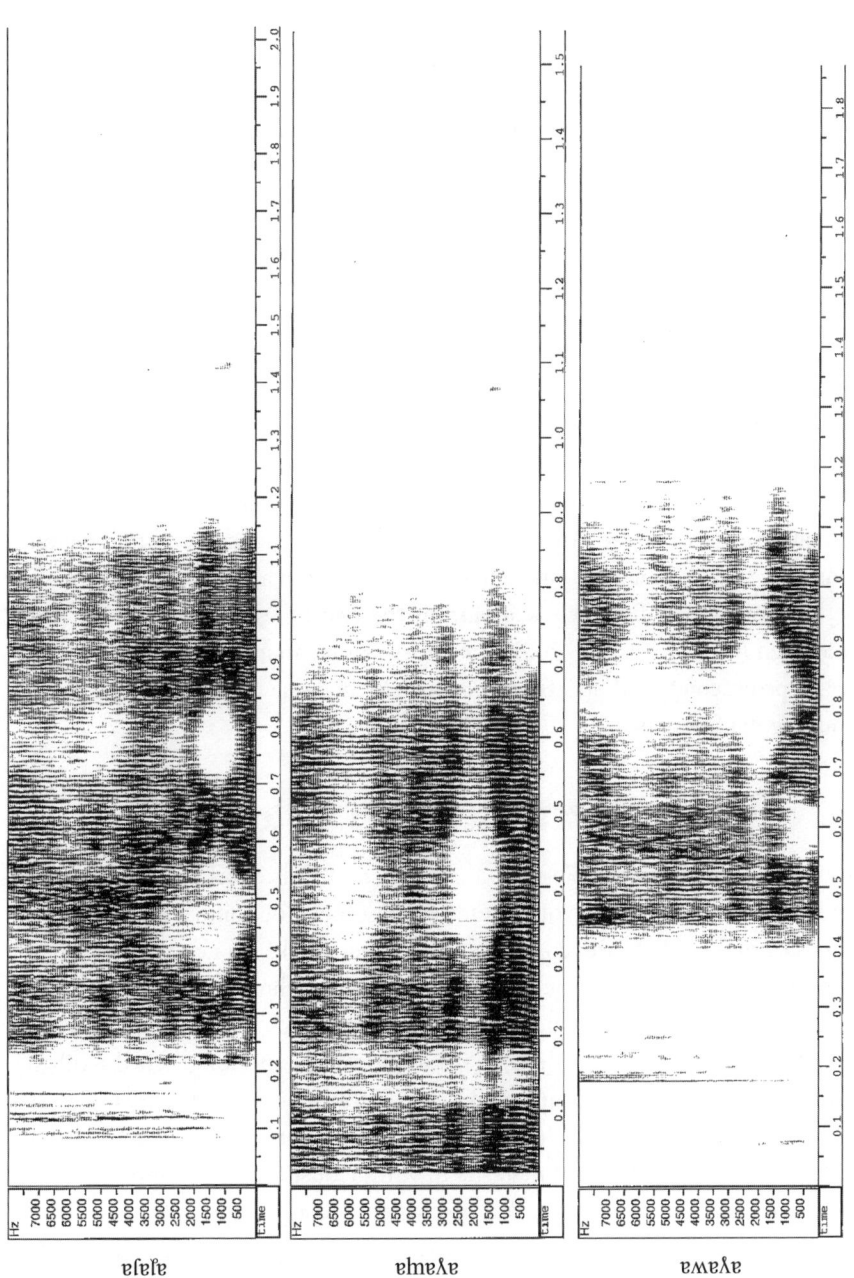

Figure 9.41 Spectrograms of [ajaja], [ayauja] and [ayawa].

transitions between vocalic and consonantal phases on the temporal dimension, but give greater detail of the frequencies, including those that make up the formants.

When the vocal cords vibrate, the shape of the resonator through which the sound is travelling produces **harmonics** of the fundamental frequency. They are whole-number multiples of the fundamantal frequency. So, if the fundamental frequency of a sound is 100 Hz, its second harmonic is at 200 Hz, its third at 300 Hz and so on. If the fundamental frequency is 123 Hz, the second harmonic is at 246 Hz, its third at 369 Hz. It is this detail that can be analyzed on a narrow-band spectrogram. Greater intensity at particular harmonic levels is what forms the formants we have been looking at throughout this chapter. A wide-band spectrogram blurs the distinctions of the harmonics and represents the formants as relatively broad horizontal bands. Compare the two spectrograms in Figure 9.42. The top one is wide-band, the bottom one narrow-band; both are of the utterance [ðə ˈbed wəz ˈveɹɪ ˈhɑd] *The bed was very hard*. Notice in particular how the narrow-band spectrogram represents the intonation pattern of the utterance quite clearly. The changes in fundamental frequency that produce the pitch changes are mirrored all the way up through the harmonics. For further discussion of the two types of spectrogram, see Ladefoged ([2006], pp. 202–205). Note his warning about women's voices not always producing good spectrograms, usually because of the height of their fundamental frequency.

9.7 Practice and further reading

Practice as much as possible with a computer software package for acoustic analysis. Record your own voice and those of others for comparison with the examples provided in this chapter and in other books on acoustic analysis. Remember that one drawback to all instrumental phonetic investigation is that it can rarely deal with naturally occurring speech. Even the process of recording puts speakers on their guard linguistically speaking. On the other hand, natural speech occurs in adverse surroundings from the point of view of the phonetician or phonologist interested in minute details. However, try using both scripted and unscripted material in your acoustic analyses and see what the results are like. Since I do not discuss the acoustic correlates of all the sound types I discussed in Chapters Two and Three, try recording and analyzing clicks, ejectives, voiceless vocoids and/or voiceless nasal stops, for example. The important thing is to experiment and see what happens.

Acoustic Phonetics 223

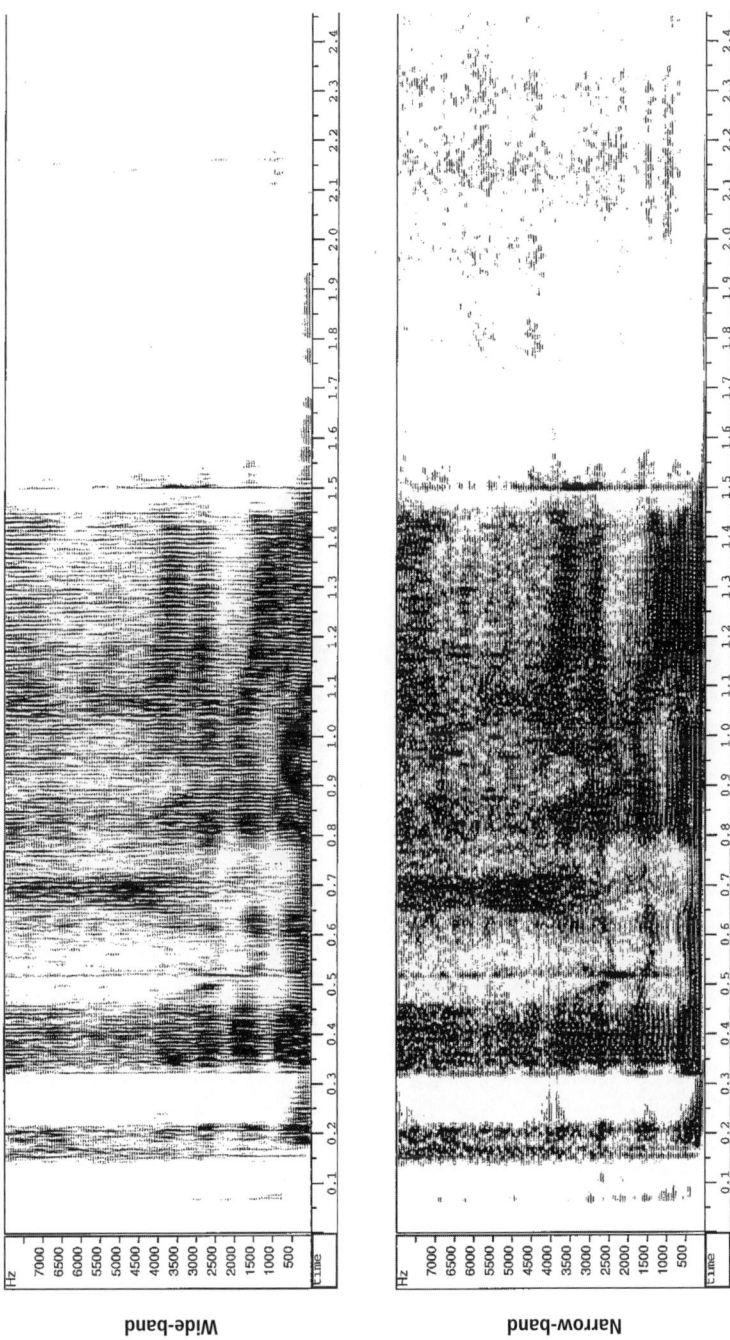

Figure 9.42 Wide-band and narrow-band spectrograms of [ðə ˈbed wəz ˈveɪɪ ˈhad].

224 A Critical Introduction to Phonetics

Besides the brief introduction to acoustic phonetics in Silverman (2006), the following give a more detailed account: Ball and Rahilly (1999), Clark and Yallop (1995), Ladefoged (2006). The most comprehensive and technical books are Ladefoged (1996) and Johnson (1997). Hewlett and Beck (2006) provide an excellent introduction to acoustic phonetics and other types of instrumental phonetics, for example, laryngoscopy, ultrasound imaging and electropalatography.

Glossary of Phonetic Terms

Cross-references within the glossary are given in **bold**.

acoustic phonetics   the study of the physical nature of sound waves in relation to human speech

advanced   a vocoid articulation in which the body of the tongue is advanced from the rear periphery of the vowel area

affrication (also **delayed release**)   the parting of the articulators relatively slowly following a stop causing a short phase of local audible friction

airstream   any air used in the articulation of language

alveolar   describes sounds in which the **tip** or **blade** of the tongue is placed against the **alveolar ridge**, for example, [t d s z]

alveolar ridge (also **teeth-ridge**)   the boney protuberance at the start of the roof of the mouth into which the teeth are set

alveolo-palatal   describes sounds in which more of the **front** of the tongue is placed against the **palate** in comparison with **palatoalveolar** articulations

ambisyllabicity   a phonological term referring to sounds that are interpreted as being both the coda of one **syllable** and the onset of the next

amplitude   the loudness of a sound

anticipatory assimilation (also **regressive assimilation**)   **assimilation** where a sound shares a feature or features with the following one(s)

anti-formant   an energy trough rather than an energy peak produced in nasal **stops** by the effect of the stoppage in the oral (side) chamber, which causes the acoustic energy to reduce the energy levels in the larynx-to-nose (main) chamber

aperiodic wave   a sound wave that has no repeated cycle, such as those produced by **fricatives**

apical any articulation involving the use of the **tip** of the tongue

approximant (also **frictionless continuant**) a sound produced by narrowing the opening through which the airstream passes by putting the articulators together (approximating them) without any contact at the point of narrowing

articulator a part of the vocal apparatus that is used in the production of linguistic sounds, for example, the teeth, the lips, the tongue

articulatory phonetics the study of the way in which human beings produce linguistic sounds

assimilation a term that refers to cases where there are alternative pronunciations of the same lexical item and where a phonetic feature is shared by a number of contiguous **syllable** places, for example, place of articulation, nasality

auditory phonetics the study of the ways in which speech affects and is interpreted by the hearer

back (of the tongue; also **dorsum**) the part of the tongue immediately below the **velum**; see Figure 2.9

bilabial describes articulations in which both lips are used, for example, [p b m]

blade (of the tongue; also **lamina**) the part of the tongue immediately behind the **tip**; see Figure 2.9

breathy voice (see **murmur**)

cardinal vowels the set of idealized **vocoid** articulations proposed by the British phonetician, Daniel Jones

cavity friction the slight amount of friction caused by air flowing over any object in a cavity, in the case of phonetics all the 'clutter' in the mouth

centralized a vocoid articulation in which the body of the tongue is in the central part of the vowel area

click a sound produced with the **back** of the tongue against the **velum** and a closure made somewhere in advance of this obstruction; the air from outside can be drawn into the intervening space by first depressing the centre of the tongue to reduce the air-pressure in the remaining cavity and then removing the outer closure

Glossary of Phonetic Terms

closure   the initial phase of a **stop** during which the articulators are brought together

coda   the final position of a **syllable**; it may be simple or complex, and may not occur in all syllables

contoid   a sound whose articulation depends on some contact between the articulators

creak (also **creaky voice**)   the type of **phonation** in which **vocal cords** are only open at one end and are vibrated very slowly

degree of occlusion (also **manner of articulation**)   the extent to which the articulators obstruct the airstream

delayed release   (see **affrication**)

dental   describes sounds in which the **tip** or **blade** of the tongue is placed on the back surface of the top teeth or between the teeth, for example, [θ ð]

diacritic   mark situated above, below or to the side of a main symbol, for example, [̥ ̈ ̃ ̩]

diphthong   a vocoid articulation that involves a movement of the tongue from one position to another, for example, [aɪ aʊ oʊ ɪə]; see Figure 2.19

dorsal   any sound articulated with the **back** of the tongue

duration   the period of time any phonetic feature lasts in the speech continuum

egressive pulmonic air   air expelled from the lungs for linguistic purposes

ejective   a sound produced by trapping air between a closed **glottis** and an oral closure, with the nasal cavities shut off, raising the **larynx**, thereby increasing the air pressure in the oral cavity; on release of the oral stop air is expelled out of the mouth

epiglottis   the small upward-pointing flap at the extreme base of the tongue; see Figure 2.9

faucal opening   the opening between the tonsils at the back of the oral cavity

flap   a sound produced by the rapid forward movement of an articulator (usually the tongue **tip**) striking another articulator as it passes

foot the stretch of syllables from one main **stress** up to, but not including the next, so feet differ in their make-up depending on the number and type of syllables involved

formant an overtone of a sound wave at a resonating **frequency** caused by a structure in the vocal tract, for example, the position of the tongue; **vocoids** are characterized by their formant structure

formant chart a chart on which the measurements of the first **formant** of a **vocoid** is plotted against the second **formant**

formant transitions changes in the **formant** structure of a section of speech

frequency the rate at which the peaks of **pressure fluctuations** occur in terms of numbers of complete opening and closing movements of the **vocal cords**; it is measured in cycles per second or **Hertz**

fricative a sound produced by holding the articulators almost together but with a very small gap between them to allow the airstream to escape; when the air passes through the narrow gap, it is subject to turbulence, which produces local audible friction

frictionless continuant (see **approximant**)

front (of the tongue) the part of the tongue immediately below the **hard palate**; see Figure 2.9

fundamental frequency the level of **frequency** produced by the rate of vibration of the **vocal cords**

glottalic airstream air trapped between the **glottis** and some oral closure; it can be compressed by raising the glottis or reduced by lowering the glottis; it is used in the production of **implosives** and **ejectives**

glottal reinforcement a glottal closure produced at the same time as a **supraglottal** one; if glottally reinforced stops are released, the glottal closure is released slightly before the oral one

glottal stop the complete closure of the **vocal cords**, completely obstructing the flow of air through the **glottis**

glottis the part of the windpipe that goes through the **larynx**

hard palate (also just **palate**) the bony part of the roof of the mouth back from the alveolar ridge

harmonic   whole-number multiple of the **fundamental frequency**

Hertz   the unit of measurement of cycles per second

hold   the defining and essential phase of a **stop** during which the articulators are held together

homophony   the situation in which two or more words sound the same

homorganic   made at the same place of articulation, for example, [mb ts]

implosive   a sound produced by trapping air between a closed **glottis** and an oral closure, with the nasal cavities shut off, lowering the **larynx**, thereby lowering the air pressure in the oral cavity; on release of the oral stop air is drawn into the mouth

information structure   the distribution of what the speaker considers to be old (given) and new information for the hearer in a sentence

interdental   describes a sound produced with the **tip** of the tongue between the teeth

intervocalic   adjective meaning occurring between vowels

intonation pitch   changes within an utterance which have a variety of functions, for example, the speaker's attitude, the indication of a particular type of communication such as a question or a warning

labialization   lip-rounding

labiodental   describes sounds produced by placing the top teeth just inside the bottom lip, for example, [f v]

laminal   made with the **blade** of the tongue

larynx   the casing made of cartilage and muscle around the windpipe; see Figure 2.2

lateral   a sound in which the airstream escapes along the side(s) of the tongue, for example, [l ɫ]

lateral release   release of a stop by lowering the sides of the tongue away from the upper molars

manner of articulation   (see **degree of occlusion**)

monophthong   a steady-state vocoid articulation

mora a timing unit of relatively constant duration, which can be made up of consonants and/or vowels; Japanese is a **moraic** language

murmur (also **breathy voice**) the type of **phonation** in which the vocal cords are kept apart, but closer together than for **voicelessness**; the force of the airflow causes vibration of a different kind from **voice**

nasal release the release of a stop mechanism through the nasal cavities (but see section 2.9.1)

nasopharynx the upper part of the **pharynx** (throat) near the entrance to the nasal cavities

nucleus the core element of a **syllable**; typically, but not exclusively, a **vocoid** articulation

obstruent one of the class of **stops** and **fricatives**, the sounds produced with a major obstruction in the mouth

onset the initial position of a **syllable**; it may be simple or complex, and may not occur in all syllables

palate (see **hard palate**)

palatal describes sounds in which the **front** of the tongue is used to articulate sounds by raising it into contact with the **palate**, for example, [ç ɲ]

palatalization front **resonance** caused by raising the **front** of the tongue

palatoalveolar describes sounds in which the **tip** of the tongue is placed on the back of the **alveolar ridge** and the blade on the front of the **palate**, for example, [ʃ ʒ tʃ dʒ]

parameter an individual component of articulation relating to one particular mechanism, for example, **phonation**

periodic wave a sound wave that has a repeating cycle such as those produced by **vocoids**

peripheral vowel a vocoid articulation produced on the peripheries of the vowel diagram, for example, the **cardinal vowels**

perseverative assimilation (see **progressive assimilation**)

pharyngeal describes sounds in which the **root** of the tongue is retracted to enable the extreme back of it to touch the **pharynx** wall

pharyngealization back **resonance** produced by a back tongue position and retraction of the tongue **root**, causing pharyngeal narrowing

pharynx the throat

phonation the resultant effects that the different positions of the **vocal cords** have on speech, including **voice** and **voicelessness**

phoneme not a phonetic term; the minimal distinctive unit of segmental phonology, established by means of meaningful contrasts

phonotactics a phonological term referring to the possible combinations of sounds in a **syllable** in a particular language

pitch the relative level at which the hearer places a sound on a scale; acoustically it is related to the level of the **fundamental frequency**

place of articulation the general term for the different combinations of the oral active and passive articulators

plosive a **stop** which is released

pressure fluctuations disturbance of the molecules in the air caused by sounds (of any kind); when the fluctuations reach the hearer, they cause her/his eardrum to move

progressive assimilation (also **perseverative assimilation**) assimilation where a sound shares a feature or features with the preceding one(s)

proprioceptive observation the technique of learning to observe and be aware of what you, as a speaker, are doing while speaking

prosodic features phonetic features of speech which occur over a considerable stretch of the speech continuum, for example, **intonation**

pulmonic relating to the lungs

regressive assimilation (see **anticipatory assimilation**)

release the final phase of a **plosive**, which may be absent from other types of **stop**

resonance a feature of sounds determined by the positioning of the body of the tongue on the front-back dimension, involving the bulk of the tongue being positioned under the palate or the velum; see also **palatalization, velarization** and **pharyngealization**

resonator   any container used to modify a sound source; it makes the sound more complex and in the case of speech the sound source is the vibrating **vocal cords** and the resonator is made up of the throat and the oral cavity with or without the nasal cavities

retracted   a vocoid articulation in which the body of the tongue is retracted from the front periphery of the vowel area

retroflex   describes sounds in which the tongue **tip** is flexed backwards so that the under surface is towards the roof of the mouth. Contact is made with the area just behind the **alveolar ridge** or just in front of the **palate**

rhyme   the **nucleus** of a **syllable** + its **coda**

root (of the tongue; also **radix**)   the base of the tongue at the back of the oral cavity that forms part of the wall of the **pharynx**

sibilant   a fricative with strong turbulent noise at a pitch range between 2500 Hz and 8000 Hz, for example, [s z ʃ ʒ]

sine wave   a simple periodic wave with energy at a single **frequency**

soft palate   (see **velum**)

sound wave   movement of the molecules of the air together and then apart in various ways

spirant   (see **fricative**)

stop   a complete stoppage of the air in the oral cavity

stress   an auditory property that enables the hearer to pick out a **syllable** which has been produced with greater articulatory effort

subglottal   adjective meaning situated or occurring beneath the **vocal cords**

supraglottal   adjective referring to any articulation or air above the **glottis** in the oral cavity

syllable   there is no satisfactory purely phonetic definition of the syllable, although it is clearly an organizational unit of both phonetic and phonological relevance

tap   a sound produced usually by the rapid upward movement of the **tip** of the tongue to strike against the roof of the mouth following by its rapid return downwards; the **uvula** can be struck on the **back** of the tongue in a similar fashion

teeth-ridge (see **alveolar ridge**)

tip (of the tongue; also **apex**) the extreme front part of the tongue; see Figure 2.9

tone a **pitch** that is used to convey meaning in a word or a sentence

tonic stress the main sentence **stress**, accompanied by a marked change of **pitch**

trachea the windpipe

trill a sound made up of a series of strikes by an articulator against another one; in alveolar trills the tongue **tip** is put in a position behind the **teeth-ridge** so that it bangs repeatedly against it in the egressive airstream

triphthong a vocoid articulation that involves two movements in different directions, for example, [aɪə aʊə]; see Figure 2.20

uvula the small soft part that hangs down into the **faucal opening** as a continuation of the **velum**

uvular describes sounds in which the **uvula** is brought into contact with the extreme back part of the tongue

velar used to describe sounds in which there is contact between the **back** of the tongue and the velum, for example, [k g x ŋ]

velaric airstream air trapped between a **velar** closure and a closure in advance of this; it is used to produce **clicks**

velarization back **resonance** caused by raising the **back** of the tongue

velic closure the closure of the **velum** against the back wall of the **pharynx** in order to shut off the nasal cavities

velum (also **soft palate**) the soft section of the roof of the mouth towards the back of the oral cavity

vocal cords (also **vocal folds**) two muscular flaps within the **larynx** which can be moved into various positions to interfere with the air flowing through the **glottis**

vocal tract the air passages above the **larynx**

vocoid a generic term which includes the **approximants** as well as what are typically referred to as vowels; none of the members of this set have any contact between the articulators

voice the feature of **phonation** produced by holding the **vocal cords** close together to produce their vibration in the **airstream**

voicelessness the feature of **phonation** produced by having the **vocal cords** wide apart, allowing the air to flow freely through the glottis

vowel diagram a conventionalized trapezoidal representation of the area in the mouth in which non-approximant vocoids are produced

References

Abercrombie, D. (1965) *Studies in phonetics and linguistics.* London: Oxford University Press.

Abercrombie, D. (1967) *Elements of general phonetics.* Edinburgh: Edinburgh University Press.

Agutter, A. (1988) 'The not-so-Scottish Vowel Length Rule.' In Anderson, J. M. and MacLeod, N. (eds.) *Edinburgh studies in the English language.* Edinburgh: John Donald Publishers, pp. 120–132.

Appelbaum, I. (1999) 'The dogma of isomorphism: a case study from speech perception.' *Philosophy of Science* 66: S250–S259.

Archangeli, D. and Pulleyblank, D. (1994) *Grounded phonology.* Cambridge, MA: MIT Press.

Ball, M. J. (1993) *Phonetics for speech pathology.* London: Whurr.

Ball, M. J. and Lowry, O. M. (2001) *Methods in clinical phonetics.* London: Whurr.

Ball, M. J. and Rahilly, J. (1999) *Phonetics, the science of speech.* London: Arnold.

Beal, J. (1999) *English pronunciation in the eighteenth century.* Oxford: Oxford University Press.

Bendor-Samuel, J. T. (1960) 'Segmentation in the phonological analysis of Terena.' *Word* 16: 348–355. (Also in Palmer, [1970] pp. 214–221.)

Bertelson, P., Morais, J., Alegria, J. and Content, A. (1985) 'Phonetic analysis capacity and learning to read.' *Nature* 313: 73–74.

Boase-Beier, J. and Lodge, K. R. (2003) *The German language: a linguistic introduction.* Oxford: Blackwell.

Brazil, D., Coulthard, M. and Johns, C. (1980) *Discourse intonation and language teaching.* London: Longman.

Browman, C. P. and Goldstein, L. M. (1986) 'Towards an articulatory phonology.' *Phonology Yearbook* 3: 219–252.

Browman, C. P. and Goldstein, L. M. (1989) 'Articulatory gestures as phonological units.' *Phonology* 6: 201–251.

Brown, G. (1977) *Listening to spoken English.* London: Longman.

Carter, P. (2003) 'Extrinsic phonetic interpretation: spectral variation in English liquids.' In Local, J. K., Ogden, R. A. and Temple, R. (eds.) *Papers in laboratory phonology VI.* Cambridge: Cambridge University Press, pp. 237–252.

Clark, J. and Yallop, C. (1995) *An introduction to phonetics and phonology.* (2nd edition) Oxford: Blackwell.

Cruttenden, A. (2001) *Gimson's introduction to the pronunciation of English.* London: Arnold.

Davenport, M. and Hannahs, S. J. (2005) *Introducing phonetics and phonology.* (2nd edition) London: Hodder Arnold.

Dell, F. (1980) *Generative phonology and French phonology.* Cambridge: Cambridge University Press.

Docherty, G. and Foulkes, P. (2000) 'Speaker, speech and knowledge of sounds.' In Burton-Roberts, N., Carr, P. and Docherty, G. (eds.) *Phonological knowledge.* Oxford: Oxford University Press, pp. 161–184.

Gimson, A. C. (1962) *An introduction to the pronunciation of English*. London: Arnold.

Gussenhoven, C. and Jacobs, H. (2005) *Understanding phonology*. (2nd edition) London: Hodder Arnold.

Gussmann, E. (2002) *Phonology*. Cambridge: Cambridge University Press.

Halliday, M. A. K. (1967) *Intonation and grammar in British English*. The Hague: Mouton.

Harris, J. *English sound structure*. Oxford: Blackwell.

Hashim, A. and Lodge, K.R. (1988) 'The phonological processes of Malay: a preliminary statement.' *UEA Papers in Linguistics* 28: 1–28.

Hewlett, N. and Beck, J. (2006) *An introduction to the science of phonetics*. Mahwah, NJ: Lawrence Erlbaum Associates.

Hughes, A., Trudgill, P. and Watt, D. (2005) *English, accents & dialects*. London: Hodder Arnold.

IPA (1949) *The principles of the International Phonetic Association*. London: IPA.

Johnson, K. (1997) *Acoustic and auditory phonetics*. Oxford: Blackwell.

Jones, D. (1956) *The pronunciation of English*. (4th edition) Cambridge: Cambridge University Press.

Kelly, J. and Local, J. K. (1986) 'Long-domain resonance patterns in English.' In *International conference on speech input/output; techniques and applications*. Conference publication no. 258, London: IEE, pp. 304–309.

Kelly, J. and Local, J. K. (1989) *Doing phonology*. Manchester: Manchester University Press.

Kenstowicz, M. (1994) *Phonology in generative grammar*. Oxford: Blackwell.

Kohler, K. J. (1995) *Einführung in die deutsche Phonetik*. (2nd edition) Berlin: Schmidt.

Ladefoged, P. (1996) *Elements of acoustic phonetics*. (2nd edition) Chicago: University of Chicago Press.

Ladefoged, P. (2006) *A course in phonetics*. (5th edition) Boston, MA: Thomson Wadsworth.

Lass, R. (1976) *English phonology and phonological theory*. Cambridge: Cambridge University Press.

Lass, R. (1984) *Phonology*. Cambridge: Cambridge University Press.

Laver, J. (1994) *Principles of phonetics*. Cambridge: Cambridge University Press.

Lindau, M., Jacobson, L. and Ladefoged, P. (1973) 'The feature advanced tongue root.' *UCLA Working Papers in Phonetics* 22: 76–94.

Local, J. K. (1992) 'Modelling assimilation in a non-segmental rule-free phonology.' In Docherty, G. and Ladd, D. R. (eds.) *Papers in laboratory phonology II*. Cambridge: Cambridge University Press, pp. 190–223.

Local, J. K. and Lodge, K. R. (2004) 'Some impressionistic and acoustic observations on the phonetics of [ATR] harmony in a speaker of a dialect of Kalenjin.' *Journal of the International Phonetic Association* 34: 1–16.

Lodge, K. R. (1983) 'The acquisition of phonology: a Stockport sample.' *Lingua* 61: 335–351.

Lodge, K. R. (1984) *Studies in the phonology of colloquial English*. London: Croom Helm.

Lodge, K. R. (2003) 'A declarative treatment of the phonetics and phonology of German rhymal /r/.' *Lingua* 113: 931–951.

Lodge, K. R. (2007) 'Timing, segmental status and aspiration in Icelandic.' *Transactions of the Philological Society* 105: 66–104.

References

Lodge, K. R. (to appear) *Fundamental issues in phonology: sameness and difference.* Edinburgh: Edinburgh University Press.

Lodge, K. R., Local, J. K. and Harlow, S. (in prep.) 'Challenges for intrinsic phonetic interpretation and the domains of harmony in Tugen.'.

Macken, M. A. (1995) 'Phonological acquisition.' In Goldsmith, J. A. *The handbook of phonological theory.* Oxford: Blackwell, pp. 671–696.

Mann, V. A. (1986) 'Phonological awareness: the role of reading experience.' *Cognition* 24: 65–92.

Maris, M. Y. (1980). *The Malay sound system.* Kuala Lumpur: Penerbit Fajar Bakti.

Morais, J. (1991) 'Phonological awareness: a bridge between language and literacy.' In Sawyer, D. J. and Fox, B. J. (eds.) *Phonological awareness in reading: the evolution of current perspectives.* Berlin: Springer-Verlag, pp. 31–71.

Morais, J., Bertelson, P., Cary, L. and Alegria, J. (1986) 'Literacy training and speech segmentation.' *Cognition* 24: 45–64.

Morais, J., Cary, L., Alegria, J. and Bertelson, P. (1979) 'Does awareness of speech as a sequence of phones arise spontaneously?' *Cognition* 7: 323–331.

Muthwii, M. (1994) Variability in language use: a study of Kalenjin speakers of English and Kiswahili in Kenya. Unpublished PhD thesis, University of East Anglia, Norwich.

Nolan, F., Holst, T. and Kühnert, B. (1996) 'Modelling [s] to [ʃ] accommodation in English.' *Journal of Phonetics* 24: 113–137.

Odden, D. (2005) *Introducing phonology.* Cambridge: Cambridge University Press.

Ogden, R. A. (1999) 'A declarative account of strong and weak auxiliaries in English.' *Phonology* 16: 55–92.

Ohala, J. J. (1992) 'The segment: primitive or derived?' In Docherty, G. and Ladd, D. R. (eds.) *Papers in laboratory phonology II.* Cambridge: Cambridge University Press, pp. 166–183.

Orton, H. and Halliday, F. (1962–1963). *Survey of English Dialects: basic material, volume 2.* Leeds: E. J. Arnold.

Palmer, F. R. (1970) *Prosodic analysis.* London: Oxford University Press.

Pike, K. L. (1943) *Phonetics.* Ann Arbor: University of Michigan Press.

Pring, J. T. (1950) *A grammar of Modern Greek on a phonetic basis.* London: University of London Press.

Read, C., Yun-Fei, Z., Hong-Yin, N. and Bao-Qing, D. (1986) 'The ability to manipulate speech sounds depends on knowing alphabetic writing.' *Cognition* 24: 31–44.

Ringen, C. and Helgason, P. (2004) 'Distinctive [voice] does not imply regressive assimilation: evidence from Swedish.' *International Journal of English Studies* 4: 53–71.

Scobbie, J. M. (2005) 'The phonetics-phonology overlap.' *Working Paper WP-1*, Edinburgh: Queen Margaret University College.

Sebba, M. (1993) *London Jamaican.* London: Longman.

Shockey, L. (2003) *Sound patterns of spoken English.* Oxford: Blackwell.

Silverman, D. (2006) *A critical introduction to phonology.* London: Continuum.

Simpson, A. (1998) 'Accounting for the phonetics of German *r* without processes.' *ZAS Papers in Linguistics* 11: 91–104.

Tench, P. (1978) 'On introducing parametric phonetics.' *Journal of the International Phonetic Association* 8: 34–46.

Tranel, B. (1987) *The sounds of French.* Cambridge: Cambridge University Press.

Trudgill, P. (1974) *Sociolinguistics.* Harmondsworth: Penguin.

Trudgill, P. (1986) *Dialects in contact.* Oxford: Blackwell.

Trudgill, P. (2002) *Sociolinguistic variation and change.* Edinburgh: Edinburgh University Press.

Tsujimura, N. (1996) *An introduction to Japanese linguistics.* Oxford: Blackwell.

Waterson, N. (1956) 'Some aspects of the phonology of the nominal forms of the Turkish word.' *Bulletin of the School of Oriental and African Studies* 18: 578–591. (Also in Palmer [1970], pp. 174–187.)

Wells, J. C. (1967) 'Specimen: Jamaican Creole.' *Le Maître Phonétique* 127: 5–6.

Wells, J. C. (1973) *Jamaican pronunciation in London.* Oxford: Basil Blackwell.

Wells, J. C. (1982) *Accents of English* (3 volumes). Cambridge: Cambridge University Press.

Zawaydeh, B. A. (2003) 'The interaction of the phonetics and phonology of gutturals.' In Local, J. K., Ogden, R. A. and Temple, R. (eds.) *Papers in laboratory phonology VI.* Cambridge: Cambridge University Press, pp. 279–292.

Index

acoustic analysis 42, 183–4
acoustic phonetics 2, 183–224
active articulators 26, 27
'Adam's apple' 15
advanced tongue root (ATR) 24–5
affrication 35
African languages, examples of pitch 113
airflow 13, 15
airstream mechanism 14–15, 46–8
allophones 69
alphabets 11
alveolar approximant 180, 181
'alveolar', pronunciation of 28
alveolar ridge 23, 27, 28
alveolar sounds 26
 t and d 86
alveolar tap 81
alveolo-palatal sounds 30
ambiguity, written and spoken 5
ambisyllabicity 128
American Phonetic Alphabet (APA) 70
amplitude 187
Ancient Egyptian hieroglyphs 11
Ancient Greek loan words in
    German 87, 132
anisomorphism 107
anticipatory assimilation 147–9
anti-formant 216
aperiodic sounds 213
apex of tongue 25
approximants 33, 36–8, 216, 218
Arabic
 consonants 91
 emphatic stops 63
 syllables 129
articles, definite and indefinite 62
articulation 14–50, 77, 141
 components 98
 manner of 33, 45, 52
 place of 26, 52, 208, 213

articulators in combination 51–66
arytenoid cartilages 15
Asian languages, examples of pitch 113
aspiration 105–6
assimilation 115, 131, 145–53
auditory phonetics 2
Australian pitch raising 176

back of tongue (dorsum) 25
bilabial click 48
bilabial sounds 27
blade of tongue (lamina) 25
Brazilian-Amazonian jungle
    language 24
breathing pattern 14–15
breathy voice 19–20
British English 16, 17, 68
Burmese voiceless nasals 54

cardinal vowels 39, 40–1
categorical interpretation 56
Caucasian languages 22
cavity friction 62
Chinese writing system 11, 100
citation form 135, 157–8
clicks 15, 47–8
closed syllable 80
closure 34
Cockney 177
coda 9, 124, 125
coda obstruents, English 106
Comaltepec Chinantec 10
comparison of accents 173–4
concatenation 135–6
connected speech phenomena 145–58
consonants 38, 176–7
 and vowels 62
continuous speech 135–60
contoid articulations 206–16
contoids 54

contoid/vocoid, terms 38
creaky voice 20–1
cues to meaning in speech 4
Cufic alphabet 11
Cyrillic alphabet 11
Czech
  stress in 119
  syllables 129
  trills 46
  word 125

dearticulation 155–6
  of laterals 179
delayed release 35
'deletion' examples 156–8
dental clicks 48
dental fricatives 57
dental sounds 28
diacritics 33, 42
diphthongs 42, 44
  central 74–5, 78
  front-closing 73
  rising, in French 85
disyllabic words 135–8
Down's syndrome 24
drama 12
duration 112, 119–21, 125, 126

East Anglia 167–8
egressive pulmonic airstream 15, 53
ejectives 15, 47, 177
electronic tone 188
emotional involvement 115
enclitic 119
English
  phonological structure 8
  stress patterns, list 117
  varieties 150, 161–82
  vowel system 49, 71
epiglottis 14, 22, 24
'Eve's wedding ring' 15

face-to-face context of speech 7
falling diphthongs 42–3
faucal opening 21

foot 131–2
forensic linguistics 12
formant and anti-formant 184
formant chart 195, 196, 198
  English short vowels 204
  vocoids 195
formants and frequencies 190–205
fortis 49
fortition 153–4
French
  nasal vowels 84
  pronunciation 83–5
  stress 118–19
  word list 85
French and English sentences 130–1
frequency 112, 187–222
fricative manner 52
fricatives 19, 30–4, 213, 216
fricatives (spirants) 36
  in German 86
friction 35
frictionless continuants 37
front of tongue (dorsum) 25
fundamental frequency of utterance 5–6,
  190, 222

General American 68, 81–3
German 86–9
  pronunciation 86–9
  stress and rhythm 132
  trills 46
  vowels 86–7
  word list 88
glide 49
glottal activity, Chong 104, 106
glottal closure 55
glottal fricative 62
glottalic airstream 15
glottal reinforcement 17, 86, 155, 176–7
glottal stops 16, 33, 177
  as definite article 56–7, 177–8
glottis 15, 17, 18
gradient interpretation 56
Greek alphabet 11
Greek, Modern 89–90

Index

h sound 176
Habsburg royal house 27
harmonics 218, 222
harmony languages 151
Hertz (Hz) measurement of frequency 112, 187
High German sound shift 154
high pitch 113
hold 34
homophony 9, 84
horizontal axis (abscissa) 195
hypercorrectness 163

Icelandic 49
implicit meanings 7
implosives 15, 46–7
Indian English 170
information structure 113, 114
'insertion' examples 157–8
International Phonetic Association (IPA) 11, 39, 41
  chart x, 52, 54, 55, 59
'interpersonal meaning' 2
intervocalic sounds 17
intonation 2, 3, 4–8, 80, 112, 114
isomorphism 11, 12

Jamaican Creole 169–70
Japanese 43
  high vowels 62
  moraic language 129
  syllable structure 129
Jones, Daniel, phonetician 39, 41

Kalenjin, Nilotic language, Kenya 152
Kenyan English 170–1

labialization 61
labiodental approximant 180–1
labiodental sounds 27
labio-lingual articulations 24
labiovelar articulations 53
Lancashire 17, 164, 177–8
laryngeoscopy 50
larynx 14–16

laterals 45, 52
  approximants 45
  in English 44, 69, 77, 78, 179
  fricatives 45, 57–8, 100–1
  release 35
Latin 83
  and German stress 132
  loan words in German 87
left-to-right assimilation 147–9
lenis 49
lenition 153–4, 181–2
lexical alveolar nasal 146
lexical entry form 135
lexical incidence 78, 169, 170
liaison 130
  in French and English 157
linguistic structure 10
linguistic systems, study of 8
lips 13, 14, 25–7
  position 41, 61, 108
  rounding 40, 61, 141
  spreading 40, 141
  vocoid articulation 40
Liverpool accent 107
  lenition 182
London Jamaican 170
London speakers 179
long-domain features 107–8
loudness 185
lowered positions 60, 61
lowering of pitch 113
lungs 13, 14–15

magnetic resonance imaging (MRI) 50
Malay 90–3
  loan and replacement consonants 91
  word list 93
Mandarin Chinese 112, 113
  tones, table 113
Margi labiodental flap 46, 51
Middle English 80, 167
  velar fricative 171–2
Modern Greek
  assimilation 149–50
  stress in 119

monophthongs 42, 44, 72
　French 84
　German 88
　Jamaican 169
　Scottish English 166, 167
monosyllables, English 129
mora, timing unit 129
moraic language, Japanese 133
mouth 13, 14
murmur 19–20

narrow-band spectrograms 218, 222
nasal assimilation
　English 150
　German 150
nasal contoids 216
nasal fricatives 55
nasality 52, 146, 200
　in English 77, 78, 145–6
　in Malay 92–3, 111
nasalization
　of vocoids 41, 82, 174
nasal stop 30, 31, 34–5, 53–5, 216
nasal versus oral sounds 22, 216–17
nasopharynx 22
neutral position of lips 25, 26
non-obstruents 57–8
non-pulmonic air 63–4
nonsense words 94
Norfolk 17, 177
northern English 56–7, 162–3
Norwich 167–8, 177
nose 14
NP (noun phrase) 5
nuclear vowel 106, 124
nucleus 124, 125

obstruents 36
occlusion, degrees of 33
onset 9, 124, 125
open syllables 80
oral articulators
　active 26
　passive 26

oral versus nasal sounds 22, 216–17
oral stop 30, 35, 53–5, 207–13
ordinate 195
organs of speech 2
overlap, articulatory 101–7

palatal 30–1
palatal nasal 83
palatalization 63
palate 27
　soft, hard 22, 29
palatoalveolar clicks 30, 35, 48
palatography 50
parametric interplay 64–6, 135–45
parametric view of speech 64–6, 98–101
passive articulators 26, 27
perseverative assimilation 147–9
pharyngealization 44, 63
pharyngeal sounds 33
pharynx 14, 21–2
phonation 16, 52, 55, 64
phonemes 9
phones 10
phonetic duration 120–1
phonetics and phonology 8–11
phonetic structure of real speech 98–109
phonological length 120
phonotactics 127
Pirahã labio-lingual flick 51
pitch 19, 112–15, 185–9
place assimilation 147–50
place of articulation 26, 52, 208, 213
plosive 34
Polish, stress in 119
post-alveolar sounds 29
postaspiration 105
post-tonic position in German 88
PRAAT (computer program) 185
preaspiration 105, 106
pre-palatal sounds 29
pressure fluctuations 2, 185
pre-tonic position 88
prognathous jaw 27
progressive assimilation 147–9

Index

proprioceptive observation 23
prosodic features 110–34
pseudo-phonetic terms 48–9

radix 21, 25
raised positions 60, 61
'received pronunciation' (RP) 70–1
   speakers, radio and television 158
   transcription for 120
regional accents 162
regressive assimilation 147–9
release 34–5
resonance 44–5, 111, 126, 179, 218–19
   types of 62–3
resonator 189
retracted tongue root (RTR) 24–5, 49
retroflex sounds 29, 45, 213
rhotacized vocoid articulations 81
rhoticity 81, 164–5
rhyme 9, 124
rhythm 112, 130–3
rising diphthongs 43
rising intonation 114, 115
rock music rhythms 133
Roman alphabet 11
root of tongue (radix) 21, 25
rounded position of lips 25, 26, 61, 198–9

schwa 75–7, 173, 191–2
   absence of 77–9
   British English examples 41
   French examples 41
   German 87
Scotland, vowel systems in 166–7
Scots Gaelic 44, 129–30
Scots, East Fife 153
Scottish Vowel Length Rule (SVLR) 166
segmentation 11–12, 98–109, 139
Semitic languages 49
semivowel 37, 49
sibilants 36, 126, 213
Sindhi 48

sine wave
   complex 190
   constant 188, 189
   fading (diagram) 188
singing 12
smoothing 168
sound waves 2, 185–7
   aperiodic 187
   periodic 187–90
sounds, deletion and insertion 101–2
Spanish, syllables 129
spectrograms 128, 190–4, 196–212, 213–16, 217–22
speech
   continous 135–59
   objective description of 1, 2
   transience of 2
   versus writing 2–8
speech therapy 12
spoken language 3, 4, 5
spread vowels in Turkish 151
Standard British English (SBE) 70–81
steady states 207
stops 33–8, 207–8
stress 112, 116–19
   in English compound words 118
   on final syllable 85
stressed syllables 76–7
subglottal 18
suffixation in Turkish 152
supraglottal 18
supraglottal closure 16, 47
Swedish 86
syllabic consonants 78
syllable boundaries 127, 128
syllable structure 124–25
syllables 112, 121–30

taps and trills 45–6, 58
teeth 27
tense/lax 49
thyroid cartilage 15
tone group 114–15, 131–2
tone languages 112, 113

Index

tongue 23–5, 27
tongue tip 25
tonic stress 114
trachea 15
transcription 67–94
  broad 69
  exercises 158–9
  narrow 69
  samples
    in English 78–9
    in French 85
    in German 88
    in Malay 91–3
    Modern Greek 90
transitions, changes in formant structure 207
trills 45–6
triphthong 42, 43, 44, 75, 76
Trique, Otomanguean language 101
Turkish 43
  vowel harmony 108, 151, 152

ultrasound images 50
uvula 32
uvular approximant 180
uvular fricative 83
uvular trill in German 86

velaric airstream 15, 47–8
velarization 44, 63, 155
velar nasal stop 48
velar sounds 31–2
velic activity 52
velum 13–15, 22, 23, 27
  velar, velic and velaric 32
vibration of vocal cords 19, 105, 112, 187
vocal cord activity 56
  timing 104–7
vocal cords 13, 56
  closed and open 18
  glottis and 15–21
  vibrating 18–19

vocal tract closure 34
vocoid articulation 39, 40, 44, 125, 151
vocoid phase 206
vocoid positions, sample 59–61
vocoids 37–8
  close (high) 80
  lip position and 58, 59
  open (low) 80
  resonance and 44
  voiceless 41, 59, 62
voice assimilation in French 150
voiced sounds 18–19
voiced obstruents, German restriction on 86
voiced uvular trill 69–70
voiceless nasals 54–5
voicelessness 17, 18, 56
voiceless vocoids 61–2
vowels
  checked and unchecked 80–1
  close or high 39, 40
  diagram 138
  differences between GA and SBE 80, 81
  duration 80
  front, back, and central 32
  German long and short 87
  'long' and 'short' 80–1
  Modern Greek 89
  moving 43–4

Wavesurfer (computer program) 185
Welsh 45
whisper 21
wide-band and narrow-band spectrograms 218, 222, 223
word boundaries 131
writing systems, non-alphabetic 100
written language 2–4

Yorkshire 17, 177–8
young speakers of English 174–5